YOU

SHOT

MY

DOG

AND

I LOVE

YOU

YOU
SHOT
MY
DOG
AND
I LOVE
YOU

ANONYMOUS

MERCIER PRESS

MERCIER PRESS

Cork

www.mercierpress.ie

© The Author, 2019

ISBN: 978 1 78117 721 1

A CIP record for this title is available from the British Library.

Printed and bound in the EU.

To my firstborn son, for showing me
I was on the right road all along.

'Every truth unspoken is a lie.'

– my father

AUTHOR'S NOTE

This account of my early life is based on my own recollections and those of particular family members. However, names and certain identifying details have been changed to protect the privacy of both the innocent and the guilty. And, moreover, to protect myself.

CONTENTS

DUBLIN 1982

I knew I was in deep shit. And this time there appeared to be no way out. A rather hefty woman had trundled over to the side door of the post office and, while looking me straight in the eye, closed it purposefully. She then reached for the keys in her pocket. From the periphery of my one good eye I could see that the only available teller was beginning to close down her station, despite the fact that it was still early in the morning. Something was terribly wrong.

Time seemed to pause while I looked for a credible means of escape, but I could see none. The largely wooden, decaying interior of the building had only one exit, the very same portal that my mother had just used and which the hefty staff member now appeared to be locking.

For a moment I entertained the notion that I might be suffering from some sort of delusion or paranoia. Perhaps the women's behaviour had nothing to do with me? Maybe they were just going about their daily routine and I was imagining this perceived threat? With that in mind I decided to form a queue of one in front of the teller. But she cast me a look as if to say: 'I don't fucking think so, sonny.'

The look she gave me was unmistakable. We'd been rumbled.

Word must have circulated about a mother-and-son team working the Dublin area, and neither of these women gave the impression that they were about to let themselves be scammed by a twelve-year-old boy. I became acutely aware that if, by some miracle, I got out of this predicament, we would have to leave Dublin, and soon. The jig was up.

***

Extraordinary days begin like any other and this day had been no exception. We had no inkling of what was to come as we drove towards the port area of the city that morning. As we hadn't 'done' that part of the city yet, my parents were keen to be early birds. This meant starting before lunchtime, which was unusual. Prior to this, we had generally begun our light-fingered antics much later in the day, giving the staff plenty of time to become tired and invariably let their guard down. Late afternoons were considered best.

On this pivotal day, however, we were out on the prowl early, perhaps too early for such shenanigans. It struck me that we might well be the first customers through the door, which surely was not wise? To add insult to injury, my dad had decided that both my mother and I were to go into the first post office and make two separate withdrawals, one after another. This was not normal practice either, especially at smaller branches – mostly due to the fact that my mother and I bore a striking resemblance to one another and, no matter how well we acted, it would be blindingly obvious to all present that we were related. My dad seemed unconcerned by this, but, then again, why would he be? He may have been a master forger and getaway driver, but he never committed any actual face-to-face crimes. He was, however, the brains of the outfit, so I put my faith in him and did as I was told.

As it was now over a month into our endeavours, both my mother and I had become quite adept at our technique. On such rare occasions at this, she would always enter first, while I lagged behind, making sure not to enter before her transaction was almost complete. On this sunny April morn, my mother was particularly quick and left the premises in record time with her spoils, leaving the counter free for the next in line: little old me.

But clearly the staff's suspicions had already been aroused. As the hefty woman fumbled with her keys and the teller reached for the counter blind, I knew that they were on to us. Still, I felt that I had little choice but to go through the motions. After all, I had a mission to complete.

I thought that if I was convincing enough then maybe I could quash their misgivings. My legs propelled me to the counter with considerable gusto, disregarding the teller's facial expression and ignoring the fact that she was clearly battening down the hatches. I placed my account book down firmly and, in what I hoped was the most trustworthy of voices, blurted out, 'I'd like to withdraw thirty pounds, please.'

Not only did I bear an uncanny resemblance to this woman's previous customer, but I was also taking out the exact same amount. The look on the teller's face made my stomach churn. I knew the additional line I had prepared about it being my birthday wasn't going to fly.

A sense of panic grew within my small frame. A mirror behind the counter reflected the frosted glass front of the post office, allowing me to make out something blue moving slowly along the street outside. It appeared to be the same colour as our getaway car, although I could not be certain. It looked as if my parents were absconding without me.

The teller ignored my request, choosing to stare me out instead. It was time to get out of there. Two outcomes beckoned: freedom or incarceration. So, abandoning my play altogether, I turned and charged towards the door, which was still being guarded by the key-holder. I summoned all the aggression I could muster and screamed: 'Open the fucking door.' She point-blank refused, standing firm.

'Open the fucking door,' I yelled again. The teller, offended by my colourful language, was now waving my account book and heading in my direction, no doubt to help detain me.

A combination of fear and adrenaline awakened a brute strength. I pushed the key-holder out of the way and grabbed the door handle. To my astonishment, it was still unlocked. Hey presto! The door swung open and I bolted. I ran as fast as I could, looking for my parents while trying not to panic. I could hear the women shouting after me, but luckily neither of them attempted pursuit. I was sure, however, that the guards would not be too far behind.

As I turned the corner, I could see my dad's car in the middle distance, driving away, albeit slowly. I saw two heads inside, confirming that my mother was safe. I kept running, shouting for them to stop in a volume that burned my lungs, the cold morning air slicing the back of my throat. Anxiety and excitement were essential fuel for my young legs as I galloped ever faster, gaining on the car with every stride. My parents must have heard my cries and the car began to slow a little – not to a complete stop, but just enough to allow me to jump in. I threw myself into the back of the moving vehicle, relieved.

Once my dad saw that I was safely inside the car, he hit the accelerator hard. There was a screeching sound accompanied by the stench of burning rubber, which immediately irritated my nostrils. Both my mum and I were pinned to the back seat as he showed off his impressive getaway skills. It was not dissimilar to being in a plane during take-off, only without the seat belts. We were unsure if anyone had taken down our number plate, but the car had to be ditched regardless, just in case. I had to be temporarily ditched too. The guards were sure to be looking for a couple with a young boy, so I had to be dropped off somewhere at my earliest inconvenience.

After a number of speedy twists and turns around some rarely used back roads, the car came to a sudden stop. My dad turned around and beckoned at me to get out, pointing in the direction of the local canal. He suggested that I follow it westward, back through the area in which we lived. He reminded me, however, that under no circumstances was I to approach our house. I was to stick meticulously to the plan we had made for an occasion such as this.

He asked me if I understood what had to be done and I told him I did. He leaned over and pulled shut the car door behind me, then informed me through the glass in muffled tones that they had to get going. They intended to set fire to the car and destroy their clothes. Before I could utter a word, the engine revved violently and my parents were gone. I could just about make out my mother waving at me from within the vanishing car. I was about to wave back, but before I could raise my arm a cloud of gravel and dust enveloped me. They were gone.

With a few pounds in my pocket, I headed in the direction my dad had suggested, looking over my shoulder the whole time. I was fully aware that under no circumstances could I afford to get caught. Once I reached the canal I removed my jacket and threw it into the stagnant water, the tartan lining becoming ever more entangled in weeds and beer cans as it faded into the darkness below. I then turned my T-shirt inside out, roughed up my hair and started to walk a little differently. I had to believe I was an entirely different person if I was to convince others. I succumbed to this new character with relish, soon feeling like I was someone other than myself.

Although the canal led all the way home, I did not want to be obvious and simply follow it blindly. For all I knew the guards were looking for me with the women from the post office in tow. If I was spotted, they were sure to recognise me, regardless of my efforts to disguise myself. So I decided to take the side streets in a zig-zag pattern, constantly crossing the putrid canal every few minutes. I had a good sense of direction and before long I was back in my local area, close to home.

As I was under strict instructions not to go to our flat, I paced the surrounding streets in circles – in effect, casing the joint. I was keen to know if the guards had found our abode, thinking it not inconceivable that they might well be searching the place right there and then. As I moved closer, I half-expected uniforms to emerge with arms full of my dad's forgery paraphernalia.

When the door did in fact open, it was not the guards who emerged. Surprisingly, it was my parents. They were each carrying a large bag and acting pretty normal for two people skirting arrest. I was tempted to make contact but decided it was best not to approach them yet, instead sticking to the plan my dad had drummed into me.

That plan (should things go awry as they most certainly did on this fateful day) was for us to meet at a specific location at a designated time. As I still had a couple of hours to kill before our meeting, and I now assumed my time in Dublin was limited, I decided to take a final walk around the city centre, enjoying all my old haunts one last time.

***

It was hard to say goodbye to a city that had so recently become my home. I was fond of Dublin, mostly because it reminded me of London. Although only twelve years old, I already had an affinity with big cities. The larger population helped stave off the feeling of isolation I'd often had while living in rural Ireland.

As I walked down O'Connell Street, I replayed that morning's events, trying to pinpoint the exact moment the women became suspicious. Was it something I did? Maybe I was too obvious? Did I inadvertently make eye contact with my mother as we crossed paths? The potential reasons were many, but I concluded they were of no importance now. All that mattered was that I had escaped and, by doing so, had avoided borstal or possible jail time within the Irish penal system.

After a brief wander, I arrived at the designated meeting point: Bewley's Tea House. It was a beautiful old building, smack bang in the middle of a bustling shopping street. My parents would dine there often, mostly in order for my dad to reach his weekly cake quota. On one such occasion, it had been decided that it would be the perfect location for us to regroup if something went wrong. So there I perched, at the right time and in the right place. Unfortunately there was no sign whatsoever of my parents.

Bewley's was not usually the kind of place in which a young boy could hog a table, but one of the waitresses was kind enough to look the other way. For a good while she let me be, but eventually she came over to ask if I wanted to order anything. I had very limited funds and did not want to spend the little cash I had on an unnecessary beverage. I told her I was expecting my parents at any moment and she agreed to let me wait a little longer, but told me that if they didn't turn up soon, she would need the table back.

It wasn't long before it became painfully obvious that my parents weren't coming. I had stuck to the plan meticulously and could not understand why they had not done likewise. I wondered if perhaps they had visited Bewley's earlier and hadn't seen me? If so, they would no doubt have assumed that I'd been apprehended. If that was the case, they were sure to leave Dublin without me.

I was pondering various scenarios when I received an abrupt tap on the shoulder. It was the manager. He was clearly suspicious of a young boy sitting on his own and made no secret of his desire for me to leave. I had been taking up valuable dining space for far too long and my time was up. I left without issue, nodding my thanks to the waitress as I descended the steep staircase onto the busy street below.

By now it was late afternoon and little sun remained. As I navigated my way through the streets, it dawned on me that a decision had been made on my behalf. I would have to disobey my dad's explicit instructions and risk returning to the flat. I had little choice. I had barely any money and nowhere else to run. As I walked back through the city I had to face the distinct possibility that I may well be on my own. It was a terrible realisation and I felt abandoned.

The evening air was chilly and I was ill-equipped for it, due to being jacket-less after the morning's shenanigans. No matter what time of year it was, it always seemed to be cold in Ireland; at least London had warm stretches during the summer. On the way home I made a tentative plan to leave for England the following day. Whose door I would knock on after my arrival remained something of a mystery, although I was fairly sure the skills I had learned from my parents would enable me to gain free passage back to Blighty in no time.

However, before I could commit to such a thing, I had to find out if I was, in fact, on my own. Could my parents really have left Dublin without me?

I knew that it wasn't safe to simply walk up to the front door, so I surveyed the house, keeping an eye out for any suspicious guard-like activity. I decided to position myself in a doorway opposite the end of our street to observe any movement. The squat beige house in which we lived was wedged into a terrace of similar buildings that continued in uniform towards the horizon. Our house had three outward-facing windows, but on this dark evening they shed no light.

I sat in the cold for some time. There were no comings or goings whatsoever. I kept my eyes peeled, but it soon dawned on me that nothing out of the ordinary was occurring. I was finding the temperature a little hard to bear and needed the warmth only four walls could give.

I got up from my hiding place, crossed the busy road and crept along the narrow pavement until I reached our front door. I slid my key into the lock, trying not to make any noise. The entrance gave way to a pitch-black hallway. All was piercingly quiet. Not a single light burned in the entire building.

I made my way upstairs to my bedroom (which, uncharacteristically, was separate from my parents' living quarters below), avoiding the squeaky floorboards as I went. I opened the door and fell onto my bed, exhausted from the day's events. Sleep very nearly overtook me, but I resisted; this was no time to let my guard down. I was also exceptionally hungry, but alas, all our food was locked away in my parents' flat downstairs, and that was a key with which I had never been entrusted.

In my room everything was exactly as I'd left it, the only difference being the amplified silence. Had it always been this quiet? As the night stretched on, the nothingness was only broken by the clanging of hangers inside a small, brown wardrobe, caused by the passing of any vaguely powerful vehicle. It was abundantly clear that no one had been in my room since I'd left that morning, neither my parents nor the guards. If the law had paid a visit, I was sure that my room would have been turned upside down.

After a while, I moved from the bed to the window ledge, peering down at the street. The house was relatively small and even though I was on the first floor it never really seemed that high up. I soon became lost in thought. With every passing reflection my eyelids grew heavier and fighting the urge to sleep became more difficult. However, my attention was soon drawn to a strange noise coming from outside. I could hear the distinct sound of metal on metal, and it seemed to be getting closer with every clang.

I had given up all hope of seeing my parents. I was therefore mystified by what unfolded in the street below. First my dad came into view, accent first, followed closely by my mother. Both of them appeared to be riding brand new bicycles and they were bickering avidly. My dad spotted me perched on the windowsill and waved up with surprising enthusiasm.

I was baffled. My parents were fully kitted out with camping gear, each of them wearing a bulging steel-frame rucksack complete with sleeping bags attached at the bottom. My dad also had an enormous tent strapped to the underside of his rucksack with bungy cords. It all looked extremely heavy and cumbersome. Once he dismounted, I noticed that his bike was still pressed firmly against the asphalt. The weight of overfilled saddlebags clinging to his back wheel gave the impression that it had a flat tyre. What on earth could they be carrying?

The clanging I had heard from afar was soon explained; it was my mother. Attached to the back of her rucksack was a selection of aluminium pots and pans, which swung from side to side, creating a sort of tinny rhythm in time with her pedalling.

It was difficult to know how to react to what I was witnessing. My dad seemed genuinely pleased to find that I was still at large. My mother, however, gave the initial impression that my being home and free was an inconvenience. Apparently it was my dad who had insisted on one final check of the house before they left for France.

'France?'

The look on my face must have been one of complete bewilderment. Why were they both suddenly equipped for a two-wheeled adventure? It wasn't part of any plan I'd been made aware of.

My mum was still astride her bicycle out on the street when my dad came bounding up the stairs. Up until that point, it felt like I had been watching this farce play out in slow motion; it was only when my bedroom door flew open that I finally snapped out of the trance. My dad was beaming and I half-expected a hug. This would have been the prime moment in our joint existence to deliver one, but alas it was not in his nature. Instead there were a few seconds of awkwardness and confusion followed by, 'Jesus, we thought you'd been caught', while he hovered uncomfortably in the doorway.

My father explained that they were convinced I'd been picked up by the guards, probably close to where they dropped me off that morning. Believing this to be the case, they'd decided it was best to abscond under the cover of night. But this tall tale made me somewhat suspicious. Was I some sort of patsy in all this? Had they expected me to fail from the outset? Were they hoping that my apprehension would be enough of a distraction for the guards to ensure their escape? This would certainly explain why they never bothered to show up at the tea house.

My mother had clearly become irritated with waiting outside and dragged her bicycle loudly through the hallway into their flat. It seemed that my avoiding arrest had ruined their immediate plans. I felt like excess baggage that they had hoped to shed.

My dad asked me if I had seen the letter they'd left for me. 'What letter?' I enquired. It was then that he ushered me out of my room towards a small table at the foot of the stairs, the kind that becomes overgrown with pizza menus and the unwanted post of previous tenants. Atop the pile was a small white envelope with my name on it. My dad picked it up and handed it to me.

Inside the envelope was a scruffy piece of paper with holes torn along the top. It was an insignificant scrap of notepaper that just happened to contain the first words to ever make me cry. It was an incredibly difficult read, not least because my dad's spiky handwriting could have benefitted from subtitles.

The letter explained that they were taking the night ferry to Cherbourg. They wished me luck and stated that if by some miracle I had not been apprehended, it would be best for me to make my way across the Irish Sea to my grandparents' house in London. There wasn't any money in the envelope, so how they expected me to make that particular voyage was one of life's little mysteries.

My mum had written the slightly more legible sign-off at the bottom: 'We won't forget you, son; we will come for you, love Mum & Dad'.

I looked up to see my dad's misguided smile. He was waiting for some sort of reaction, but I was finding it difficult to swallow. I folded the letter ever so carefully and slid it back into the envelope, my heart just a little more broken than before.

LONDON

1970-77

CHAPTER 1

HITTING THE SKIDS

I first filled my tiny lungs with the dying breaths of the 'Swinging Sixties', an era to which I have no affinity whatsoever. I like to think, however, that at least it meant that I was privy to a couple of momentous events, one being the subject of everyone's favourite conspiracy theory: the moon landing. My mother informed me that she watched it live on television, so I must have borne witness to Neil Armstrong's ever-quotable words, albeit from the muffled womb. I also technically attended my parents' nuptials, which apparently took place worryingly close to my first day on earth. Although there is no photographic evidence to prove this union actually took place, due to my dad's phobia of lenses, I am told that it was exactly five weeks prior to my arrival.

I was delivered in the very same ward in which my mother was born just seventeen years earlier, into a family of Irish-named 'Englanders' living in London. My twenty-year-old father was from Ireland. So, although a Londoner by birth, I was soon made aware that all roads led directly to a mysterious land called Ireland.

Shortly after I was born my parents decided to become squatters. Our chosen flat was situated within a clump of post-war, red-brick buildings a mere stone's throw from Big Ben, Westminster and many of the sights that tourists flock to on a daily basis. Like many buildings in that part of London at the time, ours was in a state of partial disrepair. Some of my earliest memories are of passing row after row of boarded-up homes while in the comfort of my perambulator. Many of the buildings were simply left in a semi-demolished state after being bombed during the Second World War. There was no rush to renovate as the city's population was somewhat smaller than it is today; not every nook and cranny was occupied as it is now.

My dad told me that around this time, many builders were offered up to two houses completely free by the council. London's housing authorities were simply handing them over to renovators in order to boost the local economy and reinvigorate neglected areas. The only caveat was that each home had to be brought up to a decent living standard. Upon completion and the passing of relevant checks, the developers were given the deeds. My dad, being a bricklayer and plasterer, was therefore in possession of the very skills necessary for such an endeavour. If only he had taken this route instead of the one he actually chose, then our lives would no doubt have been vastly different, especially considering that we would have owned two homes in London that would be worth millions of pounds in today's market.

My mother and I had initially lived with my grandparents in their small terraced house before I was whisked away to the squat that my parents had furnished with stolen treasures. My grandparents disliked my dad intensely and did not trust him one iota. They were fully aware that he was up to no good with his brothers and suspected that he was dragging my mother into mischief. Little did they know that it was, in fact, my mother who often instigated their exploits.

Once my grandparents discovered that I was living in a squat, they became concerned for my welfare. It was therefore decided that my nan would pay us a surprise visit, so she could see our living conditions first-hand. On her arrival, the door was yanked open by my mother, whom my nan suspected was high. She was also perturbed to find me asleep on the floor, swaddled in nothing more than a thin, crumpled blanket. My parents seemed unaware that I should have been getting my slumber in a crib or cot, feeling that a hard wooden floor would suffice. It's hard to know if this was due to neglect or just the inexperience of youth.

At that point my parents were dabbling with drugs and Southern Comfort, even going so far as to put a selection of hallucinogens into my bottle to witness the effects for their own amusement. I only know about this because my mum made no attempt to hide it when I was older, often speaking openly about their experiments with my milk supply. Her only regret was apparently the time she added a small amount of speed to my formula to see how long it would take me to fall asleep.

I have often wondered if all this could really be true. What kind of person would want their baby to stay awake longer, after all? Surely the opposite is preferable. It seems so incredibly stupid, but stupid they were. Add a dash of crime and a pinch of violence to the mix and you have a cocktail that was only ever going to end badly.

***

My dad's smile has always been difficult to read. On rare occasions it would surface in the same way that it would on a regular person's face: as an honest reaction to something joyful. Sometimes it could be seen creeping from one cheek to the other, riding on ripples of self-pride, usually while he was recounting his and my mother's wrongdoings. Mostly, however, it was a precursor to something else. It was very much a facial expression of his that I learned to fear. A smile from my dad often indicated that something terrible was about to happen.

One of my earliest recollections is of my father sporting very short-cropped hair, towering above me and wearing a sinister grin. Although I was very young, this memory is still accompanied by a feeling of uneasiness. Further proof, for me at least, that from the outset there was never any real trust between us.

Of course it's impossible to pinpoint the exact moment when a child's memory banks begin recording, burning images and events into their sub-conscious for access at a later date. Most children's earliest recollection is of something enjoyable: nursery, for example, a trip to the seaside, or a birthday party with friends. Mine, however, is the flashing lights of an ambulance and being carried into the back of said ambulance while some sort of argument was taking place around me. It was a frantic situation, which is why I believe this moment is firmly etched into my brain recorder.

Sometime in my first year, my dad became so enraged that he punched me square in the face, sending me flying across the room. Injured and crying, I was taken by ambulance to a nearby hospital where it was discovered I had suffered a fractured skull. My nan arrived soon after and was horrified by my injuries. She always used to tell me that this event took place when I was around five months old. My mum, however, disputes this, claiming that it was slightly later.

Whatever age I was, it was a truly abhorrent act. I have since put it down to an over-consumption of alcohol and drugs. After all, this was around the time that my dad climbed up onto a nearby roof claiming he would jump, all because he believed himself to be both indestructible and a piece of fruit, notably an orange.

The trauma of this event and the stress on my small body must have switched something on in my head. Since that day, no doubt to my parents' continued annoyance, I have been able to recall every similar incident with utmost clarity. The older I got, the clearer the memories would become. Of course I cannot remember much else, but these types of events seem to have stuck with me regardless of my age.

After this incident, it soon became apparent that there was something very wrong with my right eye. Once the swelling went down, it emerged that I had lost most of the sight in that particular eyeball. Accompanying this newfound loss of sight was a number of severe nosebleeds, which would continue throughout my childhood. I have often been told that I may well have had a dodgy eye and nose in the first place, but, even if that were true, my dad's actions certainly exacerbated the problem.

My grandparents were quite rightly perturbed. As a result of the rising tension, an altercation occurred between my dad and granddad. I have heard the story from both sides, but I like to believe that my granddad gave my dad a thorough thrashing and not the other way around. As I have witnessed only cowardice from my father, I can't imagine him actually engaging in a fight with another fully grown man.

***

The next couple of years saw my parents living the high life. They were, in their own words, 'millionaires' by today's standards. They were defrauding post offices and committing other crimes in and around London. They were joined on their escapades by my dad's youngest brother, George, and his wife, Colleen, and, occasionally, by his two older brothers, Archie and Finn.

Archie was, according to my dad, 'one bad bastard'. The story he likes to impart to illustrate Archie's temperament happened during my dad's first few days in London, fresh off the boat from Ireland. Archie was showing him around North London, when, out of nowhere, he completely lost the plot. Apparently they were having quite a cordial chat when suddenly Archie spotted someone looking at him in a way he didn't appreciate. Before my dad knew what was happening, Archie had pulled out a knife and was shoving it between the guy's teeth, rocking it from side to side until the poor fellow had what is colloquially known as 'a Glasgow smile'. This was for nothing other than a look.

My dad swears that until that moment he had no idea just how violent his brother could be. I have my suspicions that my father remained afraid of him for the rest of his life, until Archie passed away in his fifties. Not to speak ill of the dead, but Archie was considered by many to be something of a lunatic.

In the early 1970s it was relatively easy to commit fraud if you had a good system, and they did. They had devised a plan that worked incredibly well, its genius being its simplicity. It was all about opening accounts, making fake deposits and then withdrawing the non-existent funds. They would spend their days opening post office accounts in and around London using various fake names and depositing a single pound into each. Little identification was needed at the time for such things, which meant that many accounts could be opened daily with great ease. Each time they were successful they would receive a post office book pertaining to that fake name. Once an official post office franking stamp had been illegally obtained, my dad and George would work through the night entering fake deposits into each account. Various handwriting styles and signatures were used to give each entry a look of authenticity; add a thump of the official post office stamp and, hey presto, they were suddenly in the possession of accounts that, on paper at least, appeared to be full of cash. Once this phase was complete it was time to withdraw the monies that were never there in the first place.

My mother and Colleen were cast as the actors in the piece. My mum was a natural, a veritable master of the con. If any suspicion arose, she would simply ask a random question, typically something like: 'What time do you close?' Basically, anything that would distract the thought process of the teller. This is a method hypnotists still use today and I can personally vouch for its effectiveness.

My dad's older siblings were busy with their own criminal enterprises. Archie was the more experienced villain, running a separate operation in North London where he was apparently something of a feared gangland leader. He would occasionally help out with my dad's outfit, but there was some concern that he would go too far, being that he had a tendency to do whatever needed to be done, regardless of outcome.

Even David, my dad's oldest brother, who wasn't part of either gang, was a cat burglar at the time. It seems that crookedness was very much in the blood.

The last brother was the elusive Finn. Even though we would go on to live in the very same street in Ireland, I only met him once, and it was brief. I can recall standing at his front door, him peering from behind it and speaking softly. I spent the entire episode trying to make out shapes in the darkness. In later years, my dad rarely spoke to or of him, which I always found quite peculiar. Finn was a big fan of the booze and would often drink himself into oblivion. Bizarrely, regardless of his early debauchery, as my father grew older he seemed to frown upon such things. I am pretty sure he abstained from both alcohol and drugs after the age of about thirty.

But in early 1970s London the alcohol and drugs were still in full flow. My parents were young, foolish and loaded. They were having a grand old time at everybody else's expense. One thing is for certain; they were outrageously irresponsible for a couple with a child. In retrospect they were probably too young to be raising an infant.

As my parents' activities became more apparent and my dad's abusive outbursts more regular, my grandparents decided they had to act. They could not have known it at the time, but everything was about to come to a head without them having to lift a finger.

In late 1972 my dad was arrested and charged with conspiracy to defraud. This was less to do with his own antics and more to do with the company he was keeping. He managed to make bail, but instead of staying put and going to court, he decided to jump bail and go to Paris for the weekend. So, with my mum, Colleen and George in tow, he dumped me with the grandparents, drove directly to Dover and caught a ferry to France. It was quite a flashy thing to do in those days. Apart from my granddad's wartime travels, none of the family had ever left Britain and Ireland.

The Paris adventure remains something of a mystery, but I know that they ascended the Eiffel Tower for the obligatory tourist photo, ate in fancy restaurants and stayed in the best hotels, and why not? They had more money than they knew what to do with.

Once back in England, they picked up the car they'd left in Dover and began their journey home, but instead of heading directly to London to face the music, they decided to make a short detour along the coast to the small seaside town of Deal. This seemingly insignificant decision would prove to be a titanic error.

They parked the car, found a decent-enough-looking café, sat down and ordered a hearty lunch. Fresh from their Paris adventure, spirits were still running high and they were easily the loudest people in the room, which brought unwanted attention. According to my mum, George was particularly vocal and not exactly subtle either, especially when it came to paying the bill. He foolishly produced a large wad of notes from his pocket, right under the nose of the café owner, which instantly aroused her suspicions.

When they left, she followed them and took down their number plate, passing it on to the police. There had been a spate of local robberies over the weekend and she was sure that they were the culprits. She was mistaken, of course, but the die had been cast.

Moments later, a police car with flashing lights appeared in my dad's rear-view mirror. He cranked the gears and launched into full getaway mode, hitting the narrow streets of Deal at high speed. He would later say that if you want to commit a crime, 'don't do it in Kent, as there is no way out of that fucking place'. He gave it his best shot, however, flying around tiny back streets while being chased at first by one police car, then two, then many.

At one point he slowed down in order to let the others out, but they refused to leave. It was all for one and one for all as they sped forward.

Eventually my father managed to wriggle his way out of Deal, getting onto the road for Canterbury, but alas they were now in a full-on, movie-like police chase. This continued for the best part of an hour, which can only be a testament to my dad's driving skills. They were, of course, blissfully unaware that they were being chased for a crime they did not commit. They were convinced that they'd been compromised, which left them with little option but to try and outrun the police, the alternative being prison.

With a sea of screaming sirens behind them, my dad veered off the main road and into the town of Canterbury, in the hope of somehow losing the police. Unfortunately he was unable to traverse the complex inner sanctum of the old town's ancient streets and soon found himself on the verge of losing control of the speeding vehicle. With his passengers bracing for the worst, he decided the only course of action was to crash directly into a nearby brick wall. They were travelling so fast that he felt any other action would send the car into an uncontrollable flip and most likely kill all involved. Seconds before the crash my dad accidentally clipped the side of a bread van, sending various baked goods flying high into the air. A sky full of dancing bread products was the last thing he saw in the rear-view mirror before impact.

Once the dust had settled, my mum and Colleen found themselves trapped in the back, their legs wedged between the front seats and the twisted shell of the now-wrecked car. My dad and George were miraculously spared injury, despite being in the front, so they decided to make a run for it. They were of course rounded up within minutes.

The police were dumbfounded when they cracked open the boot to find a stash of fake post office books, forgery paraphernalia and thousands of pounds in cash. It was very much the end of the road. After a short trial, my dad was sentenced to seven years in prison. George received a similar term. Archie, who was apprehended later, for both his ties to my dad's outfit and his own exploits, was sentenced to spend the remainder of the decade in prison further up the country.

The women were a tad luckier. My mum and Colleen both received suspended sentences due to the fact that they both had young children. Still, my mum was now very much alone. She confided in me later that she had been seriously considering leaving my dad just before they were caught, and was thoroughly irritated that she now had no choice but to wait for him. At the time it was considered very bad form to abandon your partner while they served their time. Unfortunately my mum's luck was about to get even worse.

My grandparents decided to enact a plan they had been concocting for some time. They considered their daughter foolish to have shackled herself to a violent thug, who not only had harmed their first grandchild, but was now in jail for the next seven years. Admittedly, it was they who had forced my mother's hand in marrying him in the first place. She was pregnant, and that's just what people did in those days; to have a bastard was simply unacceptable. I assume, however, that by this point they had realised that giving in to that kind of thinking had been a gross error in judgement.

(Conversely, years later, I stumbled upon my grandparents' marriage certificate and was astonished to find that they only got married shortly before their sixth child was born, which made my mother and most of her siblings actual bastards!)

No longer content to sit back and watch my poor treatment, they decided to take charge of the situation. The next time my mother left me in their care they planned to make their move, and it was to be a pretty shitty one.

My mother soon gave them an opportunity to strike. Whenever she went to visit my dad in prison, my grandparents became babysitters. As the front door closed behind her on the day in question, the poor girl had no idea what was about to follow.

Upon returning that same evening, my mother was given some distressing news. She was told that she had lost custody of her child and that her parents were going to raise me instead. As she stood bewildered in the hallway, my grandparents deliberately blocked me from view as I ignored her cries of 'Come here, son.' Once I was out of earshot, she was told that, in her absence, they had made me 'a ward of court'. They were now my official guardians and she had lost all her rights as a mother.

This must have been tough for my mother, especially as she was actually living with my grandparents at the time. We all went to sleep in the same house that night, but the plates of my mother's world had suffered a tectonic shift. She was still exceptionally young and, although she had made numerous stupid mistakes, the very thought of what she had to endure that evening saddens me deeply. When I was eventually told about this episode as a teenager, I was furious with my grandparents for orchestrating such an unscrupulous move against their own daughter. They obviously thought they were protecting me, and they were probably right, but it still seemed just nasty to me.

Eventually the strain of her parents' actions became too much and my mother returned to the inner-city squat. Just a few weeks earlier she had been gallivanting around Paris without a care, living like a *de facto* queen. Now she was in a dingy London flat, alone, with her husband in jail and her three-year-old son removed from her care. It must have been truly awful. She was barely twenty-one years old.

My mum may have been somewhat inept, but she was the only mother I had. To lose that bond at such an early age was incredibly painful and I'm sorry to say that it later led to a lot of bad behaviour on my part, especially towards my grandparents.

CHAPTER 2

SEMI-DETACHED

With my dad in jail and my mum living alone in a squat, I was now firmly installed at my grandparents' house in North London. My life had taken a turn for the normal and I soon got used to a world without my parents. My new family consisted of my nan and granddad, plus their youngest daughter, Carol, who, although she was my aunt, was just seven years older than me. Moreover, their other children had only recently fled the coop and were young enough to still be dropping by, all too often.

I always seemed to have a favourite uncle, and in those early days this alternated between my uncles Joe and Tim. I would run towards them excitedly whenever they paid us a visit. Upon arrival, Joe would always shout 'Zippy!', a nickname he affectionately gave me when he noticed my penchant for incessant talking. Tim would simply grab me, turn me upside down and begin tickling me half to death, an interaction I enjoyed at first but soon learned to hate, as it often led to me wetting myself. Occasionally my uncles would stay late into the evening, allowing me to fall asleep listening to their indistinct voices coming from the living room below.

Either the drugs administered via my baby bottle were now finally having an adverse effect, or things were just getting plain weird on their own. Either way I was beginning to get spooked. Opposite ours was a house that boasted a distinct round window, and within its circular frame I would sometimes spot the silhouette of a young woman who possessed the longest and straightest ginger hair imaginable. The mere sight of her moving slowly within that ornate glass hoop was enough to scare me into hiding underneath my bed.

There were many images akin to this that gave me the willies as a youngster, the biggest culprit being the BBC test card. This was a still image that would be broadcast continually whenever the channel was off air, and had a disturbing image of a somewhat demonic-looking girl playing noughts and crosses with her raggedy clown doll. There was something about how she was poised before that chalkboard that I found unsettling. The way in which it hung there on the TV, unmoving, accompanied by a single high-pitched tone, was just plain creepy. In the age of twenty-four-hour television, subsequent generations have thankfully been spared seeing such things before bed.

One night, I awoke with a start. I had been asleep for a good while, so I assumed it was the middle of the night, but what I saw and heard confused me greatly. I rubbed my eyes as streaks of coloured light danced around my bedroom in the moonlight. Loud music was somehow playing within my room and voices were coming from inside the walls. To add to the weirdness, I watched as the wallpaper began melting from the walls, dripping to the floor where it pooled like candle wax. My heart was beating so fast that I could hear it. It was time to get the F out of dodge.

I jumped down from the bed and ran out of the room, deliberately not looking back. I clambered down the stairs, almost tumbling. I could hear recognisable voices coming from the living room – perhaps it wasn't as late as I'd initially thought? I figured if I made it to the voices all would be well.

Near to the bottom of the stairs, however, I came to a sudden stop. The bamboo painting of a stork that hung so proudly in our hallway looked different somehow. As I stared at that stout-billed image something odd happened: the Chinese letters that ran down its right side began to change shape. What the hell was going on here? I knew I was awake, it wasn't a dream, I could tell the difference.

I jumped over those last few steps and bolted through the door into the room with the voices. I threw myself onto the lap of the person closest to the door, which just happened to be Joe. 'Zippy!' he exclaimed.

Zippy was safe at last.

When I wasn't hiding under the bed or tripping my tits off, I was out exploring. Behind our house were a number of buildings that were in a state of utter disrepair. My particular favourite was one just a few doors down, which had rubble for rooms and a creaky half staircase that I liked to frequent.

I was in said house one afternoon when the front door opened and in walked an old man and a small white dog. He was acting very much like a fellow returning from an afternoon stroll, hanging his coat on the rusty brass hook on the back of the door and setting down his umbrella against the crumbling plaster. I assumed he was a squatter like my mother and greeted him with a friendly hello. He nonchalantly turned around, refusing to look me in the eye, and asked what I was doing in his house. I explained that I was exploring. He paused before responding, 'I think you had better leave now', at which his dog gave out a little bark as if in agreement.

I was about to answer when there was a knock at the front door. I figured it was Carol coming to join me, so I ran over to open it, protesting to the old man as I went. Carol's first words were 'Who are you talking to?' I turned around and pointed into the now-empty house. They were gone. There was no sign of the old man or his canine friend. She assumed I was messing around and continued playing as normal. I was confused. Did I imagine the entire episode? I guess I had quite the imagination.

My world was still very small. With the exception of the neglected buildings near the house, I rarely got further than the big red doorstep that my nan cleaned so obsessively. While she scrubbed that step thoroughly, I would play in the street with my plastic toolkit, disassembling my go-kart and anything else I could get my mitts on. However, on occasion, if

I promised to be well behaved, I would get to accompany her to buy dog food. Now I realise that doesn't exactly sound like a thrilling expedition, but I relished any chance to escape the street on which I lived, so a trip to the local shops was actually quite exciting.

I would accompany my nan to a parade of shops nearby where she would purchase a shallow tin of horse meat for the dogs. It was called Fido meat, a devilishly red concoction that smelled revolting.

We had two dogs and I loved them both, not that I understood what love was exactly. I saw little distinction between humans and animals at that age and considered them to be part of the family. In particular, I enjoyed the warmth they generated and would often snuggle up to them for comfort on damp winter evenings.

One afternoon, however, I woke up to the fact that they were wild animals. I was playing outside when I accidentally stood on the tail of the bigger dog. He turned on me instantly, his large pointy fangs nipping at my calves. I was shocked at how our passive dog had become such a bloodthirsty wolf in a matter of seconds. I never quite trusted him after that, but then again I never stepped on another dog either. My nan's reaction of course was to whack me round the head with a rolled-up newspaper. Standard.

***

Living with my parents in the squat soon became a faded memory and I had little concept of anything beyond the immediate neighbourhood of my grandparents' house. I only became aware of the outside world again thanks to my mother. She would visit, occasionally, taking me out for the afternoon. These visits were the most exhilarating events of my young life. I loved nothing more than getting on the bus with her and heading off to mysteriously named places like Camden Town and Notting Hill. They weren't very far away, but from my perspective they were akin to distant lands.

Having an inquisitive nature led me to ask an awful lot of questions, which could sometimes get a little embarrassing for my mother. I did not yet possess any kind of buffer and would often say whatever came into my head, regardless of location or circumstance. Being in public made little difference; in fact, I might have enjoyed the audience. On the bus home one evening, to her horror, I allegedly blurted out loudly: 'When's my dad getting out of jail?' Then, while pointing at a stranger, I asked, 'Mum, why is that man black?'

I'm not sure if my mum had some money stashed away from her fraudulent days, or if she had another scam going on; all I know is she had plenty of money and wasn't afraid to spend it. She bought me tons of cool threads during this period and I was suddenly a very well-dressed little boy. I can recall walking through the door of my grandparents' house looking pretty dapper in bright-red tartan trousers and a matching scarf.

Our outings, however, came with a curfew. My mum was under strict instructions to bring me home before dark, something she occasionally, intentionally, forgot. Most notable was an afternoon spent in the company of some real-life hippies in a North London squat. I can still see them now: puffing on thin joints, wearing their collective John Lennon glasses, staring in awe at the colour television set one of them had somehow acquired. It was very much the talking point of the gathering. I had never seen a colour TV either and was aware that it was something special. Can you imagine such a thing? Seriously, sometimes I feel as if I was born in the 1800s!

Whenever my mum left me back at my grandparents, I would feel abandoned. I didn't quite understand why I felt this way, as I rarely thought of her when she wasn't around. However, whenever I watched her leave I would grow angry and resentful towards those around me, over time becoming something of a problem child. I was, of course, way too young to understand the intricacies of the complex situation I was caught up in, but I knew one thing: I was immensely pissed off.

After the visit to the hippies' flat, the next time I saw my mother she was on crutches. I was aware that there had been an incident as she hadn't visited in a while, but I did not know the details. I only found out some time later that she had very nearly been murdered.

My mother was at her sister-in-law Colleen's flat when a man wielding a knife burst through the door and tried to attack the two of them. He had just stabbed someone else in the same building, so I have to assume he entered with an already bloodied knife. A terrified Colleen managed to escape, although, bizarrely, she left her kids locked in the bedroom. My mum was not quite so lucky, subsequently finding herself trapped in the first-floor flat with Mr Stabby McStabby heading towards her. She felt certain that she was about to be killed.

As he lunged at her in the living room, she pushed over various items in the hope of blocking his path, while simultaneously looking for a viable exit. Unfortunately there was only one way out, and it was downward. After dancing around the furniture, she ended up outside on the small balcony. The man then let out a blood-curdling scream as he charged towards her, knife outstretched. But it was too late. She had already jumped.

The impact was severe, but it was preferable to a madman's knife. The attacker thankfully fled, but the break my mother suffered was serious. She remained on crutches for many months and to this day walks with a partial limp. I became extremely protective of my mother over the following years and I wonder if seeing her on crutches, looking vulnerable, ignited that particular spark.

While she was recovering from her ordeal, there was another worrying incident involving her, this time at my grandparents' house. It was during this altercation that I first feared for my mother's safety and realised in the process just how powerless I was.

One afternoon, during one of my mum's visits, we were outside in the front garden, when out of nowhere came the sound of screeching tyres. A van came hurtling around the corner into our street and stopped abruptly outside the front gate. The driver slammed the door and stormed angrily around to the front of the vehicle, hurling abuse at my mother with each stride. He was heading straight for her, getting closer with each poisonous word.

The man looked creepy. He was almost completely bald with just a few inches of cotton-thin hair clinging to each side of his lemon-shaped head. He was sporting a delusional comb-over, which only added to his menace. His clothes were dusty and tan brown. He fumbled with the latch of the gate, spitting out curse words and revealing his nicotine-yellow teeth. He clearly intended to hurt my mother, but all I could do was stand beside her, feeling feeble. I wanted so desperately to protect her but was too young to be of any use.

'Why don't you fuck off?' said my mum, her standard response to such situations, which of course only inflamed the already tense atmosphere. The man then broke through the gate and I braced myself; I was sure that my mum was about to get very badly hurt right in front of me.

It was then that the front door flew open, revealing two angry uncles. They had heard the commotion and come running to protect their sister. They told the man to leave or they would 'kick the shit out of him'. Spooked, he turned on his heels and left under a torrent of abuse, getting back in his van and driving off into the cloudy sunset. I still have no idea what that incident was about and I seem to be the only person who remembers it.

Until that day I had no idea that people could simply turn up at your door and cause trouble like that. I guess I was yet to fully learn that the world could be a dangerous place. Feeling helpless troubled me greatly, but I soon realised that there were a lot of things that I would just have to get used to. Feeling powerless was just one of them.

***

Sometime in the middle of 1974 the house began to fill up with furniture, all of it brand new and covered in thick plastic. My grandparents had decided to move to an up-and-coming suburb east of the city.

During those final days in North London something strange occurred. The entire family was present and everyone was in fine spirits. There was a sort of celebration taking place, which I can only assume was held to toast their move, while raising a glass to the old house that had served them so well. New furniture was cluttering up every spare inch, making the house difficult to navigate. Eventually, the party moved upstairs to the front bedroom and the conversation became progressively louder the more everyone drank. A brand-spanking-new white sofa sat awkwardly in the middle of the room, but nobody dared sit on it for fear of ruining it before the big move. Next to it stood a dark-glass coffee table, its legs temporarily protected by corrugated cardboard and cellophane.

It was while my family was standing in this room that something odd supposedly happened. Again I stress: allegedly. Both my granddad and Tanya (my uncle Joe's future wife) swore they saw it. Apparently the glass table became awash with letters, a slow-moving, illegible scrawl that neither of them could quite make out, but later decided was English, written upside down in mirror image. It vanished before they had a chance to fully understand it, but both agreed it was some kind of warning. My granddad and Tanya then asked if the others present had seen anything odd. They most definitely had not. The rest of the family thought they were either messing around or had perhaps consumed too much party sauce.

Deflated that nobody had witnessed their vision, they both then looked up to see my mother standing silent and still, but not as her twenty-two-year-old self. Instead, she appeared as an older woman, dressed head-to-toe in black with one visible rotten tooth. My granddad later told me they got the distinct impression that she was alone, possibly grieving.

Well, that's quite the story, I thought, disbelieving every word of it, no matter how many times it was relayed to me throughout my childhood. That is until about a decade or so later, when my mother opened her mouth, and there it was. Right there in her gob stood a solitary black tooth.

It should be stated quite clearly that I am not a believer in the paranormal. Although I have witnessed many questionable events first-hand, I prefer to look for scientific explanations wherever possible. I do, however, believe anything is technically possible, considering that we are essentially hairless chimps clinging to a rock as it catapults itself through space. Being proved wrong is no bad thing, but I have yet to see anything tangible with my own eyes to make me believe in such things. But hey, even the atheist hopes they're wrong, right?

A few days after this party, I found myself inside the cab of the removal lorry. Uncle Tim had been given the privilege of driving us to our new house and I was going to travel the entire way with him in the front seat. To say that I was excited would have been an understatement. I was both intrigued by the process of moving and thrilled to be going somewhere new. The lorry contained glass-bottomed corners through which I could see the road below, and throughout the journey I crawled right down into them to look down at the road markings passing by. Tim switched on the radio just in time for Elton John's 'Goodbye Yellow Brick Road' to kick in as we pulled away. We both sang along to the high parts, waving as we went.

CHAPTER 3

LEGOLAND

In our new East London suburb, houses were laid out over a much wider area than in North London. Our previous home had seemed to merge into the building next door, but here everything appeared separate and spacious. Gone were the claustrophobic cobbled streets of old, replaced by open skies and tree-lined avenues in which to roam. It was wondrous. Our new house was quite small inside, but typical for the period; it also resembled every other dwelling on the street exactly. My granddad attempted to make his mark by building a small rockery in the front garden, but alas the neighbours found it unsightly and demanded it be removed. Uniform, it seemed, was very much in vogue.

I was now attending my first proper school, which was so close that I could roll out of bed and practically land in the classroom. It was odd being out of the house for the entire day and I wasn't sure I liked it. What I did like, though, were girls, and I made sure I was near one at all times, preferably one called Jennifer. I had put my arm around her one morning in class, which resulted in me 'feeling kind of funny'. It was a nice sensation, one which I attempted to repeat with some vigour. My newfound passion, however, soon landed me in hot water with the teachers, most notably when I decided to take the game of kiss chase to a new level. I thought it was perfectly acceptable to chase any girl I fancied around the playground in an attempt to kiss her, regardless of whether she was into it or not. *What could possibly be wrong with that?* I thought.

I soon developed quite the imagination and no sooner had I started school than I became convinced that a secret railway ran underneath my classroom. While looking through a grill of leaves at playtime, I was sure I heard a rattling sound, followed by something seeming to speed by beneath my feet in the darkness. It gave me quite the start. I was utterly convinced it was a phantom train. I gathered my friends and went back to investigate, but we could never find anything concrete.

I would often come up with this sort of adventure in order to try to 'solve' a mystery. During one such escapade, I ended up falling off a tree stump quite hard, which resulted in a rather bad injury to my knee. As the blood poured out, I became queasy and had to be accompanied to the school nurse. I can still smell the iodine she applied that morning, turning my knee a strange sort of yellow.

Another outlet for my imagination was LEGO. I was a big fan of those coloured, interlocking shapes and as my sixth birthday approached I became very excited at the prospect of getting my hands on some new pieces.

My nan organised a birthday party, inviting a few of my classmates to the house, but I wasn't too keen on the idea. I was resigned to the fact that I had to see these snotty-nosed kids at school, but that didn't mean I wanted them running around my actual house. As they began to arrive, I was sulking, busying myself by making toy farmyard animals dance to songs such as 'Bohemian Rhapsody', a newfound favourite pastime, using records borrowed from my granddad's record collection.

The melancholy lifted in time for the present-opening ritual, my fingers excitedly ripping the thin wrapping paper to shreds. And lo and behold, LEGO! I gained a number of new blocks and set about playing with them pronto, but on my own, of course.

The party was going pretty well until my nan suggested that I share some of my new Danish plastic with the other children. *Yeah right, I don't think so*, I thought, and carried on regardless. I was quite protective of my belongings and since I'd seen the other kids picking their noses, I didn't want their bogeys all over my nice new LEGO.

It also bothered me that the other kids were building structures with no colour co-ordination whatsoever out of my older LEGO blocks, stacking random blocks atop each other without regard. There was clearly a lack of discipline in their creative efforts and I had no intention of letting them get their grubby, unskilled hands on my brand new blocks, not on my watch.

My nan, spotting my continued refusal to share, insisted that I divvy out my new bricks. At the time I had a rather large green LEGO base in my hand and thought, 'Right, okay, if you want me to share, fine, I'll share.' I stood up, calmly walked over to the sideboard, retrieved a large pair of scissors and then set about cutting the LEGO base in half. It didn't quite work at first so I had to bend it back and forth in order to get it to finally snap. I did this completely out of view of the others, then casually walked back over to one of the kids in attendance and handed him the brutalised LEGO base, right in front of my nan. 'There you go,' I said, sat back down and carried on as before.

My nan was livid, but I felt justified in that moment. Destroying my own toys to prove a point was the only way I knew to show her how upset I was about being forced to share.

It sounds ridiculous now, of course, but at the time I didn't really enjoy hanging out with other kids, much less sharing my things with them. I was definitely a little spoiled by my grandparents, but it wasn't just that. I can still remember thinking that they should use their own toys and not come round to my house and put their dirty mitts all over mine. It just felt plain rude to me.

My mum arrived later that day, improving my mood dramatically. I missed her dearly, as her visits were rare. Every time she visited it felt like Christmas. As the party appeared to be winding down, she asked if she could perhaps take me out for a while. My nan reluctantly agreed but forcefully reminded her not to stray too far and to bring me back before nightfall. So off we trotted. Me and my mum. I was happier than I had been all day.

I assumed we were simply going to the local shops, but once we got to the main road we immediately hopped on a bus. It was only when we were on the tube, heading towards Central London, that I realised something was amiss. But my mum seemed calm and didn't appear to be bothered, so neither was I.

We continued to travel for about an hour, eventually ending up at my aunt Colleen's flat under cover of darkness. The first thing I spotted was a small set of drums in the corner, apparently a recent present for my cousin who had also just celebrated a birthday. From my perspective this seemed like an extravagant gift. 'Are they rich?' I wondered. My mum and Colleen chatted the night away, drinking, smoking and laughing into the wee hours. When they spotted my eyes getting heavy, I was given a pop-up bed in which to slumber. It was situated right there in the sitting room, so I ended up falling asleep to the sound of their voices. I was acutely aware that this was not where I was supposed to be and that it was bound to cause a problem upon my return – if I was, in fact, returning.

The following day, after breakfast, we headed back to my grandparents' house as if nothing out of the ordinary had occurred. Again my mum appeared completely calm. 'Is she playing some sort of game?' I wondered.

It became apparent just how serious the situation was the moment we approached the house. The front door was slightly ajar and inside I could see two policemen talking with my grandparents. The second we were spotted my nan came running towards me, while the police chased my mother, who had legged it. She was quickly apprehended and taken into custody. As she was no longer my legal guardian, her actions were tantamount to kidnapping. There was a great deal of shouting as they led her away. It was all extremely upsetting.

Although I was very young, I was taken aside and told I had to promise to never go anywhere with my mother ever again, as she could no longer be trusted. I was told that she regularly took drugs and that her erratic behaviour was a direct danger to my well-being; anything could have happened, apparently. If I wanted to be safe I had to promise to stay with my grandparents and never stray. The vibe I was picking up seemed to suggest that I was somehow complicit in my own disappearance, which I did not appreciate.

This was the day when I became aware of my 'ward of court' status and the sad fact that the state was effectively my parent. I had never even heard the term before that morning. I was informed that my grandparents were my current guardians but that the situation could easily change should I misbehave or become unruly. If for some reason my grandparents felt they could no longer tolerate my behaviour, I could be taken into care. This was shocking news and something I would be threatened with throughout my childhood.

So there I stood, a just-six-year-old boy, forced into promising not to see his own mother. It was an impossible situation. All I ever wanted was to be with my mum; she was fun and I adored her. From that day forth, I felt imprisoned in my grandparents' house. Living with them became a punishment. Admittedly, I had no idea what kind of person my mother was – she was clearly a little selfish and could be inconsiderate – but my connection to her felt incredibly strong. I longed to run away and find her, but I had no idea where she lived. It was all so bloody tragic, now that I think about it.

CHAPTER 4

BALANCING ACT

I have never been a religious individual. However, around the time of my sixth birthday, my nan got it into her head that I should pray nightly before bed. My slumber was henceforth delayed by the recital of the scariest verse imaginable for a young child. With elbows dug deep into my mattress, hands clasped firmly together and eyelids squeezed, I would ask a supposedly benevolent God to spare my soul:

> *Now I lay me down to sleep,*
> *I pray the Lord my soul to keep,*
> *If I should die before I wake,*
> *I pray the Lord my soul to take.*
> *Amen.*

This used to scare the living bejesus out of me. Until I started saying this prayer aloud, it had never crossed my mind that I might one day die. It gave me a sense of mortality that I could have done without for a few more years at least. This newfound demand to pray was strange too, given that neither of my grandparents seemed particularly religious. The only time I had been inside a church was for my own misguided christening.

My granddad, in particular, had been suspicious of the clergy for most of his life. He would proudly recount stories of how he'd chased priests away from the house whenever they came to the door. Often they would demand that my mum and her siblings attend Mass, to which he would reply, 'Fuck off', while apparently chasing them down the garden path with a poker, or some other household weaponry. Therefore, I have to assume that the God stuff was coming solely from my nan, who had been brought up a tad more devout.

On Christmas Eve 1975 I became over-excited at the prospect of receiving presents and refused to go to bed. I was watching Dick Emery on television and laughing loudly when I noticed that my nan had become unusually irritated. She then uttered the worst sentence I had ever heard up to that point: 'If you don't go to bed right now, you will die in the middle of the night.'

That stopped me in my tracks. She had my attention.

She then explained that God was watching and would not allow me to wake up the next day if I didn't start behaving myself and go to bed. I didn't need telling twice. I ran upstairs at lightning speed and threw myself under the covers. I wasn't taking any chances. My nan followed soon after to check if I was actually in bed, and I recall asking her if I would in fact be okay, as I was now understandably terrified of dying in the night. What if I couldn't fall asleep? Would God punish me for that? She refused to answer; instead she simply turned off the light, closed the door and left. Admittedly I was being a brat, but it was a pretty awful thing to say to a young child.

With all this God talk, I started to have some very odd dreams, often incorporating my nan's dire warning. In one, a man without a face was banging nails into a fence with his bare hands. I approached cautiously to ask what he was doing, but, just as he was about to speak, I woke up. I told my nan about it and she explained to me nonchalantly that it was obviously Jesus. He had clearly come to tell me to 'mend my ways'. It was that simple.

From that moment on I prayed avidly. I became a little self-conscious in the knowledge that I was constantly being observed and judged by an invisible being and that everything I did was of consequence. It felt like an invasion of privacy, but there wasn't much I could do about it. God was watching.

I prayed for many things, but mostly I prayed for harm to come to a boy who lived opposite me. His name was Dave and he was a bully. Not only was he older than me, he was massive. He was what you might call a lummox. He would often wait for me after school and accost me before I could get to my front door. No matter what I did to avoid him, he would always manage to catch me, whereby he would sit on top of me and punch my torso. If I tried to outsmart him by walking home the long way round, he would somehow fathom that I'd changed my route and be waiting behind a random hedgerow. I could not stand that fat bastard. He made my life a fucking misery.

Thankfully, it soon became clear that, while my prayers were not going to be answered via harm, it seemed they had been heard. Although we'd left North London just eighteen months earlier, cardboard boxes once again began arriving at the house. My grandparents had found a dwelling they preferred a couple of miles away in a more open setting. The shops were a lot closer and the house was more spacious, plus it had a much bigger back garden. It was so large that my grandparents installed a swing, just for little old me. This was a grandiose move and I felt incredibly spoiled.

Once we moved in, I sat on that swing every day, trying to get as high as I possibly could without flying off. I would sing while I swung, making up silly songs, amusing myself for hours. I loved it.

There always seemed to be a number of large black slugs around my swing, but my nan soon got rid of them. She appeared with a giant tub of salt one afternoon and started sprinkling it onto the poor mites. I watched as they shrivelled up and died right there at my feet. I thought it was an unnecessarily cruel act and ran inside, grossed out. My nan scooped them up, calling them 'black bastards' in the process. She was clearly racist when it came to slugs.

We had a very kind neighbour at the time, a widower who grew various vegetables and herbs in his garden. One of the things he liked to grow was mint and he would hand my granddad a bushel over the fence every Sunday without fail. My granddad would finely chop it and turn it into mint sauce for the Sunday dinner. I couldn't get enough of the stuff. My granddad was very much the cook, though my nan did help out a bit. Every Sunday we would sit around the table together and consume nothing short of a feast. For four decades, to my granddad's continual dismay, my nan would serve him a large portion of Brussels sprouts. He detested them and would remind her every week, but she would plonk a ladleful of those bad boys on his plate regardless. I am sure she was doing it on purpose, just to wind him up. It kind of became a thing. The best part of the meal, however, was my granddad's Yorkshire puddings. They were legendary.

Inevitably, I had to move school, and my days were now being spent at the nearby infant school. The playground was enormous compared to my previous school, plus they had a lot more toys to play with. At break time a vast selection would be laid out for us all to use, my absolute favourite being the big bike. I was one of the few kids who could ride without stabilisers, thanks to my granddad, so I tried to get my hands on it as often as possible. This led to me developing something of a competitive streak. When the bell rang I would push the other kids out of the way to rush to the playground so I could get to the big bike before anyone else. Most of the time I managed this feat, until the teachers began to notice my hogging of said bicycle and forced me to share, which I, of course, hated. Watching other kids' attempts at balancing frustrated me so much that I had to look away.

I clearly preferred solo experiences over shared activities. Riding around the playground gave me a much-needed feeling of separation. For a few minutes a day I was able to do my own thing without interference. There was nothing on earth I liked anywhere near as much as riding that bicycle. Although I was going round in circles, it still felt like a step towards freedom.

My time at this school was short-lived, however, as I became somewhat unruly. One of the teachers reprimanded me for something forgettable and her tone upset me. I thought she was being particularly unfair and took instant offence. Therefore, I decided to seek vengeance.

During that same day's lunch break, I walked across the playground towards her office, picking up a discarded red brick mid stroll. She was sifting through a selection of folders on her desk when our eyes met through the window. The next thing she saw was shards of glass flying and a brick landing squarely on her desk with an almighty thud. She was more than a little surprised. I then turned and calmly walked away. I wasn't bothered at all by what I had done. I felt completely justified.

My nan was immediately summoned to the school. I was given a dressing down and ordered to pay five pounds towards the repair of the window. It was to come out of my daily sweets money, five pence a day for a hundred days. (My nan did reduce my funds for a few days but gave in soon after.)

As for the school window, I can only assume that my grandparents paid for it up front. I'm sure five pounds would have seriously cut into their finances in those days. It was clear that I was becoming a bit of a handful.

CHAPTER 5

MEETING MY MAKER

My father did not believe I was his son. My mother spent many years trying to convince him that I was, in fact, his offspring, but he point-blank refused to believe her. Trust me, I no more wanted to be his son than he wanted to be my father. For a time I suspected that his friend, Brendan, could have been my real dad. I used to imagine that one day Brendan would turn up to save me from my impostor of a father's clutches. No such luck; we were stuck with each other.

My mother did have a brief relationship with Brendan shortly before my dad came on the scene, so my suspicions were not completely unfounded. Once they broke up my mother simply moved on to the next guy in line: my father. What she saw in a shaven-headed thief with a penchant for raw crumpets is a mystery.

I have since recovered a photograph of myself, aged four, that was sent to my dad while he was in jail. My mum later explained that it was the picture she sent to him in order to prove that I was in fact his son. He had often accused her of sleeping around while they were together, and she hoped he would finally see the resemblance in the photo and believe her once and for all. The message on the reverse side reads:

> *Dear Husband*
> *This is our, 'your' son.*
> *I love you*

Maybe this explains his early animosity towards me. He perhaps assumed that I was the result of an indiscretion on my mother's part and saw me as a reminder of that infidelity.

During the blazing hot summer of 1976 my dad walked free from prison. He had kept his head down, earning himself an early release for good behaviour. I heard the news via my grandparents, but I paid it no regard. I had little memory of him and could not have cared less. I was aware of his existence, of course, but, as I had only heard bad things, he rarely entered my thoughts. My father was a complete stranger, an unknown quantity. Even the idea of having a dad was now a peculiar concept.

Nine months had passed since my mother took me on that little birthday excursion and relations were finally beginning to thaw. She was visiting more often and on one occasion she asked if she could take me to the nearby shops. She claimed that she wanted to buy me a treat. My nan tentatively agreed, telling her to neither stray too far nor be too long. It must have been pretty demoralising to be told what you can and can't do with your own child, but at the same time I can certainly now understand my nan's reticence.

Just a few yards from the front door we came to a stop. My mum asked me to stand still and wait. The prospect of sweets meant that I was keen to get to the shops as soon as possible and so I protested. My mother told me that she had a surprise for me, but it had to remain a secret. I agreed, as long as we could go to those pesky shops afterwards. To be honest, I'd have agreed to anything for the promise of confectionery. She reiterated that on no account could I tell a soul, especially my grandparents. Again I agreed. I was pretty sure I could keep my mouth shut about whatever it was she was banging on about.

It was then that I saw him. My mum was waving at an odd-looking fellow approaching from the other side of the road. I remained stationary as this strange man with long hair approached my mother and embraced her. He then came over to me, leaned in and said something in an accent I could not understand. I did not get a very good vibe from him at all; in fact, he made me nervous. I certainly didn't trust him and of course I had no clue that he was my father. My only memory of my dad was of a shaven-headed, thin-lipped thug staring down at me with odd intent. This guy looked nothing like that. In fact, he resembled one of the three musketeers. My mum later told me that it was after this meeting that he finally believed I was his son. He took one look at me, saw the family nose and that was that.

This secret rendezvous lasted just a few minutes, ending with a quick kiss for my mother before he hot-footed it back to wherever he'd come from. My mum was still waving to him as he shrank to a thin, black line, before vanishing into the summer heat.

'Who was that?' I asked.

My mum paused for a second before uttering four unforgettable words: 'That was your father.'

I was both taken aback and excited by what had just occurred. My mum reminded me to keep schtum as we turned and headed back towards the house. I was a little miffed that we weren't actually bothering to go to the shops and wondered why on earth I should honour the deal when she hadn't delivered on her promise of sweets. Still, I had no intention of getting my mum into trouble and was sure I could hold my tongue.

Alas, as soon as I walked into the living room, excitement took over. I blurted out the line that would guarantee my mother would never be able to take me anywhere again. 'I just saw my dad!' I exclaimed.

My nan and granddad were livid and my mum was suitably horrified. A row erupted and she was thrown out of the house and told to stay away for good.

I guess I wasn't the kind of person who could keep a secret after all.

***

My mum sort of gave up after that and she and my dad moved to Ireland. I blamed myself. If I hadn't opened my big mouth perhaps she wouldn't be living hundreds of miles away. I missed her terribly. Although I had no concept of who my parents really were, I wanted to live with them regardless. Being a nan kid was in no way an advantage and I was jealous of my schoolmates' apparently normal lives.

At times, my frustration and anger couldn't help but bubble over. One evening, my favourite television programme, *Top of the Pops*, was on. I would often watch this with my aunt Carol, usually before my nan arrived home from work. I was an avid fan and looked forward to Thursday evenings for this very reason. On this particular evening, just as the show was about to start, Carol demanded that I go to my room. She wanted to watch on her own. I immediately took offence and refused to leave. However, Carol managed to manhandle me upstairs and into my room, then closed the door.

Once inside I became enraged and could not control my growing anger. Suddenly, without regard, I punched my window in frustration. The glass shattered in all directions and it was then that I heard a voice swearing in the street below. I peered down in horror to see my nan picking pieces of glass off her coat. The shards had fallen onto her and had scattered along the entire garden path. She was pretty unimpressed, especially as she was getting home from a hard day's work.

I felt no pain whatsoever until I noticed my arm was covered in blood. This was due to the huge piece of glass sticking into the flesh of my right hand. It had gone in one side and out the other, and it was beginning to smart, to say the least.

My nan came bounding upstairs, entered my room and began hitting me around the head with her bag. Still, I was a tad more concerned about my hand, which was bleeding. A lot. Our family didn't really do hospitals, so there were no stitches in my childhood, only plasters.

I regretted punching the window, but it was too late for sorry. My nan was seriously pissed off as she stood in my room, screaming at me with glass in her hair.

My behaviour was spiralling downward and I felt like I had very little control over it. One thing was certain: I was becoming one angry little boy.

CHAPTER 6

ALL ETIQUETTE, NO CHARM

In the early summer of 1976 I did a very bad thing. I was visiting an aunt and uncle when an abhorrent event occurred. Although I was just six years old at the time, it is in no way an excuse for what happened.

Lenny was my mother's oldest brother and just happened to be married to my father's oldest sister, Aoife. Confused? I realise it all sounds incredibly incestuous, but I assure you it is more common than you would think. Lenny was a friendly man with a timid nature and I was particularly fond of him during this period. Whenever he visited he didn't attempt to tickle me to the point of wetting myself, something I was beginning to get a little sick of. Neither did he call me names like Zippy, an initially amusing remark that was also getting a little old. I had the utmost respect for Lenny. He would often take me out in his work lorry for the day and we would drive around delivering all kinds of goods until the sun went down. I enjoyed his company immensely.

Lenny was given a particularly hard time by my granddad while growing up and it showed in his demeanour. He never quite managed to garner his father's approval and in many ways ended up gaining the mantle of the black sheep of the family. His wife is my dad's older sister and, although I know little of her, I have always thought her to be one of the kinder members of their clan. I even adapted a song called 'Fuzzy Wuzzy' to describe her hair at the time. I used to make myself laugh out loud by singing this lyric while climbing ever higher on my swing in the back yard:

Fuzzy Wuzzy was a bear,
Fuzzy Wuzzy had no hair,
Fuzzy Wuzzy wasn't fuzzy was he?
He cut his hair off and gave it to Aoife.

I guess you had to be there.

The weekend in question began with Lenny coming to pick me up in his car. It wasn't too long after my mum had sprung the surprise meeting with my dad on me, and both Lenny and Aoife were aware of the trouble I had caused my parents; they weren't best pleased. Once I got to their house they were very vocal about the grief I had caused by opening my big mouth. I had single-handedly managed to ostracise his sister and her brother (stay with me) in one fell swoop. So it was under this cloud of awkwardness that we embarked on our weekend together. I liked them both very much, but on this occasion I was pissed off at them for making me feel bad about something I felt had nothing to do with either of them.

Their flat was in the middle of a huge housing estate, the kind where the exit out of the rabbit warren is never obvious, and I felt a little trapped within its confines. The whole area was uniform and dull and seemed a world away from the street I lived on. No sooner had I settled in than I caused them, and myself, unforgettable anguish. I am a little patchy when it comes to the exact details surrounding this incident and I've since been told that I built it up to be far worse than it actually was. Still, the memory is pretty hard to shake.

This is what I know: I was wandering around the estate on my own, feeling irritated, when I came across a baby in a pram. Yes, it's going to be that bad. I was immediately overcome with a desire to inflict harm upon this poor mite. I got a feeling in my teeth not unlike when you burn your gums on hot tea and I became a little tingly. The next thing I knew I was hitting the baby.

Lord knows why I did this. I cannot fathom why I committed such a reprehensible act. Regardless of age, I should have known better. It seemed that wherever I went, drama followed. However, it was nearly always of my own creation.

My memory of the aftermath is hazy, but I recall some sort of commotion involving the parents of the baby, before I was dragged back to the flat by my uncle.

It was obvious that I was in dire straits. Lenny and Aoife were looking at me differently – not just angry, but also a little scared. What the hell would I do next? After a verbal thrashing, the weekend was cut short and I was promptly returned to my grandparents that same evening. There was a lot of shouting at the house that night and I was sent to bed without food. My nan and granddad were disgusted by my behaviour and did not want to see my face.

I tried to understand why I had been so violent, but concluded that it was simply an urge I could not resist. I wanted to cause pain because I could, and I acted upon that want. I was an animal that day.

**

It was after this disturbing event that things became rather serious. My grandparents felt they could no longer control my behaviour, so it was decided I would spend the rest of that particular summer away from my family.

I had often been threatened with being taken into care, though this was not quite that, apparently. My grandparents had contacted a day centre for troubled children not too far away and it was agreed that I would be taken in. At first I would spend just a couple of days there to see how I got on, and then, if all went well, I would spend the remainder of the summer with this 'surrogate family', learning how to behave properly.

This was very bad news. I was suddenly facing my worst nightmare. I became convinced that I was, in fact, being taken into care and they simply weren't telling me. My suspicions were aroused further when I asked my nan how long I would be away and she refused to give me a straight answer, avoiding the question completely.

The centre itself was a bit like a small school masquerading as a home and it was very much a family affair. There was a mother and a father figure and a whole bunch of foster kids, some of whom were strays like me, while a few others were from care homes. This was a very different environment to what I was used to and it was pretty scary.

The father was a stern individual, who shouted at me every chance he got. Mostly he seemed to have a problem with the way I used my knife and fork. In his opinion, I was using my cutlery the wrong way round. So I had to endure ridiculous lessons in manners and etiquette, which I could not have given two shits about. Another gripe of his was lip smacking. If I so much as made one saliva-based sound with my mouth during mealtime, he would scream across the table at me, and heaven forbid that one of my elbows land upon the tabletop, as that would turn him blue with anger. I could not fathom why he was getting so excited about such unimportant things. Personally I thought the man to be something of a maniac.

The other kids were about as keen on me as I was on them and, unsurprisingly, I failed miserably when it came to fitting in. As it was effectively a juvenile detention centre, the kids were of varying ages and the older ones very much ruled the roost. The older kids would constantly bully the younger kids and make our lives a living hell. It was a terrible state of affairs and I made plans to run away at the earliest opportunity, though I had no idea where I would run to exactly.

It was a horrid cocktail of troubled youngsters masquerading as a nuclear family and I despised it with my entire being. Weeks passed, but there was zero contact from my family. There were no visits, phone calls or letters, nada. It was a blackout. I was encouraged to accept and embrace my new family, which made my anger rise. *This is not my family,* I thought.

I was getting the distinct impression that I had been abandoned and was probably never going home again. Was I now in care? It was terrible not knowing. The entire episode was, of course, my own doing, but the knowledge that I had single-handedly caused my own downfall was hard to bear.

As the weeks rolled by, I got into a groove and did what was asked of me, albeit reluctantly. The other kids had begun whispering about a trip to the seaside and I became intrigued. It transpired that, as a reward for our good behaviour, we were to be taken on holiday during the last week of summer. *That doesn't sound too bad,* I thought. The location was to be the rather mysterious-sounding Butlin's in Skegness, a hundred or so miles north of London.

We travelled by coach for a few hours, arriving at Butlin's by late afternoon. The holiday park looked like the epitome of fun. There were numerous rides and shows, and loads to do. Best of all there was a futuristic monorail that ran above the entire resort. It was a far cry from the boredom of the day centre and I instantly became upbeat.

By the time we arrived at our allocated chalets most of the beds were already taken and the few remaining options were snatched up by the older kids the second we entered. I ended up with the last possible option: a small, unmade bed near the door. It didn't even have any sheets on it. Not a problem. One of the workers went off to retrieve my bedding, returning moments later with two sheets. The next thing I knew my roommates were pointing at me and laughing. At Butlin's, the boys' beds were made up with blue sheets and the girls' beds with pink. Unfortunately for me the man had returned with the only sheets available: bright-pink ones. The other kids took the piss out of me continually that night, but I thought it nonsensical. Why should it matter what colour your bloody sheets were?

I enjoyed my time in Skegness and it definitely felt like a reward of sorts. There was a new rumour going around in those final days, but this time it only applied to a few of us. The non-lifers, myself included, were apparently going home after the holiday. I became excited but also nervous. I hadn't seen my family for some time and wondered how they would react upon my return.

We went back to London in the same coach, but instead of dropping us at the day centre, it ended its journey in a dusty car park. Through the muddied glass I could see my nan waiting for me. It was true. I was going home. Thank the Lord!

I had acquired a *Planet of the Apes* mask while in Skegness and had become rather attached to it, wearing it constantly. I loved the way it mimicked my jaw movement. However, when my nan saw me disembark from the coach with said mask around my neck, she ripped it from my person and threw it directly into a nearby bin. As she dragged me off towards the car, she reminded me how she'd explicitly told me that I wasn't allowed a monkey mask. Apparently, I had asked for one previously. We travelled back in complete silence that day. It was not the greatest of homecomings.

However, I had survived my prison sentence and was grateful to finally be going home. I learned a valuable lesson that summer and vowed to behave myself from that moment on. I was convinced that I had experienced the worst of times and things could only get better.

CHAPTER 7

UNDER THE INFLUENCE

1977 was very much the year in which I first travelled properly, and by properly I mean across a body of water. I found myself in Ireland twice in the space of just six months. The first time I visited Ireland was with my nan, shortly after the Queen's Silver Jubilee celebrations. Somehow, despite the family mistrust, it was agreed that we would travel together to visit my parents for a whole fortnight. My granddad abstained due to his intense hatred of my father, but my nan missed her faraway daughter and felt the need to reach out.

And so it was that I found myself aboard a bus hurtling through the patchwork-quilt landscape that is the Welsh countryside, heading for an overnight ferry that was set to take a whopping twelve hours. I experienced my fair share of nightmares regarding Ireland prior to the trip, mostly consisting of people running around in balaclavas with guns drawn while bombs exploded nearby. The news had obviously managed to seep into my subconscious, although I had clearly failed to grasp the divide between the North and the South of the country.

The overnight ferry was extremely rough and took its toll on my untravelled stomach. I spent most of the night on deck fighting seasickness – and failing miserably. I finally drifted off and in the morning awoke to see the motherland off the starboard side. My initial impression was of a lush green and empty land. I had never seen another country before. Well, besides Wales.

When we arrived in port my parents were waiting. My dad had recently purchased a Ford Cortina, a car that was quite chic at the time. It was a sweet ride and dark-green in colour; everything in Ireland appeared to be green. My parents had recently made the switch back to automobiles after being thrown from their respective mopeds over the course of a couple of days. Thankfully they sustained only cuts and bruises, but it was enough to put them off riding motorbikes for good. However, being inside the relative safety of the car was no guarantee of survival either, not with my dad at the helm. He appeared to be honing his getaway skills on those perilous mountain roads as we drove towards my parents' house. I guess no one had told him that it was okay to slow down.

Their house was a long, white bungalow that sat atop a steep hill on the outskirts of a small town. The only way for my dad to get the car up onto the driveway was first to let the passengers out, thereby reducing the weight, then rev the engine to the max and release. The car would sort of take off until it got to the top of the verge, whereby my dad would slam on the brakes, causing him to lunge forward, almost hitting his head on the windscreen.

I was now in my dad's birthplace. As I took in the view, I noticed an odd smell in the air; I could even taste it in my mouth. It appeared to be a combination of rancid yoghurt and burning faeces. My mum explained that the culprit was a nearby factory.

I got settled in and soon enough we received our first inquisitive visitor, Padraig. I couldn't understand a word he was saying, as I had never heard such a thick accent before. He had a good rapport with my mother, I noticed, and she treated him like a son. At first I thought he was my cousin but later found out that he was, in fact, my dad's half-brother and therefore my uncle. It was quite confusing, as he was only slightly older than me. I was then told I had numerous uncles and aunts in town, some even younger.

Behind the house was a hill and on this hill were cows – lots of cows. Testing out a new friendship, Padraig and I decided to roll down said hill. On one of our rolls, I hit a giant cowpat at high speed. The impact, coupled with my velocity, made that turd-mine explode all over us. I was covered head to toe in cow dung, as was Padraig. Although it stank terribly, we found it pretty funny and wandered back to the house in hysterics. It was definitely nice to be out in the open, connected to nature like that (perhaps a little too connected). I certainly didn't get much cattle shit on me in London.

During our stay it became apparent to all just how sheltered I had actually become, no doubt as a direct result of my nan's coddling ways. It was a quality she bestowed solely on me, having allegedly been a very different kind of mother to her own offspring.

One particular incident springs to mind. I was on the lavatory doing what is colloquially known as a number two. Once I had dropped anchor I called out 'Naa-ann' in a big loud voice. She immediately came running, as always, and began to wipe my bottom. At this, my mum and dad showed actual revulsion.

I remain convinced that this one action sealed my fate for many years to come. My parents had often expressed the view that I'd been spoiled and this was just the ammunition they needed to prove their point. They urged my nan to cease her toilet duties immediately as I was at this point seven-and-a-half years old. In their view, what she was doing was quite disgusting and just plain weird, which, of course, it was. She reluctantly conceded and afterwards explained to me that from now on I would have to perform that particular act alone. In my parents' eyes I was somehow complicit in this, enjoying being molly-coddled (which, in retrospect, I guess I was).

Still, I was angry at my parents for making me feel bad, and this time I took my anger out on something they cared about: their dog.

Soon after the number two incident, I was in my parents' garage when in walked their tiny dog, barking. He was trying to get my attention so I would throw his saliva-infused ball at the wall, something I knew he enjoyed. At first, I obliged, throwing it with enough force to release a bit of dog phlegm. The hound jumped into the air to retrieve his spit sack before coming back to me, panting, in the hope of more attention. When I bent down to retrieve said ball, he refused to drop the damn thing, instead opting for growling. This frustrated me greatly, so for reasons I will never quite understand, I picked him up and hurled him at the garage door instead. He yelped and tried to escape, but I soon caught him and did it again.

Once it dawned on me what I was actually doing, I sort of woke up within myself and felt instant remorse. I ran over to the poor thing, picked him up and apologised profusely.

As I sat consoling him, with tears of guilt running down my cheeks, I could not understand why I had behaved so horribly. It made no sense. I loved dogs and animals in general. At home I would refuse to step on a single ant in the garden, so why was I now inflicting pain on this poor beast? Did a part of me enjoy it, perhaps?

It was the first time that I grasped the notion of there being two versions of myself: a conscientious, ethical me, and the devilish me. However, in moments of heightened anger or frustration, I could not seem to control which one was in charge – sometimes the devil just took the wheel.

***

Six months passed after that upsetting event and I found myself due back in Ireland for part of my Christmas holidays. I was going to arrive by aeroplane with my *de facto* sister, Carol. It was the first flight of my life and prior to leaving I became both excited and fearful at the prospect. I simply could not comprehend being 'in the sky'.

Somehow my mother had persuaded my grandparents to send me to Ireland for the holidays with just my sixteen-year-old aunt as insurance. Carol was under strict instructions to bring me home with her in the New

Year or there would be consequences. Unfortunately for my young aunt, as soon as my mother got me alone, the hard sell began. I was informed that if, for instance, I wanted to stay in Ireland, I could. The fact that I didn't have to go back to London in the New Year if I didn't want to was a revelation. I had no idea I had any choice in the matter. It appeared that the ball had very much landed in my court.

Over the next few days, my mum took me around the town, visiting relatives, showing me the school I could go to and all the things she would buy me if I did indeed decide to stay. This included a rather beautiful, tan-coloured satchel, which, to be honest, sealed the deal. She even went so far as to open an account for me at the local Bank of Ireland, whereby I received a money box in the shape of a little van, which I instantly treasured. Everything seemed so incredibly positive that it didn't take long for me to fall in love with the idea of staying. After all, I loathed my life in London, plus being both 'a ward of court' and a nan kid irritated me greatly. Staying in Ireland appeared to be the perfect solution to all my ills. I had always fantasised about living with my parents, and now, if I wanted to, I could.

Of course, I had my concerns. I was troubled by how much my staying in Ireland might upset my grandparents and I was worried about the trouble that Carol would invariably get into if she were to arrive home without me. But I had made my decision. Ireland would be my new home. It seemed to me to be the logical choice. At last I would be like other kids – living with my young parents instead of a couple of old codgers.

Although my dad was basically a stranger, I found him to be incredibly friendly at first and witnessed no signs of violence whatsoever. He was so nice to me that I assumed the stories I had been told about him were lies told to keep us apart. Although I was clearly being manipulated, the decision to stay was mine alone and I have no one else to blame but myself for what happened next. Not once did my mum do anything to force me to stay – the decision rested squarely on my shoulders. If I wanted to stay,

I could; if not, I could simply return to London with Carol as planned. I was greedy and became distracted by the shiny thing that was a new life in Ireland. In retrospect, I think I was also swayed by the idea of living in another country. I was half-Irish, after all, and perhaps it was time for me to find out about the other half of myself.

I waited for Carol to go to bed before telling my mum the good news. She was beyond pleased. Staying true to her word, she took me shopping the very next day and bought me the satchel I'd had my eye on, plus some stationery items and a bunch of new clothes, some of which were suitable attire for the new school I would be attending.

As we were due to fly home in a matter of days, it was obvious to Carol that something was afoot once we returned home with our purchases. Instead of giving her the runaround, my mum told her straight. It was the exact nightmare scenario that Carol was afraid would happen. Some terse words were exchanged before it became physical. At one point it got so heated that my mum actually punched Carol full in the face, sending her flying over the back of the sofa. This was not good. My mum threw Carol out of the house that night, telling her she was no longer welcome. I felt terrible.

What the hell had I done? I didn't see Carol for more than two years after that explosive night. Apparently she went to stay with my relatives in town until her flight home a few days later.

***

I have very rarely spent time alone with my father. However, during my first week of living in Ireland, he insisted on taking me to the local graveyard, as he had something important he wanted to show me. The graveyard was next to my new school and unlike any I had seen before. It was cluttered with ancient tombs in varying states of disrepair interspersed with Celtic crosses overgrown with moss and weeds. After a while we came to a stop at a newish-looking plot. I soon noticed that the surname on the headstone was my own.

My dad explained that it was the grave of his half-sister, Hannah, who had died the previous year. She would have been almost the same age as me, had she survived. I'd never even heard her name before and was surprised to find out about this relative who had died so suddenly while so young.

The story of her demise was truly horrific. It was a regular evening at the family home and Hannah was playing in the back garden surrounded by her many brothers and sisters. On a whim she decided it would be fun to jump over the back wall. Unfortunately, behind their house was a yard where a company kept much of its stock on wooden pallets. This meant there was a constant flow of vehicles in the vicinity. The second she landed on the ground, she was hit by the full force of one of these and killed instantly. This was shocking enough, but it turned out that my father was the first person over the wall after her, and it was he who had retrieved the body. That must have been tough.

Once I learned of her terrible fate I felt an odd sort of connection to her and began visiting her grave often, mostly after school. Each time I would 'talk' to her for a little while before heading home. It was strange, but I felt as if I missed her, even though we had never met.

The New Year celebrations had drawn to a close, but my mum and dad remained in full party mode. It has to be remembered that they were still in their twenties, so there was plenty of Southern Comfort being drunk and a fair amount of cannabis inhaled. My dad had gone so far as to engineer a Swan Vestas matchbox into a smoking device, which he used nightly.

Due to their consumption of stimuli, I became the butt of many unfunny pranks. I can still recall the night my mother offered me what appeared to be a toffee bar covered in chocolate. Dinner that night had been a tad on the microscopic side and I was still peckish, so I bit into it with relish. I gagged as the taste hit my tongue. It was beeswax. I was spitting out wax while they rolled around in hysterics. I was less than impressed. Were these my parents or a couple of children?

I hadn't been living in Ireland very long before my dad offered me drugs. He brought his pipe into the lounge one evening and asked me if I wanted to try it. I was eight years old and curious, so I said yes. I doubt I was aware of its effects at the time; I probably just assumed it was some kind of cigarette. He handed it to me and I took a small puff. It hit me immediately. Razor-sharp cold air slammed into the back of my throat and I felt funny. I did not like it one bit and handed it straight back to my grinning father.

Unfortunately this was not my only run-in with cannabis that week. A few nights later my parents decided to go out until late, catching a movie before heading to one of the many pubs in town for drinks. Before leaving they set me up in the lounge for the night, pulling out the sofa bed and placing some snacks and a big bottle of pop nearby. They switched on the television as they left and what should be on but my favourite TV programme at the time, *The Late Late Show*. I was a happy bunny, looking forward to my solo night in. As I was getting comfortable, my dad reappeared. He leaned in and asked me conspiratorially if I wanted some dope. Now, even though I didn't like it the first time, I figured I would give it another go, for his sake. Perhaps it would make me seem cooler in his eyes. So invariably I said, 'Yeah, sure.' With that he retrieved his pipe, showed me once again how it worked and disappeared into the evening.

I was now on my own with a cannabis pipe and a whole evening to kill. I guess it was akin to the first time you get drunk on your own, except this wasn't booze. Why he was giving me this stuff at eight years of age I will never understand.

I took a few tokes and this time I didn't mind it so much. I enjoyed the tingly feeling it gave me but not the sharpness of breath that began to hurt my throat again. I had a few more puffs while I watched Gay Byrne and relaxed into the evening.

Being partially blind in one eye has its disadvantages and whether it was the drugs or my lack of spatial awareness, I ended up knocking the entire bottle of pop all over the sofa bed. The sheets were ruined, a bright-orange stain was forming and I began to panic. I was sure that my mum would be furious if she saw the mess I'd made, so I started to pull the sheets from the bed in order to clean them.

Suddenly, out of the corner of my good eye, I noticed something odd. The bottle of pop was still there, perfectly full and upright on the table. 'What the?' I was very confused. Apparently I had hallucinated the entire episode. The sheets were fine, as was the bottle.

***

My new school lay on the edge of town and was a boys-only establishment. I had never attended a segregated school before and found the whole concept bizarre. In Ireland, at that time, the girls were almost exclusively taught by nun-run institutions and the boys were taught by Christian Brothers; it all seemed quite medieval for a modern boy from London.

The most glaringly obvious difference was the curriculum. For instance, one of the compulsory subjects in my new school was Gaelic, to which I took an instant dislike. I refused point-blank to learn it; in my mind I was primarily English, not Irish, and therefore I didn't need to learn such ridiculous wordage. *When would I use that anyway?* I thought.

There was one other subject in which I found it difficult to participate at first: Irish dancing. Yes, dancing was on the curriculum. To some, this was a fun class, but not to me. My eight-year-old self was highly self-conscious and a lack of co-ordination left me feeling both embarrassed and irritated. However, over time I did improve ever so slightly and, dare I say it, I even came to enjoy it a little. Still, all that leg kicking was a bit much.

Home life was changing rapidly. The promises my mum had made were gradually evaporating and my parents began revealing their darker sides. I soon acquired various household chores, most of which I was too young to manage. After school I would be made to scrub floors, wash dishes and clean dirty clothes, while still having to find time for homework. I appeared to be starring in a male adaptation of *Cinderella*. My parents would go out on the town, leaving me a long list of chores to be completed in their absence. It occurred to me during this time that perhaps they had persuaded me to stay in Ireland simply to have a slave of sorts.

One of the more difficult tasks was scrubbing my dad's work jeans. This had to be done with a nailbrush and a lot of soap. He was working as a bricklayer at the time, so his jeans were often covered in sand and cement. I was instructed to remove all of the hard bits using the brush, then wash and rinse everything by hand in a bucket. I gave it my best shot, but, no matter how I tried, I could not get all the dirt out, let alone the water. I simply wasn't strong enough. On one such occasion I did the best I could, then hung everything out to dry high above the range. When my parents returned home they scrutinised my work, finding fault in almost everything I'd done. My dad took one look at his jeans and swore profusely. He then dragged me right over to them, putting my nose against the denim while asking me if I thought they were clean. I said yes I did. And for that I received my very first beating.

I had never been hit like that before, only the odd slap here and there from my grandparents. This was different. It was vicious. The emotional damage was instant and I felt scared for my safety. 'What have I gotten myself into?' I wondered.

I went to sleep that night, bruised and shocked, and in the full knowledge that I had made a terrible mistake.

CHAPTER 8

ANIMAL CRUELTY

Months after deciding to stay in Ireland, I still found the idea of having so many family members living close by to be a bit of an oddity. In London, my family was scattered all over the city, sometimes hours away. Here everyone – my cousins, aunts, uncles and my Irish granddad, Sean – all lived side by side in a grey-green cul-de-sac. Although related, they were still complete strangers to me. They would often take the piss out of me by calling me what I first thought was an 'Egypt', their accents so broad that I could barely understand a word. I later learned they were in fact calling me an 'eejit', meaning idiot.

Sean may have been my granddad, but I certainly never called him by that moniker. That particular connection just wasn't there. I understood him even less than the rest. Initially, I was certain he didn't like me; however, a chance to change his mind soon presented itself when he asked me to find some chairs for his house, promising to pay ten pence for each usable seat acquired. So off I trotted around town in search of said chairs and returned a few hours later with a small selection for his perusal. He took them all and paid up in full. I had proved I could be of use and he seemed impressed. Progress was made.

The differences between my life in London and here were becoming more obvious. In London our dogs were named Pom and Patch, while friends had dogs called things like Spot and Patch. Here in Ireland things were different. Sean had two dogs with very literal names. One was a scruffy black dog simply called Blackie. Then there was a white fluffy dog whose name was, ahem, Whitey. I kid you not. I always hoped he would acquire a brown one, just to complete the set. Conversely, my mum had recently been given a gorgeous puppy and thankfully gave him the relatively sensible name of Gypsy.

In England, although we were far from wealthy, I had plenty of LEGO and Fuzzy-Felts to play with, but here in Ireland children seemed to have an awful lot less. Nobody I knew had actual toys or clothes that weren't hand-me-downs or shared. Often I saw kids without shoes or socks and was aware that even underwear could be considered a luxury. It was a different world. I would often play in the street with my similarly aged relatives, as there was little to keep us entertained in our respective homes.

I'm not sure that I completely understood where food came from before living in Ireland, especially meat, but, once in Éire, I was to be sheltered from this knowledge no longer. Whenever we visited Sean's house there was always a pig's head on the table, which led to many awkward interactions. During one of these first visits he carved off a thick slice of pig snout and threw it in my direction. I caught it with the grip of a bad juggler, wondering what he expected me to do with it. I could see nasal hairs still attached, for Pete's sake! Obviously I refused to eat it, much to his disdain. He would also occasionally carve off an ear and munch on it while talking to us.

Sean's abode was very much a house of boiled bacon and pig's feet stew. I hated pork as a child and I think I'm finally starting to understand why. I did, however, enjoy the fact that he always had potatoes on hand, literally. Although they were cooked, he only ever seemed to eat them once they had cooled down. He would often throw me a cold spud, which I would consume with vigour. I loved spuds and this sudden cold-potato eating was great fun. No knives, no forks, just hands. It was the opposite of the unnecessary etiquette drummed into me back in London.

There wasn't much in Sean's sparse front room, just himself and a chair that was slowly making its way towards the Earth's core. Four distinct circles could be seen where the chair legs had dug into the bare concrete over time. There was a small radio on a shelf, plus the aforementioned pig's head on the table, and that was about it. In addition, there was a tiny piece of wall space dedicated to his favourite visual stimulus: the *Daily Star* topless calendar. Somehow my mum managed to secure him a copy of this every year from England. He would always insist on paying for it and, when he did, an enormous wad of cash would emerge from his left pocket.

Sean always seemed to have money in his pocket, and lots of it. I never quite understood where it all came from, as I rarely saw him leave the house. Although he had the funds, he didn't seem to spend very much. I don't think he was tight; I suspect that he was just a simple man with basic needs.

My dad conveyed many horrors to me regarding his father, but considering the source I can only believe what I witnessed with my own eyes. I had never recognised Sean as the man my dad described, but on one fateful day I did catch a brief and awful glimpse.

All the children in the house slept in the same room upstairs, and in that room were two medium-sized double beds, one for the girls and one for the boys. I only ever slept over at Sean's house once, and once was enough. The only place for me to sleep was in the boys' bed, so I squeezed myself against a couple of half-uncles and a cousin and tried to get settled. There were four of us in total under one itchy brown blanket. It was very uncomfortable and I could not believe that my relatives had to live this way. I felt thoroughly spoiled, having my own bed back home.

As the girls' bed was on the other side of the same room, there was one restriction. They were not allowed in our bed and vice versa. However, that night, one of the girls decided to stray. Her name was Orla and she lay at the foot of our bed talking briefly before returning to her own shared scratchy blanket. We were all very young and it was of course an innocent encounter, but someone still let slip that she had got under the covers with the boys.

I returned to the house later the next day, having forgotten something from my sleepover. I wish I hadn't bothered. I opened the door to Orla's screams. She was crawling around the floor in a semi-foetal position while Sean beat her with an iron poker. As he lashed at her torso, he noticed me at the door. Our eyes met and he paused briefly. Orla was begging him to stop and for me to intervene. I was appalled but could not react.

Sean then barked at me to get out; he wanted to continue his barbaric act in private. I tried to leave, although my legs refused to co-operate at first. The fact that this was happening because she had climbed into the boys' bed was absurd; it was such an over-reaction. A young girl being battered and bruised like that was by far the most brutal thing I had ever seen up to that juncture.

***

One of the best things about living in my father's hometown was its proximity to the sea. In England we had to take trains to get to the seaside; here all you had to do was drive for a couple of miles. You could be sitting on a deserted beach looking out at the vast Atlantic Ocean in a matter of minutes. But just as I was getting used to life in this little Irish town, my parents decided it was time to relocate. They were bored and wanted to move to a bigger town, which lay twenty or so miles away. I knew the distance well, as we would often drive there at weekends to do our weekly shop. I would count down those long miles, clenching my stomach muscles the entire way, hoping not to puke. (Since moving to Ireland I had developed terrible carsickness.)

For me this move meant that there would be yet another change of schools and this time I was set to attend the rather ominous-sounding Christian Brothers Primary School. Gulp! I had heard very bad things about 'the Brothers' and immediately began to worry. Being sent there in the first place seemed a little hypocritical, considering both my parents claimed to be firm non-believers. They did, however, believe that the Brothers' particular form of discipline might do some good in further weaning me from my supposedly molly-coddled English ways.

Our new flat was in an old farm building two miles north of town. It was an ancient building and although it had been refurbished into flats, it still bore the imagery of its past, namely horses. From the gatepost to the door handle you were never too far from a brass equestrian adornment. The immediate area was very green and at the back of the property stood a wood, meaning you could literally look out the kitchen window and see woodland animals frolicking around in the mist. Unfortunately the most common animals on show were rodents. Our flat being slightly beneath ground level meant that the woodland floor was at head height. It could be a little disconcerting looking a giant rat square in the eye over breakfast.

The biggest downside, however, was the flat's distance from the nearest shop. It was quite the trek. My mum would often send me to the super-market for various vague items, never being totally clear regarding her requirements, saying things like 'Go and get some bread.' I would then, of course, ask, 'What type of bread?', to which she would reply, 'Cop on and use your brain.' I would then have to walk to the distant shop, where I would be confronted with the choice of white or brown. I used to get par-ticularly confused about what to do at this point, worrying that whichever choice I made would be the wrong one, and invariably it was. As I didn't have the power of telepathy, I would often return home with the wrong item and receive several smacks around the head for my alleged stupidity. I would then be sent all the way back to exchange it for whatever variant she wanted in the first place.

I despised her for this and felt that she was deliberately giving me the runaround. Of course, over time I learned which items she preferred, but I was so pissed off by this point that I would sometimes choose the wrong items on purpose just to annoy her. Her slaps were small fry compared to my dad's punches and I would often laugh internally as she attempted to hurt me. Sure, I was getting hit, but it was on my own terms. In a way, I felt like I was getting my own back. Her failed attempts to hurt me also exposed a weakness that I enjoyed witnessing. With every blow I felt stronger, my hatred for her growing tenfold.

From this contempt came a sinister ritual. I would take one of the coins from the money she gave me to buy groceries and toss it high into the air, often over an open drain or cattle grill. I decided that if the coin fell in, then she would die. I believed it had absolute power at the time. I loathed her for making me feel inept, though of course I didn't really want her to die. She was my mum and I loved her just as much as I hated her. The few times when the money actually fell in, I ran home at speed, terrified that I had in fact 'killed her'.

To add to my already shit life, school was a complete nightmare. The faculty was run with iron fists by the Christian Brothers. From day one it was apparent that they really loved hitting kids, especially ones with English accents who didn't believe in God quite as much as they did. The fact that I wasn't brought up overly religious was obviously a problem. Admittedly I knew nothing of the Bible and its fables, but I did actually believe in God. This came solely from my nan's insistence that I pray nightly. Through pure repetition I had developed a belief system that I assumed for a brief time to be my own.

The Christian Brothers ran a devout Catholic school and although I may not have been particularly religious, I at least had to be Catholic in order to attend. But I had a dirty little secret, something I would have to keep to myself for the duration. My parents had lied to the head brother, telling him that I was baptised Catholic, when in fact I had actually been christened a Protestant, albeit in error.

I was still an infant when my nan insisted that I be baptised. So, in order to appease her, my mother simply chose the closest church to the house, made an appointment and got the deed done. My mum has since openly admitted that she remembers very little about that day, having been high for most of it. Some time afterwards, however, she realised that I had in fact been welcomed into the wrong religion. Not that it has ever bothered me, but as a result I am the only Protestant in a wholly Catholic family. So right under the Christian Brothers' noses sat an accidental Protestant.

Every lesson came with a side order of Christianity, which began to turn me off almost immediately. I found their methods particularly cruel, as they seemed to be based solely on instilling fear and guilt into us children. After I witnessed these self-appointed Brothers serve up their particular brand of folklore, something clicked inside and I began to question the very concept of God.

Any religious belief I had when starting at the Christian Brothers was thoroughly beaten out of me by the time I left. Each Brother carried an unsettling item known only as 'the strap'. It was constructed from many layers of thin leather that sat atop each other in succession. It was about an inch-and-a-half thick and when you got hit with it, you really knew about it. It was akin to being hit with ten belts at once. I had yet to receive corporal punishment in school, but not to worry, these lovely fellows were going to make up for that. They dished it out liberally, often for the most minor of indiscretions. We would feel the full force of the strap for not paying attention, getting questions wrong, talking to each other, or just being late for class.

Remarkably I even managed to receive a leathery thwack for getting stung by a bee. There I was, retrieving my jacket from the hook outside our classroom, when a bee flew down my sleeve from where it had temporarily nested and stung me right on the thumb. As I cried out, one of the Brothers came running to see what could be causing such a commotion. He grabbed hold of me, whereby I assumed he was escorting me to the school nurse, as they would have done in England. No such luck. He had a different remedy for pain: more pain. He held me down and began to hit me with the strap. I pulled myself out from underneath him and managed to get away, swearing as I ran off. *Jesus! That's it, I've had enough of this*, I thought.

I decided then and there that I could suffer these fools no more. I did not believe in their superstitious nonsense by this point and refused to listen to another word of it. I was annoyed at my nan for convincing me of God's existence and angry at my parents for making me attend a school that was akin to a sect.

As I legged it out of the school gates, I could see another poor kid being abused in a nearby classroom. *If these are God's workers*, I thought, *then I want nothing to do with God.* From that day forth I closed my ears to their divine instruction and never once faltered.

I had to return to the fold the following day, but as I no longer believed, I was no longer listening. I was simply going through the motions, waiting for the day when I could walk out of those school gates for good. Ironically, the Christian Brothers had been handed a God-fearing English boy and had managed to convert him into a fervent atheist in practically no time at all.

Cruel religious teachers were by no means my only concern during this period. I soon discovered that I was to be the subject of racism. My English accent did me no favours in late 1970s Ireland. The IRA was pretty popular in both towns in which we'd lived so far, and the English were clearly not. My mum advised me to steer clear of houses flying black flags, but on my walk home all I saw were black flags. My schoolmates even had posters of paramilitaries on their walls instead of pop stars. It was as if I were behind enemy lines.

My not being much of a fighter meant that, in the dog-eat-dog environment of the Irish playground, bullying soon ensued. Between those nasty little bastards, the Brothers and my worsening home life, I wondered if perhaps I was destined to be miserable. I realise, of course, that many children growing up in Ireland at the time experienced similar acts of violence and would no doubt regard it as somewhat inevitable considering the era. However, I feel compelled to dispute this. It's a lazy excuse and it should never have happened to any of us. They seemed particularly heartless times.

***

Once we were settled in our new flat, my mother secured a job as a petrol pump attendant at a local garage. I enjoyed visiting during her shifts and would often spend the hours after school keeping her company. Incidentally, this was to be the place where I first witnessed my mother having an epileptic fit. I had heard her mentioning how it was important that she 'take her pills', but I paid little attention to her condition until I saw firsthand how debilitating it could be.

Still, visiting my mum at the garage was almost always enjoyable. When she was in good form she was fun to be around and we would have a great time together. However, once her shift was over and we began the long walk home, her mood would sour; the closer we got to the house, the more apparent it became that we were not taking the good times home with us.

Although my parents showed signs of still being 'in love', they also seemed to despise one another. Not to defend my mother, but my dad has always been an incredibly moody bastard. The day could turn to shit by him simply walking through the door. A dark feeling would encompass the entire flat and that would be that. When this occurred my mum would become someone else entirely, more like him. And once they became terse with one another, it was time to get out of the way. They would begin by bickering, whereby they would call each other unspeakable names. This would then most likely escalate into a full-blown row. Most of the time my dad would simply walk away and go to bed in a huff, but on one memorable night he did not.

On that particular night he decided to shove her. My mother, who is not the most feminine woman, decided to shove him right back. This was unprecedented. 'Careful now,' he said, leaning over her to reiterate the point, but she'd had enough of his bullying for one day. From a cowering position, she managed to jostle him out of the way, but just as she was about to escape, my dad grabbed her by the arm. He paused for a second. Then he punched her.

This was no small tap; it was a full-on fist to the face. I could not believe what I was seeing. Although I'd always suspected he hit my mother, I had never actually seen it with my own eyes. I was also surprised that he'd exposed himself like that in front of me. My mum was now on the ground, swearing at him, calling him a 'fucking coward' among other things. He then reached down, grabbed her and threw her across the room. I could not comprehend it. All I could do was think, *please stop hurting my mum*. He then dragged her towards the kitchen by the hair, where he proceeded to beat her up, laying punch after punch into her curled-up frame until she could finally take no more.

Suddenly things got an awful lot quieter. I could hear a sort of croaky voice coming from behind the kitchen cabinet, but that was all. I decided to sneak a look. My mum was on the floor, her face soaked in tears and blood. My dad had finally stopped punching her, instead opting for strangulation. He had both hands gripped firmly around her throat and was squeezing the life out of her. She pleaded with him to stop, her voice becoming ever more faint. Instead he pulled her face a little closer to his and squeezed harder.

'Stop it,' I said, finally managing to vocalise something.

It was as if I had disturbed a lion attacking its prey. My dad's head turned suddenly, giving me a look that said, 'You're next.' I wet myself instantly. My mum was waving her hands around, urging me to run away, but I couldn't move. Finally my dad saw the sense in not killing his wife and let her go. But not before pulling her face even closer to his and saying the ominous word 'Seeee', before dropping her to the ground. I assume he meant, 'See what you made me do', but that might just be how I interpreted it.

He pushed past me before locking himself in the bedroom. I then ran over to my mum, who was still on the floor and clearly in pain. She told me to go to my room, lock the door and stay there until morning. I agreed, although I hated leaving her, especially as she was covered in bruises and red marks. As I gathered my things, she was cleaning herself up at the kitchen sink, battered. I had never seen anything quite like it. Every week in Ireland I seemed to witness something more brutal than the last.

The typical pattern that followed a falling out between my parents was weeks of not talking, followed by a sudden show of solidarity. Their reconciliation was often preceded by the arrival of a new dog, usually sprung upon my mother as a substitute for an apology. However, this incident was different – my mum wanted blood.

She was planning vengeance and wanted my help in carrying it out. I was more than happy to oblige, as I was eager to see my father suffer after what he had done to her. Revenge was served the following day. It began with my mother waking up extra early and attaching a handwritten sign onto the very back of my dad's car, just above the number plate. The car was parked with its rear tight up against the garage door, so it would be some time before my father spotted it.

The sign read: 'Fuckpig'.

My mum was keen for everyone in town to see it, so they'd know what kind of man he was. However, I was a tad concerned, as it did not seem like the greatest of plans. What if he came back and hit her again? Or me? She seemed unconcerned and could not be deterred in her quest. Hence, the Fuckpig plan was enacted shortly before dawn. But it turned out that this was merely part one of her plan for retribution.

For part two my input was required. My mum's second idea was to make the flat appear as if it had been burgled. I thought it was another odd tactic, but I figured she knew what she was doing and went along with it. First we trashed the living room, breaking ornaments and crockery as we went. It was enormous fun. We turned the sofa and armchairs upside down, threw food around the kitchen and generally made a giant mess. I was sure we'd pay a heavy price for the carnage we'd created, but neither of us cared any more. We were past the point of no return.

Once the place was suitably ransacked we both stood back and admired our handiwork. It was a pretty convincing job. My mum, suddenly realising that we were vulnerable, then insisted we flee the scene. Within minutes we were skipping into town, giggling as we went. However, behind our smiles lay some serious nerves – at least on my part.

The first person to arrive home that evening was my father. He must have been very confused by the spectacle that greeted him. My mum and I showed up much later, feigning disbelief and professing to know nothing about the state of the flat. But he was having none of it. He knew. We were rumbled and I braced myself for the inevitable.

Surprisingly, he turned to my mother and told her calmly that he was not impressed with the 'Fuckpig' sign that had been on his car all day. He seemed subdued. There were no rows and no beatings. I imagine he felt terrible about hitting her the night before and wasn't in the mood to rise to the bait. Looking downcast, he made a jam sandwich and wandered off to bed.

We both looked at each other in dismay. 'I'll get the broom,' I said.

CHAPTER 9

IN HOT WATER

My dad's brother George and his wife had recently moved from London to our town and were throwing a house-warming party, to which my parents were cordially invited. Unsurprisingly, I had no idea they were attending said shindig until the evening in question.

We were out walking when my mother sprang the news on me while simultaneously holding out a key. She informed me that they wouldn't be home until late and suggested I head back as it was getting dark. I took one look at the key and knew that it wasn't the right one, and told her so. I remembered the shape and that wasn't it. My mum barked back, telling me that of course it was the right one. I reiterated my concern and asked if perhaps she had another key on her. With that she became further irritated, telling me that 'she knew what fucking key it was' and that I was being a moron. I had a sneaky feeling that my dad suspected I might be right, but he didn't want to upset my mother, so he kept schtum. He did, however, give me a piece of paper with George's telephone number on it, telling me it was for emergencies only.

As I walked off into the darkness, he added, 'And don't turn up either.'

'How could I possibly turn up?' I wondered. I didn't even know where they lived. I walked home certain that I would not be getting into the flat that night.

I arrived at the door and tried to insert the key. It wasn't even the right size for the barrel. It was, as I suspected, the wrong bloody key. I was locked out with zero money and nowhere to go.

The real frustration was that the phone was inside the flat, so I couldn't call the number on the piece of paper even if I'd wanted to. I had but one choice: to wait. I figured they couldn't be that late, surely? I curled up on the bottom step and tried to remain hopeful. It wasn't the warmest of nights. The arched hallway was not protected by a door as such, as it was part of an old stable. It was therefore exposed to the elements. The cold breeze was a constant, but at least it was dry. I tried to keep myself occupied by doubling numbers to see how far I could get to; 2, 4, 8, 16, 32 ... I got quite high. Then it was on to capital cities of the world, but it wasn't enough, the hours were just too many. All I could do was try to stay warm and be patient. I had a prolonged sense of dread that night and felt sure that my parents would find a way to blame me for the situation I was now in. Once I'd lost all feeling in my buttocks, I noticed the sky turn a dark sort of blue. Then I heard them.

My parents staggered into the hallway, arm in arm, with a bottle in each hand, trying to remain upright. Once they'd spotted me on the stairs, they began to laugh uncontrollably, especially my mother. The first words out of her mouth were: 'You fucking idiot.' She could not comprehend why I hadn't come into town to find them.

Uh, maybe because you told me expressly not to, you fucking bitch, I thought. However, I was so very tired that I failed to vocalise an actual response. My dad showed a speck more compassion by saying, 'Jesus, don't be so ...' but he, too, thought me foolish for waiting outside all night. I have rarely been so happy to see a front door open.

***

According to my father, because I was technically missing from England, a local policeman – or 'guard', as I'd discovered they were called here – had been assigned the job of catching me and returning me to my grandparents. He was, therefore, to be avoided at all costs.

The guard's name was O'Sullivan and on occasion he would chase me while I was out on my bicycle. The first time it happened caught me by complete surprise. I was cycling into town when he ran towards me at speed, his hands pointed straight ahead like blades. He was a difficult man to outrun, but I eventually panic-pedalled my way to freedom.

I couldn't understand why he didn't simply come to my school and take me back to England from there. It all seemed a bit cloak and dagger, although the handful of times he chased me were actually quite terrifying, and I have since wondered if perhaps my dad put him up to it, just to frighten me, or to test me – to see if I actually wanted to return to my grandparents in England. I wouldn't put it past him.

I may have outrun O'Sullivan, but I was soon to encounter another obstacle on my way into town. While cycling one afternoon, I spotted some pretty girls to my left, calling out to me in unison. I became instantly distracted and so did not see the very thing they were trying to warn me about.

THA-DUMP!

All I can remember after that moment is seeing my bicycle continue up a slight hill without me. I had fallen off and was now on the ground, sporting a painful noggin and a bruised bottom. It transpired that I'd smashed into a metal traffic barrier that had been stretched out across the pavement.

The girls ran over to help, even walking me part of the way home. I was clearly concussed but did not realise it at the time. I felt extremely dizzy and wasn't making a lot of sense when I tried to speak. I felt drunk. When I eventually got back to the flat it was empty, so I went to my room for a little lie down and fell fast asleep. Admittedly, it was not the greatest of ideas.

I remained out for the count for the rest of the afternoon, finally waking up later that evening to the sound of my parents' voices coming from the kitchen. I did not want to have to explain my idiocy, so I decided not to tell them about the accident. Instead I simply entered the room silently and plonked myself on the sofa. My right eye seemed extra blurry and I couldn't quite talk or respond properly. When my mum asked if I wanted soup, I recall slurring my words. I sat in front of the television unusually quiet and watched an episode of *The Incredible Hulk* while slipping in and out of consciousness. I went back to bed soon after and forgot all about it. In retrospect, I can't help but wonder if I perhaps made my already damaged eye somehow worse that day.

***

After enduring yet another day at the hands of the Christian Brothers, I decided to do something that can only be described as reckless. Opposite the school was a small garage and on this particular day I should have chosen to walk around it and not through it. My inquisitive nature was about to take a magnificent shit on my day.

In the forecourt sat an unlocked car, and in the ignition was a set of keys. I'm sure you can guess the rest. Once I spotted those keys it was a done deal. I was overcome with an irresistible urge to turn on the ignition, just to see what would happen. I was a very curious child, often wondering about things, like what would happen if I attached two plugs to one piece of flex and plugged them in at the same time. Well, in that case the answer was an electrical fire. This, however, was an automobile, a moving vehicle. What on earth was I thinking? What happened next seemed to play out in slow motion and appeared to be happening to someone else entirely.

I reached in through the side window and turned the key. The car suddenly sprang to life and headed out of the forecourt towards oncoming traffic. I squinted in horror as it smashed straight into a passing car.

I was mortified. Although still fairly young, at eight years of age I knew this had been an imbecilic move. I was sure to pay a hefty price.

The car had been left in gear and had only staggered into the road at low speed. However, from my perspective, the crash was epic. I remained frozen in the forecourt, unable to contemplate any kind of escape. Then the owner of the car grabbed me.

He was apoplectic. He demanded to know where I lived as he ushered me with some force towards his now-battered vehicle. I instantly started lying, as I was sure I'd receive the mother of all beatings from my dad for this particular crime. I begged him to let me go, becoming more upset as the realisation of what I had done sank in. I even went so far as to tell him about my dad's wife-beating ways and how he might actually kill me for this. He was vaguely sympathetic, but how could he possibly let me go? I had ruined his car and someone had to pay.

Finally I caved in and within minutes we were heading towards our flat in the very vehicle I had just mangled. To further exacerbate the situation, we were subjected to a chorus of scraping sounds en route. This made him all the angrier, and made me feel all the more ashamed. It was a complete and utter disaster.

My dad arrived home after a hard day's work to find his son and a stranger waiting on the gravel. After some awkward pleasantries, the man proceeded to tell him what had happened while my dad listened intently, his pupils dilating more with every revelation. They chatted for a while before coming to some sort of arrangement. Then the man was gone. I followed my father into the flat without breathing. As we stood there, just the two of us in silence, I was as scared as I had ever been in my life.

As I braced for impact, my dad told me that my punishment would come later. Well, this was new. He explained that he wanted to talk to my mother first, and then together they would devise a suitable punishment for my actions. I was told that it could come at any time and that I should be ready to receive it when that time came.

He was acting way too calm for my liking; it was very unsettling. I would have much preferred to receive a beating right then and there instead of having to await my fate.

My dad's brother Archie was staying with us at the time and I suspect my dad may have preferred to wait until after Archie's departure before unleashing his wrath upon me. This waiting game was an unwelcome twist to an already terrible existence. Again I had been my own worst enemy, adding a world of pain to my own shoulders. What was wrong with me?

Archie was constantly flirting with my mother, which I did not appreciate. Still, I did quite like him; he was heaps more fun to be around than my dad. Of course at that age I had little concept of who he was as a person and was yet to spot one of the major downsides of his character: alcoholism. The clues were there, though. During his visits he would always encourage my parents to drink far too much, making them all the more erratic, which was something none of us really needed.

On the night of the car crash, my mother suggested I run myself a bath. I had never operated the bath taps before and became rather confused when the water seemed to be getting hotter rather than colder. I had turned the cold tap on to cool down what I assumed to be the hot water already in the tub, but it was getting even hotter for some reason. *That's weird*, I thought. (It later transpired that the taps were marked the wrong way around, something my parents had failed to tell me.)

Before I could fathom what was happening, my dad burst into the sauna of a room with rage in his eyes. He began shouting abuse, calling me a little cunt and asking me why I was wasting all the hot water. I was wearing the smallest of towels when he ripped it from me and picked me up. It was then that he did something truly unforgivable. He threw me into the boiling bath.

I screamed, making a sound I had never made before or since. I was in shock and I felt my skin bubble. It was so hot that I actually felt cold. My dad had a look of instant regret on his face but was still blaming me when my mum rushed in.

She let out a shriek when she saw me. 'What the fuck are you doing to him?'

My dad, realising he had gone too far, helped her fish me out of the boiling bath. My skin was a horrific shade of red. They both looked worried. I was badly burned.

Archie came bounding in to see what all the commotion was about and, upon seeing me, said something along the lines of 'Jesus, he's only a boy, for God's sake. What are you doing, man?' My dad felt ganged up on as my mum and Archie carried me from the bathroom. He retreated to his bedroom and locked the door, swearing as he went.

I was in so much pain that night that I could not sleep. Going to the hospital wasn't an option, as my parents would have had to explain what happened, which would no doubt lead to social services being called. Unless I wanted to be sent back to my grandparents, I would simply have to ride out the pain at home.

The following morning I was told that I was to be kept off school for the remainder of the term. I had assumed this would be the case, as they could hardly send me there covered in burns and scabs. It was easy enough to cover the bruises on my torso and arms with long sleeves after a beating, but burns would be difficult to hide. The Christian Brothers were a violent lot, but even they may have been taken aback by the way I looked after that incident.

For a time after this event, my father became a different person. He was kind and gentle, and showed actual remorse for his actions. I apologised for the car crash and promised to never do anything like it again. He nodded in acceptance. He bought some calamine lotion and applied it to my burns. It was the very first time he had ever touched me without it being an act of violence. In that moment I could tell that he cared about me. My dad knew that I was a fan of *Judge Dredd* and *2000 A.D.*, so in the hours after this event he returned with a large pile of comics. I suspect the entire episode was a terrible lesson for us both.

Although the bathroom incident was a hideous ordeal, at least my dad appeared to be in no mood to dish out further punishment and so, in some ways, I counted myself lucky.

This did not last long, however. Little did I know that my sentence had merely been suspended. In my mother's opinion there was unfinished business between us and she took great relish in telling me so. I was informed that, in her opinion, I had not been adequately punished for my actions. As the bath incident was essentially an accident, it didn't count.

Was she nuts? I had spent nearly two weeks in bed, writhing around in agony, and to her that wasn't punishment enough?

My mother always managed to put on a bloody good show, professing to be an innocent when it came to the physical violence I endured at the hands of my father. But here's the kicker: on rare occasions, she could be just as nasty. They may not have been her fists, but she sure knew how to direct them when she wanted to. For her next trick, however, my father's fists would not be necessary.

Once Archie had left, it was time to dish out my punishment, quite literally. This appeared to be my mum's idea, which made it all the more upsetting.

She beckoned me to sit down at the kitchen table and prepare myself. She then opened the cupboard and pulled out a full bag of yellow rice. My punishment would be to eat the entire bag raw.

'Raw?' I asked.

She nodded.

I gave her a look as if to say, 'Have you lost your tiny mind?' I couldn't possibly eat all that. I was told I would only be allowed to leave the table once the last grain had been consumed.

Her macabre game had aroused my dad's attention and he came jogging over to goad her on. I was told to eat with my hands and to drink water after each mouthful to help it down. It did not dawn on me that they were serious until all three of us were sitting around the kitchen table, their eyes locked onto mine in anticipation. This was one psychotic family unit.

My mum motioned me to begin and I took a deep breath. I reluctantly grabbed a handful of dry rice and shoved it in my mouth. It had a really strong, offish flavour that made me gag. It would not break down and I almost choked on those first few mouthfuls. Regardless, these fruitcakes seemed to be enjoying the performance, egging me on to eat more. After a few more gulps of dryness I threw up in my mouth; it was impossible to keep down. The water was actually making it harder to swallow as it was filling me up. My mum told me that I had to keep eating, otherwise I would receive a beating right there and then, to which my dad nodded in agreement. My mother handed me a spoon to help with proceedings. I tried to force more rice down my gullet without it touching the sides of my throat, but I just couldn't keep it in my stomach and threw up all over the kitchen table. This of course made them angry and I was called a 'dirty little bastard' for my sins.

I begged them to let me stop, but my mum reminded me that I had to finish the entire bag. It seemed downright impossible. She continued to bring me water and I tried my best to keep eating, but each mouthful was pure torture. Eventually I began to bloat and was throwing up after every spoonful. Things had gotten so out of hand that it was my dad who eventually called time on their sick little experiment.

With wet rice stuck to my face and vomit down my front, my mother held out yet another spoon of rice for me to eat.

'Enough, Jesus!' my dad interjected.

I think he was worried that they might end up having to take me to the hospital after all, if she continued the feeding. How on earth would they have explained an eight-and-a-half-year-old child covered in burns with a stomach full of raw rice, I wonder?

My stomach continued to swell up overnight, as intense cramps contracted my insides. It was easily the most pain I had ever felt in my stomach. That night it crossed my mind that my parents could very well be trying to kill me. At the very least, they were sick in the head.

CHAPTER 10

THE ART OF DISTRACTION

During the summer holidays I spent most of my spare time in the company of my mother. Although my trust in her was shattered, our relationship did show signs of improvement over the following weeks and months. It was during this moist Irish summer that she became bored with the status quo. She had a new obsession: food colouring. Suddenly our dinners consisted of red mash, blue chips, green bread and purple peas. Somehow my mother had single-handedly managed to make 1970s cuisine even less appetising.

When we weren't consuming multi-coloured foodstuffs, we were playing board games. However, we didn't have much in the way of choice, so one afternoon my mother decided to take me into town for a touch of light shoplifting. On a sodden summer's day, I found myself shoving goods into a shopping trolley with the intention of stealing them.

I had been privy to my mother's pilfering for quite some time, observing her skill in taking whatever she wanted, whenever she wanted. I had no idea a person could get away with such things before seeing her in action. It was an eye-opener and I had always been keen to emulate her. Like most children, I wanted my mother to be proud of me.

Luckily an opportunity presented itself that morning, when my mum suggested I take the reins and obtain that day's booty. Although I wanted to impress her, I could also hear my dad's voice in my head: 'If I you ever bring the guards to the door, I'll fucking kill you.' He had stated this often. So if I was to get involved in my mother's dodgy antics, it was imperative that I didn't get caught.

A strategy was needed – an angle, if you will. I was aware that my childlike status could be used to my advantage, as people generally tended to trust children. Furthermore, I had been told on numerous occasions that I possessed an honest face. *That's handy*, I thought.

I decided to combine my assumed innocence with a dose of distraction. I had noticed my mother engage the person she was scamming in conversation while up to no good; they would often become distracted just enough for her to get away with whatever it was she was up to. I decided I, too, would apply this technique.

On our shopping list that day was the board game *Frustration*, which my mother and I would play avidly into the wee hours. Our previous copy had been destroyed by my father while in a fierce mood – he loathed the clicking sound the dice made as it popped under a plastic dome in the centre of the board. So, perfectly within character, he smashed it to pieces right in front of us. *No problem*, I thought, *we'll just steal another one*. Even though we were replacing something my dad had destroyed, I was also on the lookout for a present for his approaching birthday, the miserable bastard.

My mum had selected the perfect shop for me to rob. It was a large department store in the centre of town, one we frequented often. They sold absolutely everything, from clothes to DIY and, of course, games. My mother would wait for me in the town square until I'd completed my mission. However, should something go awry, then I was to run like the wind and reconvene upstairs in the nearby Woolworths, which was our agreed meeting point.

I entered awkwardly through two flapping narrow doors, dragging the kind of shopping trolley you see old ladies using, with a bag on the front that zips up at the top. I must have been quite the sight. After all, not too many young boys wandered around busy department stores on their own with such receptacles. That wasn't suspicious at all.

I hung around the games' section for a while, waiting for an opportunity to arise. There were no cameras or mirrors, just the rumour of store detectives. I suspected I knew who they were, so I waited until those particular people were out of sight before making my move. I managed to nab the game we wanted without issue and was getting ready to bolt when I suddenly saw my mother through the window. She was motioning me from outside to pick up another item: *Monopoly*. I wasn't convinced I could do it again and thought she was foolish for blatantly egging me on like that. Still, I didn't want to let her down. So, after a few minutes of treading water, I grabbed a sealed *Monopoly*, shoved it into my trolley, zipped it up and walked off. As far as I could tell nobody saw a thing.

I was all set to leave when I remembered that I still needed to get something for my dad's impending birthday. A short walk along a narrow corridor took me to the other side of the building and the DIY section. I saw before me many items I was sure he would fancy. I considered my options carefully, while trying to act casual.

I should have emptied my money box and bought him a book on anger management, but instead I was leaning towards getting him a trowel.

As I picked up the bricklayer's friend I began to have doubts. *What if this trowel is crap?* I thought. *Surely he has better ones already?* I instantly decided against it and perused the shelves for an alternative. I eventually settled on a tin of paint. My dad had mentioned that he wanted to change the colour of their bedroom walls, so I was under the impression that this was the perfect gift. I was clearly a very peculiar boy.

Another peculiarity was that we generally never celebrated my dad's birthday; in fact I had only recently found out the exact date. He would always refuse to acknowledge it, getting annoyed if we dared to bring it up.

I spotted a shade of paint that I thought might do the trick, waited for the appropriate moment and dropped the tin directly into my waiting trolley, right between the two games. This time, however, I was a bit too brazen. There were quite a few sight lines in that section of the store and I didn't hide what I was doing quite as well as I could have.

Once I felt ready to leave, I rolled the trolley along the decrepit red carpet towards the door, accompanied by a niggling feeling that I was probably not going to get away with it. I could feel it in my gut. I opened the door and hoped I was wrong. It was then that I felt a strong hand grab my arm.

One of the male store detectives had seen me steal the paint from across the shop floor and was now holding on to me with one hand and the trolley with the other. There was no way to escape, so I didn't bother wrestling. I was escorted calmly to a back room and told to 'sit the feck down'. The manager came in, took one look at me and called the guards.

As the manager plonked down the handset, the ping of the receiver coincided with a knock at the door. Then, quite coincidentally, a guard entered. It may have resembled a comedy sketch, given the timing, but in this instance nobody was amused. It transpired that the officer had merely been close by and was ushered to the back office by the staff, his arrival having nothing to do with the manager's phone call whatsoever.

The guard was very friendly and in no way menacing, unlike the monsters my dad always portrayed them to be. I was sure I'd met him before, but I couldn't place when or where. He asked for my name and I lied. I was always taught to have a fake name ready, something I could believe in and stick to. It was imperative that I never give anyone my real name or address.

The problem was that this particular officer seemed to know who I was already. Therefore, all I had to do was come clean about my identity and I would be let off with a caution. The manager wasn't interested in pressing charges, he just wanted to make sure I never set foot in his shop again. The guard would simply visit the house later to conduct the caution in front of my parents and that would be that. It didn't sound too bad, so I gave in.

Once I'd spilled the beans they let me go, as promised. I was relieved to be free but still felt a sense of rising dread. Bringing the guards to the door was an unforgivable sin in my dad's eyes and I knew I would pay dearly for it. Home life had been a little easier to bear of late, but this would surely send our relationship back to the Stone Age. Then it hit me: perhaps my mum could help? After all, it was her idea to go shoplifting, not mine. Maybe she could lie and save my skin for once. I had nothing to lose so I decided to ask her outright.

My mother was pacing among the pick 'n' mix in Woolworths when I found her. She was clearly relieved to see me but unimpressed with my capture. We talked conspiratorially among the magazines about what had happened and I told her about the forthcoming visit from the law. I begged her to save my bacon and to my surprise she agreed.

My mum also had to protect herself. She knew that my dad had an inkling she might be stealing around town, which was something he frowned upon. If he found out she'd involved me as well, he would no doubt make both our lives a living hell. We had no choice but to stick together.

We went directly to a phone box and called my granddad Sean. My mum explained that she had a favour to ask, one that would require him to lie to his own son if need be. Despite this, he agreed on the spot. He adored my mother and would have done anything for her. Luckily, in this case, I came under that same protective wing. If asked, he agreed to confirm that we were visiting him, twenty or so miles away, that same afternoon. He even offered to make an official statement to that effect, if required. We hung up, walked home and waited anxiously for my dad to come home.

He arrived home in a good mood for once, singing Led Zeppelin songs at a pitch he couldn't quite reach. After a mouthful of biscuits he went for his daily workout. The strangest of sounds were emitted during these routines: grunts, wheezes and sharp intakes of breath. The only apparatus he owned was a crude rowing machine, which you could hear whizzing from any room in the flat. He would usually end with sit-ups, each of which was accompanied by a little yelp. It all sounded incredibly unappealing.

Once he'd showered, we sat down for yet another multi-coloured meal and prepared for the worst. My dad asked about our day and my mum told him that we had visited Sean. She was very convincing.

My dad was about to swallow another mouthful of pink mash when there was a knock on the door. *Here we go*, I thought. My mum gave me a look as if to say, 'Right, get ready' and walked over to the door, opening it innocently.

There he stood, the guard from earlier. He smiled, entered and started speaking in a very matter-of-fact way. He was talking openly about my apprehension earlier that day, explaining that although I had stolen expensive items, the store wasn't going to press charges. He was merely there to administer the caution, after which he'd be on his way. He smiled in my direction throughout his speech. He was clearly a nice man and I felt guilty knowing what was about to happen.

My mum interjected first, asking him, 'What the fuck are you on about?', telling him that we were not even in town that day; we had been visiting relatives in the north of the county. The poor fellow looked over at me for some sort of validation, saying something along the lines of 'Come on now son, tell the truth.' Lying through my teeth, I managed to mumble, 'I was with my mum all day, who are you again?' I was attempting to convince my dad that I'd never met the officer before, let alone been apprehended by him. My dad seemed to be falling for our concocted story.

My mum then suggested that perhaps it was another boy entirely, someone who might look a bit like me, maybe someone who was trying to frame me? I was English, after all. She even offered to phone Sean to substantiate our story. It was all very plausible.

The poor man was dumbfounded and didn't quite know what to say. He looked over to my dad for moral support, stating that I was definitely the boy he'd interrogated. He was certain of it.

My dad snapped back at him, saying something that made me feel both guilt and pride: 'Do you really think I'm going to believe the words of a fucking guard over that of my own son?' at which the guard left rather awkwardly.

Now there's a statement that would have been truly gratifying under different circumstances.

CHAPTER 11

MY ALCATRAZ (PART ONE)

Bored with living out in the sticks, my parents found a small house to rent, slap bang in the middle of town, albeit up a dark alley. It was in this building that I spent the very worst year of my life. I was still eight years old when the nightmare began. It was a truly terrible place full of only bad memories.

This house was small compared to our previous place, but its proximity to the town's amenities was a big improvement. Unfortunately the house itself was in a terrible state of disrepair. The sitting-room floor was comprised of bare concrete, sharp stones and lumps of brick all fused together. We tried to remove some of the bigger pieces with a hammer and bolster, but it was impossible to get rid of everything; there were just too many clumps of masonry attached to the floor. Instead we would just have to live with it for the duration. The house was dark, dingy and clammy. There was no hot-water supply or a bathroom to speak of, just a small toilet next to a cold tap at an odd angle atop a rusty pipe in the semi-outside area behind the kitchen. Power sockets were scarce and for heating we eventually used an old range in the lounge that had remained dormant for some time. We didn't even own a kettle. At first my mum would instead use a milk pan that sat perilously atop a single stovetop powered by a large gas bottle if she wanted so much as a cup of decaf. It was in no way a habitable abode for a family, but my dad was convinced he could bring it up to an acceptable living standard, given time. Therefore, we endured.

As if the house wasn't already dark enough, my dad decided to install a new front door. It was of the solid-wood variety and looked like it belonged in a medieval prison, especially as it blocked out all remaining sunlight. Unless we opened a wooden square in the middle to see who was calling, the lower part of the house remained completely dark. (There was one small window downstairs, but my mum had hung heavy red curtains over it in order to cover up the cracked walls and sill.) It was like living with a couple of bloody vampires.

My room was the attic, a place barely fit for storage. It did, however, have a skylight, so at least I was blessed with a view of sorts. The floor was made up of warped boards that squeaked whenever pressure was applied. My bed frame was made of wire and would make a hideous scraping noise when I turned over in the night. God knows where it came from. My parents slept in the bedroom below mine and due to this proximity any noise I made in the night was bound to wake them. I became acutely aware of this when I was told in no uncertain terms that if I woke my father I would receive a beating. He worked hard and needed his sleep.

Although we lived just off the main shopping street, I felt completely isolated. There were very few inhabited buildings nearby, as most were extremely run-down. Once I arrived home from school, a sort of darkness would envelop me as I turned into the alley and remain until I left the following morning. It was a grim place indeed.

It didn't help that from the moment we moved into that horror house my dad's persona began to change. He became even more violent and aggressive. It later transpired that during this period my father suspected that my mother was having an on/off affair with his brother Archie, which accounts for some of his behaviour – though not all. I was receiving regular beatings and they were becoming ever more severe. I was so scared of my father that I would often wet myself whenever he entered the room. For this of course I would also get beaten. It was the worst of times and I felt like we were living in our very own Amityville House.

The stress of this situation led me to start the peculiar habit of urinating behind my own headboard. If I needed to go for a wee in the night I couldn't risk waking my father, so I instead chose to piss in my own room. It was illogical, but at the time I felt there was no alternative and did it as a matter of circumstance. I figured nobody would ever find out – it wasn't as if I had schoolmates regularly coming over for visits.

However, around this time I did become friendly with a couple of sisters who lived across town and, once we were settled, my mum cordially invited them over. I was worried that they would be led upstairs to find out how disgusting I really was, but thankfully we remained downstairs.

I was not able to avoid embarrassment entirely, however. My parents knew that I fancied one of the sisters and therefore set about humiliating me. I'd had an enormous urge to kiss her a few days earlier, but when the time came I was too nervous to make any kind of move. My mum and dad had spotted my lack of prowess from afar and decided to rid me of my dilemma. They insisted I kiss them both, right there in our house. The girls started to giggle and I felt incredibly exposed. Eventually I leaned in and kissed them one by one on the lips. It was sloppy and awkward. I had hoped my first kiss would be an exciting and personal experience. Instead it was forced and humiliating. I could not believe that they had ruined that for me as well.

***

There was a building near our new house from which emanated an awful stench, as well as the most horrific of shrieks. One day I decided it was time to find out what was going on in there. I didn't actually want to enter, but my inquisitive nature got the better of me and soon enough I had a front-row seat to the sickest show on earth.

Inside were pigs, lots of pigs. I followed their route with my gaze and saw that they were being led through a maze of metal fences. At the entrance a man was inserting what looked like a pair of curling tongs into the pigs' rectums, which made them run faster towards their inevitable end. As they squashed themselves into line, the pig at the front had its head tied in a noose. This was then hooked onto a moving cable that lifted the pig off the ground at a steep angle via a series of pulleys. My eyes followed that one pig's journey as it wriggled uncontrollably, fighting for air. As it got higher there was another man on a ledge who sliced its throat open once it came within range. *Jesus, I was not expecting that!* I thought. It hung there convulsing for a few seconds, the blood pouring out of the poor thing into a barrel below, which was overflowing with the thick red plasma that had accumulated over time (which I now assume was for black pudding).

The pig then moved again, its head now hanging on by a thread. A third man stood waiting on the next platform holding a machete-style knife. He swung it hard, severing the head. The body fell to the ground, landing atop the other carcasses. The head then continued on its merry way until it was out of sight.

Sometimes we profess to be shocked when we are not; in this instance, though, 'shocked' didn't quite cut it. I was appalled, astonished, sickened even. I could not believe the utter brutality involved. It was a life-changing few minutes.

I decided to follow the line backwards and was soon outside in the front area where the pigs were roaming free before being sent into the room of doom. I decided to hang out with them for a while. They may have been oblivious to their fate, but I was not and felt an enormous urge to set them free. Instead, I simply tried to make their final moments happy ones.

Eventually one of the workers came out and insisted that I leave. I walked away knowing they would all die, and it was heartbreaking. I loved animals. I was, however, not too sure how I felt about people.

***

While walking through town one afternoon I noticed something rather odd. Either I was seeing things or there were two fully grown camels standing in the middle of the town park. Once I saw that they were tied up, I decided to go over and stroke them. They continued to chew, emitting the foulest of smells, while a number of shiny trucks pulled up alongside them. It was clear that the circus had come to town.

I visited the camels every day while the venue was being built, chatting to them about my day and so forth. Now, I realise that talking to camels may be construed as peculiar, but I was turning into quite a peculiar boy.

A few days into my hanging out with the camels, a girl appeared. She was pretty, older and spoke with a Dublin accent. Although I barely understood a word, I took an instant liking to her. However, just as we were getting to know each other, her brother gatecrashed our encounter, reminding her that they had to get to rehearsal. It transpired that they were both performers in the circus; she played Miss Piggy and her brother Kermit. As she ran off, she suggested I return the next day to watch their performance. By the time she was out of sight I had already fallen for her. That night Miss Piggy was all I could think about.

I never did find the time, or the money, to see the full show, but I did get to hang out with her and see a couple of rehearsals. It did not take long to convince myself that I was in love. I spent all my time in school daydreaming about her, finding it difficult to concentrate. I remained firmly focused on the next time I could see her in person. I was also envious of her lifestyle, not having to attend school and being able to travel around the country willy-nilly. I wished that I, too, could run away with the circus.

Later that same week, I walked enthusiastically towards the park after school. I was excited and felt tingly at the thought of seeing her. However, as I passed through the main gate I got the shock of my young life. The circus was no more. It was gone. No trace of the big top remained.

A sense of loss engulfed me. Where were they? And why had no one told me? I had a hole in my heart that evening. It was as if the circus had never existed. Whoever the girl was, I never saw her again.

***

Over the coming months the town became my playground. I had never lived in the dead centre of a bustling town before and I was enjoying the closeness of everything; nothing was far away, even the cinema was only two minutes from our front door. This cinema, however, bore little resemblance to the ones I had attended in England. It was a basic, dark room filled with a bunch of random chairs. It was incredibly uncomfortable, especially if you were watching a long film. I think this may be the reason I didn't enjoy *Star Wars*. Everyone was raving about it, but I just could not understand the appeal. I much preferred *Abba: The Movie* – now that one knew how to strike a nerve.

I spent most of my time in and around the town park. When I wasn't poaching apples from the attached orchard, I was hiding out in my favourite tree. I always found somewhere to lay low wherever I lived and in this case it was halfway up a vast willow tree in the park. I would spend hours sitting up there, listening to people as they passed. On one occasion the approaching voices belonged to my parents and I got to hear their unbridled conversation first-hand. It was great fun being invisible.

Another reason I was in the park often was my dad's insistence that I take up regular exercise. He was quite the runner and had convinced me that I should join him on his laps around the park. My parents were always telling me that I needed to lose weight, so I agreed to give it a go.

At first, it wasn't too bad. It was something my dad and I did together 'as men', each circuit of the park being about a mile in length. Then, over time, my mother started turning up. Given her limp, she, of course, couldn't take part. Instead she would shout from the sidelines, telling me to run faster and calling me names like 'fatty', which I assume were meant to spur me on. Unfortunately it did the opposite and just made me feel like shit. I quickly came to hate running. All I could think about when running around that park was 'When can I stop?'

Eventually it was decided that running would become a form of punishment. Once my parents saw how much I hated it, they realised I could be subjected to forced runs. However, instead of running a couple of circuits of the park with my dad, the number of laps I would have to complete became dependent on the severity of my wrongdoings. The more odious the crime, the more laps I would accrue. I would get terrible stitches in my sides during these punishment runs and the cold air would burn my oesophagus as I attempted an increasing number of circuits.

Near the park was the town library. It was there that I would commit my first purely solo act of lawlessness, though not before I saw something rather wonderful. On a rough piece of ground near the library was a horse, a horse that was making a peculiar array of noises from snorting to grunting and neighing wildly. It was also raising its hind legs up and down in a strange rhythm. Something was afoot. Then, without warning, a smaller horse fell out of the back of the bigger one.

Okay, well that's new! I thought.

The foal got to its legs within seconds and its mother began to sniff her offspring with her muzzle; it was amazing. I could not believe I had just seen a horse come into the world, and purely by chance. That's something I would never have seen living in London.

Shortly after that, however, I entered the library with the intention of stealing a book. I didn't really have a plan per se. Why I didn't simply join said *bibliothèque* is a question I cannot answer.

While I was casing the joint, looking for a suitable read, I noticed an unattended handbag on the ground. It was open. So much so, that I could clearly see a twenty-pound note sticking out, taunting me. The temptation was far too delicious to resist.

I shoved the note deep into my jeans pocket and briskly legged it. What a rush. My heart was pounding and I felt something brand new – a buzz, if you will – and I liked it. I didn't feel guilt, I was just excited to have cash. It was actually too much money to know what to do with. At that point in my life I probably spent less than fifty pence a day, my only vice being the odd sugar cone from the local ice-cream shop, which were only two pence each.

Instead of keeping the funds, I thought it might be more fun to blow it all on a good time. So I gathered together a bunch of loose acquaintances from school and set off to the dog track. I had zero intention of taking the money home. If I was caught with a large sum like that, I was destined to a front-row seat at the world of grief. I figured we were bound to lose it all betting, but at least we would have a good time doing so.

Before I am accused of bullshitting, I should point out that when I was a child in Ireland no one cared how old you were. You could buy cigarettes, obtain alcohol and gamble at the track; you could even ride a motorcycle if you wanted. I realise it sounds nuts now, but it's just the way it was at the time, at least going by my experience.

So there I was, not even nine years old, with a bunch of other kids, throwing stolen money after bad. I watched in awe as grown men put vast sums of money on the outcome of a dog's running ability – it seemed a ludicrous way to increase your wealth. I have never understood gambling in general. It's the one addiction to which I am certain I am immune.

I split the twenty pounds equally, and we began placing random bets. I was not expecting to win, but win I did, and not just once. I only took five pounds from my bounty but I'd soon quadrupled it back up to twenty in no time. Now what? It was actually kind of annoying. Knowing I couldn't take the money home with me, I gave even more of my cash to the others. They must have thought Christmas had come early.

Eventually I said my goodbyes and left, keeping just a couple of pounds for myself. On the long walk home I realised that I'd have been better off never taking the money in the first place. I wished that I could have gone back in time and just left that poor lady's handbag alone. It was just another crappy act on my part that I couldn't take back.

That evening I accompanied my parents to a funfair that had sprung up in the middle of town. There was an abundance of great rides including a big wheel, which I braved for the first and last time. While there, we decided to get dressed up in nineteenth-century attire for a Wild West-style photograph. We were pictured wearing outlandish costumes complete with guns and cowboy hats, like outlaws. It was the most prophetic of photographs.

***

A few days later I accompanied my dad back to his hometown to attend an Irish festival. There was everything from food, music and dancing to an array of leather products on offer, some of which were crafted before our very eyes. The festival was heavily Irish in nature, which was something I was not used to seeing, but I enjoyed it immensely. It ended up being the only fun day out with my dad that I can remember.

As the festivities began to wind down my dad suggested I get a belt. There were many beautifully designed belts on sale, but as I'd never owned one before, I found it difficult to choose. I eventually picked a brown one adorned with Celtic symbols. It had a heavy brass rectangular buckle that felt good to wear. It made me feel manly and I walked with a certain swagger after its purchase.

Bronagh had come to stay with us during this period. She was my dad's younger sister and looked almost exactly like him. At the time my dad's hair was the same length as hers, which made it impossible to tell them apart from behind. The extra company led to a fair amount of partying. Out came the booze and the drugs and I became part of the background once more.

I did not like Bronagh. She had a type of nonchalance I found hard to warm to. She would also try to emulate my parents by taking the piss out of me in front of them. This I cared for even less. Fine, if my parents wanted to insult me then so be it, but who was she to make such comments? I made tentative plans to seek revenge for her defamatory remarks before she left.

Bronagh slept in the lounge with her belongings scattered around her like a teenage boy. I bore witness to this messiness the very next morning when I appeared to be the only one awake. I crept downstairs to make breakfast and in doing so noticed her purse exposed on the counter. Again I didn't need the money, I just wanted her to pay for her insults. I picked up the purse and opened it. Inside was a wad of cash made up of both English and Irish banknotes; she seemed to have plenty, so I decided to take just five pounds. I figured it wasn't quite enough to arouse suspicion but might just be enough to cause her some grief. Then I went to school.

When I arrived home that evening my parents and Bronagh were sitting on the sofa waiting for me. My dad remained seated and gave me just one chance to come clean. If I admitted to stealing the money, then my punishment would be diminished. My blood drained. It had never crossed my mind that I'd get caught. I was convinced that the money would go unnoticed. It was quite the pickle. I refused to admit to anything. Instead I simply wet myself, which was considered admission enough.

My dad jumped off the sofa and grabbed hold of me. Before I knew what was happening I was being punched with full fists over my entire body. My mum came over and said something to him, whereby he paused briefly. I thought she was trying to stop him but alas, no. She simply wanted me to remove my urine-soaked trousers so that they didn't ruin the rug. My dad then motioned for me to remove my underpants as well and I point-blank refused. We had company, for God's sake! For this impertinence I received a dig in the ribs. Moments later I was stood in the lounge naked from the waist down with three adults looking on.

My mum was about to walk away with my jeans when my dad had an idea. 'Wait,' he said to her. An unsettling smile crossed his face.

Here we go, I thought.

He then told me to go and retrieve my belt from the wet jeans and bring it to him. At this Bronagh actually clasped her hands together in excitement. I thought she was going to bloody well clap. I begged him not to do what I thought he was about to do. Finally my mum looked worried and I could tell she wanted to stop the spectacle, but it was too late. My dad barked at me to 'cop on to myself' and 'hurry the fuck up'. So I pulled on the buckle and watched as the leather slid towards me, my fate growing ever closer with each denim loop. Once it was free, he told me to hand it to him, but I just couldn't let go of my end. I suspected what was coming was going to be pretty barbaric and held onto it for dear life. Finally, to add to my humiliation, I was told to remove my last piece of clothing, my T-shirt. I was now stark-bollock naked and terrified.

There was a slight pause. (Isn't there always?) Bronagh started egging my dad on: 'Go on!' She was clearly in the mood for a show. My mum was standing back, not taking part, but not stopping it either.

I heard the sound – a loud crack in the air – followed by a stinging sensation on my side; then the pain hit me. I assume this to be similar to a lashing. With each whip two thin lines of blood appeared on the surface of my skin, the exact same width of the belt. I tried to concentrate on this oddity rather than feel the discomfort.

Not content with the level of suffering he was dishing out, my dad decided to go one further. He began hitting me with the buckle end. Now that really fucking hurt. There was no masking the pain coming from that lump of thick brass. Although the physical pain was unbearable, by far the worst thing about this incident was that he was hitting me with the present he'd bought me just a few days earlier. Now that one good day we had together would forever be tarnished.

Through the entire attack, I watched as Bronagh laughed and applauded. Each time my dad lashed out she would give a little cry of joy. I hated her for that as much as I detested him. Sure, I stole five pounds. So what? This was savagery. It was in no way a proportional response and by far the worst beating I had ever received.

When it was over, my mum came to my aid and, on seeing the marks all over my body, told my dad he had gone too far. He disagreed and threatened her with the same. Bronagh butted in, saying I would be fine and that the bruises would fade given time. How wrong that witch was. It turns out not all bruises are physical.

Come to think of it, I was always told that I bruised easily. My mum, when explaining bodily marks, would often tell people that you only had to look at me and I would bruise; a fact that I would go on to reiterate to others for many years.

Later that same evening I heard laughter coming from the lounge, so I crept down the staircase to investigate. I descended just enough to reveal my parents and Bronagh knocking back Southern Comfort, smoking and laughing uncontrollably. Their merriment seemed particularly misplaced considering how badly I had been treated just a few hours earlier. You would be hard-pressed to know what kind of people they really were in that moment. They may well have appeared normal on the outside, but clearly there was something terribly wrong with my family.

I was soon spotted and ushered in as if nothing was out of the ordinary. I was then made to listen as my dad explained how I had brought the earlier beating upon myself, to which Bronagh heartily agreed. He then pointed out that, because I had paid for my transgression, the incident was behind us. So, if I wanted to, I could join them for the rest of the evening, no hard feelings.

Was he fucking kidding? Little did he know what was going in my mind as I watched them partying. I made a vow to enact vengeance on both my father and Bronagh as soon as the moment presented itself. This was war. If there had been rat poison in the house that night neither of those fuckers would have woken up the next morning, I can assure you of that.

CHAPTER 12

MY ALCATRAZ (PART TWO)

No sooner had Bronagh left than my dad's brother Archie appeared on the scene, visiting the house often, mostly while my dad was at work. I had no inkling of my mother's affair at the time, but it certainly explains a lot in retrospect; mainly my dad's infernal mood swings. Not only was he beating me, he was also regularly hitting my mother. Perhaps he thought I was covering for them? Strangely he never confronted Archie, who was one of the few people my dad seemed truly afraid of. I also doubt that Archie knew my dad was hurting my mother. Something tells me he would not have stood for that.

My mum seemed to spend her time either robbing the register at work or hanging out with Archie. She talked to him with an openness I had never seen before; she was clearly relaxed in his company. Archie would come by regularly and take us to the beach for entire afternoons, where my mum would insist on burying me up to my neck in sand. Compared to spending time with my dad, our days out with Archie were very pleasant. He was far more laid-back than my dad and brought some much-needed levity into our lives.

During those afternoons I would often stare out into the Atlantic Ocean, wondering who was on the opposite shore in North America. I hoped to one day be that person, looking back in the other direction. It seemed impossible from where I was lying, though, mostly because I was often up to my neck in sand.

One afternoon Archie came over to the house for one of his 'visits'.

There was no beach trip planned for that particular day, so he asked if I wouldn't mind going outside to play for a while as he wanted to spend time alone with my mother. As I left, he handed me two pounds. It remains the only time I was ever paid to disappear. This of course annoyed my mother. She told him it was too much money to give to a child and yelled after me, telling me not to spend it all. *Yeah, right,* I thought. *It's mine, and I'll do what I bloody well like with it thank you very much.*

I turned the corner and headed for the shops. I was not suspicious at all, and paid little regard as to why they wanted me out of the house. All I knew was I had money to spend and that's exactly what I was going to do.

The arcade at the end of the main street contained a number of stalls that sold inexpensive toys and sweets, and that's where I headed. Most items cost peanuts and I was soon in my element with hands full of cheap goodies. I rarely got to spend money openly and was revelling in being able to buy so much for so little. It was all rubbish of course, but it was my rubbish.

With my final pennies I bought an ice cream and walked proudly out of the arcade's rear exit. As I squinted in the bright sunlight I felt a sudden pain in my jaw. Ice cream was now splattered across my face and the cone was upside down on the ground atop my now-scattered toys. I looked up to see my dad's furious face. He had appeared out of nowhere like a man possessed. He dragged me around the back of the building and proceeded to give me a full-fisted beating. I was crying and begging him to stop, but he would only desist if another person got too close. He would tell me to act normal while he said 'Hello', accompanied by a little chuckle. Once they were out of sight, he would continue his violent act.

I could not comprehend why he was so angry with me. What could I have possibly done to make him so upset? He later told me that the beating was for disobeying my mother's wishes and spending the whole two pounds I was given by Archie, even though he couldn't possibly have known how much I had spent before hitting me in the face.

My suspicion is that he came home early to find his brother in the company of my mother. This would have pushed him over the edge. If so, the man was a fucking coward. Rather than confront his own brother for sleeping with his wife, he instead beat up his not-yet-nine-year-old son in a car park.

My dad told me to leave my broken toys on the ground, go home and tell my mother that he was going to the cinema and would not be home for dinner. As I walked away I could see him gathering up my purchases. I foolishly assumed he would bring them home after he'd gone to the movies. Not a chance. He took pride in later retelling how he'd stood at the entrance to the arcade and given away every single one of my toys to random children.

***

The Christian Brothers school was hard to endure, but as the autumn term began I kept my head down and got on with what was asked of me. At least my walk to school became far shorter once we'd moved into town. It was now but a hop and a skip along the narrow pavements. Within minutes of leaving the house I would be standing in the playground in time for the opening of the tuck shop. This was my first time attending a school with its own sweet shop attached. It was marvellous and the only positive in a world of negatives, mostly because they sold what I believe to be the greatest crisps in the world: Taytos.

One particular morning I planned to meet a friend who lived on the other side of town and walk in to school with him. It meant going the long way round, but it got me out of the house earlier, which was always a bonus. Even though I was focused on getting my tuck shop Taytos, we were both a little peckish, so we decided to pop into one of the many shops en route in search of confectionery. As I walked in something caught my eye. I wish it hadn't. It was a beautiful gold-leaf pen by Parker. I have always had a bit of a penchant for stationery and it was already becoming a bit of a problem. My nan had previously stated that I should never be left alone with Sellotape. She wasn't wrong.

The pen was calling to me. I had no choice but to go over and at least take a look. I noticed my friend was buying sweets, keeping the shopkeeper nice and busy. This inadvertently gave me an opportunity. Without thinking about the consequences, I nabbed it. The pen was in my pocket before I had time to talk myself out of it. To avoid suspicion, I walked right up to the counter and bought a few penny toffees. I took my sweet time leaving, making sure not to rush. However, I still got that chilly feeling as I walked through the door – that moment where you think you might actually get caught. Once we were outside I knew I'd gotten away with it and I was pleased. I loved my swag. Unfortunately my joy would be short-lived.

Just a few hours later I was seated in the class of a Brother who disliked me. Within the first few minutes of the lesson I made a fatal error. I pulled out the stolen pen and began writing with it. The glare from the gold must have caught his eye, as he came bounding over. He asked whose pen it was and I told him it was mine, a birthday gift. I thought it was a pretty convincing lie as I had recently had my ninth birthday, but he was having none of it. I guess it looked too expensive for someone of my standing. He gave me one last chance to tell the truth and warned me that any further lies would result in me receiving punishment. I laughed inside: 'Do your worst.'

His eyes narrowed dramatically, so I changed tack slightly. 'Okay, okay, so I found it on the way to school this morning,' I lied. At this the Brother became indignant and instructed me to wait outside until the class was over. I could not understand why he was getting so worked up about this. What was his problem?

As it was very nearly lunchtime I assumed he would reprimand me by giving me the strap or perhaps hand out a detention. I wish. Once the bell rang he dismissed his class and marched me off towards the car park. He informed me that he was taking me home. He wanted to speak to my parents. I was mortified. What the hell had I done? Was I trying to get myself killed? It was only a short drive to the house, but he still managed to insult me plenty in those few precious minutes, calling me a liar and a thief the entire way, which, although true, I found somewhat harsh.

With his fingers digging into my left arm, he knocked forcefully on my front door and for a brief moment I once again believed in deities. I prayed to whoever would listen: 'Please God, let there be nobody home.'

The door opened to a confused and irritated-looking woman – my mother. Unfortunately she was in a terrible mood. *There's a surprise!* I thought, before realising how lucky I might, in fact, be. My mother had saved me from a beating when I was arrested earlier that year. Perhaps she would do the same this time? Maybe my dad didn't need to know about any of this. I had been beaten an awful lot lately and she knew he often went too far. I was almost certain that she would protect me.

But I had a problem. While teaching me the skills of shoplifting, my mum had explained the one golden rule: if you are caught you must stick to your story, never change it and, most importantly, believe in it yourself. I had not taken her advice so far that morning, but once I was home I intended to do just that. Somehow I had to use her own logic against her, but I wasn't quite sure if I could pull it off.

The Brother explained that I had obviously stolen the pen somewhere in town but was refusing to admit it. My mum asked me straight out if that was true and I stuck to my story. I told her that I'd found it on the way to school. I had quite an embellished story by this point and I had no intention of cracking. If I could get my mum to believe me I was sure to avoid a thrashing. Nobody gets hit for finding something in the street, right?

All I had to do was remain calm and convince my mother of my lie.

Then I mistakenly glanced in her direction and crumbled. She could see right through me. She gave me a look to let me know that she knew. It was over. It was obvious to her that I was trying to bullshit my way out of the situation. The Brother left after suggesting that my father have a firm word with me. *Cheers mate!*

Once we were alone my mum gave me one final chance to come clean. Even though she knew the truth, I still stuck to my story, just as she had taught me. I was then sent to my room with a promise that I would be dealt with later. My dad would have to get the truth out of me, apparently. I did not like the sound of that.

This was not how I envisioned my day going. It was lunchtime and I still had the entire afternoon to let my fear build. My dad was going to kill me for this. I had no doubt about that. Bringing a Christian Brother to the door was akin to bringing the guards. Things at home were already appalling, and this would surely be the final straw. I prepared myself for another beating with the belt. I wouldn't say I was used to it, but I knew by then how to endure it. The punches were always painful, but I had a way of blocking most of it out, so I knew I'd be okay. *Fuck him*, I thought, *he can't hurt me any more than he already has.*

I heard the front door open and knew it was my dad coming home from work. The sound of the door closing behind him made my sphincter contract and the blood rush to my feet. I instantly felt light-headed and nauseous. The next sound I heard was their muffled whispers, followed by my mum demanding that I come downstairs.

That was the worst bit, the walking of the plank, so to speak. As I descended I could see that my dad was still in his work clothes. He was covered in concrete and his hands were grey with dust. Clearly tired from working, he appeared to be in no mood to deal with the situation with which he was now confronted. He refused to look at me while he listened intently to my mum as she explained what had happened.

I stood frozen in silence, suspecting I would not get through the evening without something terrible occurring. My dad seemed oddly detached. My mum was convinced that I was lying and was, as usual, refusing to admit the truth. *Because that's what you taught me*, I thought angrily.

My dad finally reacted. Once he'd removed his encrusted boots I knew the gloves were off. He spoke quietly and slowly. He wanted to be precise and for me to understand my options clearly. He told me that he didn't care if I lied to him, but if I continued to lie to my mother in front of him, I would be in grave danger, because apparently you don't lie to your mother. This hypocritical sense of respect for my mother always royally pissed me off. *If you respect her so much then why do you beat her all the time?* I thought.

The moment had arrived. My dad finally looked me square in the eye and asked where the pen had come from. I was told to think very carefully before giving my answer. Against my better judgement I decided the best option was to finally tell the truth, but direct that honesty towards my mum, as an apology of sorts. I thought if I came clean I would at least get some much-needed brownie points and might even avoid a beating altogether.

I should have taken my mum's original advice and stuck to my lie. As soon as I'd admitted to stealing I was under attack. My dad lifted me up by the neck and pushed me hard against the wall. I began to choke as his hand gripped my throat. He appeared to be strangling me. He held on long enough to force out the last gulps of accumulated air and I felt my eyes swell up under the pressure. He then lifted me even higher, all with just one hand, until my feet were completely off the ground. I could no longer breathe and began to spasm. It was then that I realised he might actually be killing me.

I gave in to the outcome. This was it, the day I thought would come. I was going to die right there, I was sure of it.

My mum began screaming, but it was too late, he had already decided on my fate and had no intention of letting go. His eyes were burning into mine. I did not want his distorted face to be the last thing I saw, so I tried to look away. He pushed on my throat even harder, starving my body of oxygen until I could breathe no more. At the very moment I suspect I was about to lose consciousness, he threw me to the floor, where I did, in fact, black out momentarily. I came around just in time to receive a blow to the ribs, after which my dad stormed off, swearing wildly.

My mum ran over, which I assumed was to console her beaten child. It was not. She simply wanted to remind me that I had brought it all upon myself. 'Look what you made him do,' she screamed.

I was given a scarf to cover the marks on my neck and told to wear it at all times until the redness faded. God forbid anyone should find out about the monster we lived with.

To this day I cannot explain why I didn't simply try to run away during this dark period. Deep down, I wanted to be with my parents regardless. I just always hoped things would eventually change for the better and the pain would be worth it somehow. I longed for my father to feel regret and for us to cultivate an honest future together as a family. Therefore, I clung desperately to that hope throughout all the violence and hate.

The next time I saw my father was at breakfast the following morning. I was eating cornflakes when he appeared. Usually when he resurfaced he would be in a slightly better mood, but not this time. He just walked over to me, picked up my bowl and smashed it on top of my head. The bowl broke into four distinct pieces as the milk ran down my confused cheeks and I began to cry. Cereal was strewn across my face and stuck to my hair and clothes. I'm not sure if it was nerves or her sick sense of humour, but my mother started laughing uncontrollably. My dad then came back over to me, leaned in and called me 'a little cunt', then left for work.

CHAPTER 13

THE RED-LIT ROOM

Before the cornflakes had time to dry I was summoned to the living room for a quiet word. There were to be some changes. As an extra punishment, they had decided that I would no longer be allowed in my own bedroom. My toys, pens and all personal items were now off limits. My room was subsequently locked with a brass padlock and I was relocated to the small spare room on the landing. I was to go there immediately and forfeit supper. I hadn't actually committed any acts of defiance that day, but I guess I was still paying for past crimes.

Apart from an old bed, a rusty fireplace and a flaky red light bulb, the room was completely empty. Wallpaper peeled from the walls to reveal patches of damp and the room felt cold. We had yet to use this bedroom, so my dad had never bothered to fix it up. It was, therefore, still in a state of complete disrepair. My mum had moved all my clothes into her wardrobe, so I only had access to the clothes on my back. She told me I would be given fresh attire each morning, so I didn't need any spares in my actual room. She then volunteered an awkward 'Goodnight then' before closing the door. Suddenly I was alone in a dirty, dank room.

I was not allowed books and we certainly didn't have television. I literally had no way of amusing myself or killing time in that awful space. All I could do was spend time in my own head. Once that door was closed I pondered all the stupid things I had done of late.

I was nine years into my short life and all I seemed to be doing was causing myself grief. It was time to put an end to this inane behaviour.

I made a decision right then and there to be a better son. Perhaps if I explained this to my parents and apologised profusely they would forgive me. I walked over to the door and turned the handle. It was locked. Jesus! They were locking me in now? This was an added twist to the nightmare.

I banged lightly on the door, but nobody came. I tried a few times, before coming to the conclusion that they were probably ignoring me, so I gave up. It later transpired that they had actually gone out for the evening, leaving me locked in. I thought how odd it was that just yards away from a bustling shopping street sat a young boy incarcerated in a derelict room without food or water; no one knew I was even in there. I felt completely alone in my wretched Irish life. Somehow, through my actions, I had accidentally constructed my own personal Alcatraz. Then a worrying thought crossed my mind: *What if I need a poo?*

As I wasn't allowed to see friends during this punishment period, I was kept off school for the rest of the term. Lord only knows what they told the Brothers. It was decided that my mother would become my teacher, educating me during the wee hours. She was a bit of a night owl, so it fit in with her schedule perfectly and I would often find myself trying to spell words like 'conscientiousness' at three in the morning. There was no way my mum was going to teach me in my stinky room, so it was decided that I could have a couple of hours downstairs to study each night once my dad had gone to bed.

Attending my mum's night school was a welcome relief, not unlike when prison inmates get 'time in the yard'. Once my dad was settled in his bed, my mum would appear at my door, key in hand. Once the squeaky key steel turned, I was free to learn. Eventually the rule of no books or comics was relaxed a little and my internment became bearable through escapism. Without reading material I would have surely gone mad.

My mum's dog, Gypsy, was long gone by this stage, having had the good sense to run away from the horror house early on. As a result, my mum was beginning to pine for a canine. My dad had picked up on this fact and returned home with a puppy, no doubt as an apology for something horrid he did that I never knew about. It wasn't long, however, before he lost patience and began complaining about its whimpering and high-pitched barking.

Then one night all hell broke loose. During one of my late-night classes the dog began to bark loudly. My mum and I both froze when we heard a sudden heavy thump above our heads. My dad came flying down the stairs in a fury and I shat myself a little. He exploded into the lounge, swearing at my mum, telling her that she should have kept the 'little fucker' quiet. He gave her a few slaps before coming over to me. With his twisted face close to mine, he stated that if he heard my stupid voice one more time that night he'd slit my throat. He then stormed off towards the dog while my mum screamed at me to stay in the living room. I assumed she was trying to spare me the sight of him hurting the puppy. She followed my dad into the alley, calling him a bastard as she went. I heard a yelp from the poor beast, which was followed by the slamming of the front door. He was gone and so was the dog.

My mum came back in tears, telling me to continue my studies in my room. My door remained unlocked that night, but I never once considered leaving.

The next morning's breakfast was a particularly tense experience. While munching on toast and jam, my dad casually mentioned that he'd killed the dog. He also added that if we made any more noise during the night, we would be next. I could tell when my mum was genuinely scared of him and this was one of those times. Because of this tension, my home education ended abruptly and I was forced to spend even more hours in my cell.

***

The main problem I found with being locked away was how to deal with toilet issues. I had no lavatory to speak of, not even a bucket. I could easily pee out the window, but number twos were a bit of a no-no. So, after much deliberation, I reluctantly took to shitting in the fireplace. I had limited options, after all. I would dispose of it by throwing it down into the alley below, where I hoped people would assume it came from a dog. I would then steal matches from the kitchen to remove any accompanying stench, igniting them at the window while hoping my parents didn't smell the burning. Not having toilet paper to hand was also extremely problematic. Once I had used up my comics, I took to using my underpants. I would then throw my soiled briefs onto the pub roof opposite, in the hope that they were never discovered.

Although this dirty habit only lasted a few weeks, it was hugely embarrassing to have to live this way. I was trapped like an animal for weeks, without any indication as to when my sentence would end. To make things worse I was often forced to skip my evening meal due to my supposedly being 'too fat'. There were to be no meals in the red-lit room. My stomach would hurt so much that I took to stealing food around town that I could sneak back into my room via my clothes.

My imprisonment came to an abrupt end when the landlady of the pub next door found my shitty pants adorning her roof tiles and reported the fact to my mother, who was so embarrassed that she decided to drag me to the pub to apologise for my disgusting behaviour in person. I tried to explain that I didn't exactly do it on purpose. Considering I was locked inside the room for hours on end, I'd had little choice but to use whatever was to hand. She retorted that I was a 'filthy bastard' and that my father would hear about this. I was already at my lowest ebb and knew I could not handle further violence. The situation seemed to be spiralling once more, so I tried again to explain myself, but my mother wasn't listening. Instead she kept calling me derogatory names until we were inside the pub.

Standing face to face with the landlady was anything but comfortable. I did as my mum demanded and apologised. I promised that it wouldn't happen again and that I was ashamed of my actions. My mother was clearly trying to deflect any responsibility by selling the incident as an isolated act by a disturbed child. She was so convincing that I nearly gave her a round of applause.

She then began to make light of the situation by mocking me, right in front of the landlady. That really bothered me. I had a good mind to tell the entire pub what was really going on behind closed doors just a few feet away. I had an urge to shout it from the shitty rooftops, but why would they care? Would they even be surprised? At the time I assumed that most children in Ireland were being treated in a similar fashion – which of course they weren't, but how was I to know? Based on my experiences, I honestly wondered if anyone would bat an eyelid if I blew the whistle. So I ultimately kept silent and left.

Once my dad arrived home he was told about the whole underwear on the roof debacle and I was promptly beaten. That was not a surprise, but what happened next certainly was. I got my old room back. I was suddenly allowed to sleep in my own bed and even gained access to my belongings. I was of course grateful, but also baffled. My parents explained that they thought I'd learned my lesson, but warned that I had better behave myself from now on. I assured them that I would try my best.

My dad then volunteered a promise. If I kept my side of the bargain, he would take me to the nearest city and buy me a Christmas present. Finally, things were looking up.

***

My mum became a child around this time of year and decorated the house so that, for once, it resembled a home. I was yet to experience the build-up to the festive season properly with my parents, but now that they were acting with relative normality, I had high hopes. All violence seemed to be on hold and there was even talk of me returning to school in January.

It is odd to imagine that just one year earlier I'd believed in Santa Claus. My nan and granddad had put great effort into continuing the myth just for my sake. My parents, however, thought differently and carelessly let the cat out of the bag without compunction. Of course I had suspected the obvious, but once I knew for sure, the Yuletide season seemed a little fake and harder to buy into. I was a bit young to feel quite so jaded, but in less than a year I had lost both God and Santa, so I had my reasons.

I became more excited when, as agreed, a few weeks before Christmas, we took a trip to the city in search of festive presents. I had kept out of trouble, so my reward was a gift of my own choosing.

Present-wise my dad already had something in mind. After washing down breakfast with a cola that was not Coke, we headed out into the busy streets. Suddenly my dad told me to close my eyes and led me excitedly to a random shop front. I wondered what amazing curio he could have spotted for me. Once I was in front of the window he told me to open my eyes. 'How about that?' he said with glee.

'What is it?' I asked.

'Jesus, it's a fort,' he said.

A fort? I did not want a bloody fort. 'What would I do with that exactly?' I wondered.

My mum started laughing and told him that it was far too old-fashioned. We walked on with my dad trailing behind looking deflated.

Eventually my mother became restless and wanted to head home. Now, if there is one thing I know for certain, it is that when my mother has had enough of something, you just do what she says. Trust me, it's easier. I was about to give up all hope of finding a decent present, when suddenly I spotted something spectacular. It was by far the coolest toy I'd ever seen: a model of the *Star Trek* Enterprise. The ship was attached to an arm, which in turn was attached to a heavy base. It took four huge batteries and went round and round for no apparent reason. I'm still not sure what was so appealing about it – it was easily as useless as the fort – but I wanted it. I wasn't even a *Star Trek* fan. But I loved it. My dad was disappointed that I hadn't picked his suggestion but bought it for me regardless.

Later that weekend we went for a long drive in search of a Christmas tree. My dad always tended to drive as if someone was chasing him. The fact that he was traversing dangerous mountain roads made no difference whatsoever. I became a little scared of those roads, as it often seemed like we might fly off the edge into the abyss at any given moment.

I was impressed with the way in which the Irish got their trees, though. There was no going to Woolworths for some plastic piece of tosh. They simply went into the woods and chopped down whichever one they fancied – at least that's what my dad did. It was refreshing and I liked it. When we eventually found a suitable candidate, I helped my dad cut it down with a bow saw. Then, with some degree of difficulty, we managed to get it on top of the car and drove off.

Our relationship was finally showing signs of improvement and the more I thought about it, the more I started to believe that I was to blame for most of the events that drove my dad to be violent towards me. I figured that if I stopped doing stupid things, then he would have no reason to beat me. It seemed a simple solution to end what had been an atrocious year.

***

Christmas was almost upon us when I noticed the door to a large unused cupboard had been left slightly ajar. I peeked inside and to my surprise saw a large pile of boxes. There were LEGO sets plus other festively wrapped items. Upon closer inspection I could see that they were all for me. I could not believe my luck. They had clearly arrived from England and most were from my grandparents. I became very excited at the prospect of receiving so many gifts and could barely wait for Christmas morning. It was going to be tremendous.

At midnight on Christmas Eve my mum suggested that we open just one present each. My dad had long since gone to bed, but my mum shared my love of Christmas and had therefore stayed up late, partly due to excitement. We grabbed a present each, mine being the big present bought for me by my dad. Even though I knew what was inside, it was still thrilling to hear the rip of the paper. I was aware of my other gifts from England, so I knew I had plenty coming and didn't feel bad about opening one measly box. I did think it odd that the other presents weren't yet under the tree. Still, I suspected my parents were going to surprise me with them the following day and so carried on tearing.

I pulled out my *Star Trek* Enterprise, clipped it together and had it up and running in no time. It was fantastic and I remained very happy with my choice. Santa or not, this was a great Christmas. My mum ended up opening two of her presents and between us I guess we were making a bit too much noise.

Suddenly above our heads came a familiar aggressive thud, followed by stomping feet heading down the staircase. We gave each other an uneasy look.

My dad burst into the room. He was as mad as I had ever seen him. He grabbed my mother and struck her. She fell to the floor, cursing at him through her tears. He was screaming at her about making too much noise while he was sleeping. He then saw my *Star Trek* toy and was pissed off that I'd opened it early. For that very reason he picked it up and threw it against the wall. He then went over to where it landed and stomped on it with brute force. That was that then. I also got a few slaps, but he was gone as fast as he'd arrived. In a matter of seconds our festive spirit had been completely quashed.

Christmas was cancelled that year. My dad stayed in his room for the duration and I never saw the presents from England again. I could hardly ask about them, as I wasn't supposed to have seen them in the first place. Not wanting to get a beating for snooping, I kept my mouth firmly shut in that regard.

In the New Year, my dad volunteered an explanation out of the blue. Rather cruelly he told me that my grandparents and other relatives had sent me a box of presents from England. Upon opening the box my mum and dad deemed many of the presents unsuitable, allegedly for being too childish. Therefore, instead of handing over my bounty, they had decided to give them away to my younger relatives. *Well, isn't that just dandy?* I thought.

In January my dad took me out. He wanted me to try something called a Knickerbocker Glory at one of the many cafés in town. It was obvious that he was trying to say sorry for ruining Christmas. The dessert was delicious, but I wasn't falling for that crap any more. It had been an astonishingly bad year and the damage was done. I knew it and he knew it.

It was a little late for ice cream.

CHAPTER 14

THE PITFALLS OF TRUSTING YOUR MOTHER

The first few months of 1979 passed by in much the same way as the previous year. The house in the town centre seemed to bring out the worst in everyone and violence was commonplace. I continued my reluctant studies at the Christian Brothers' school and tried to avoid the daily thrashing. There seemed to be no end in sight for this horrid life.

Then I found out that my mother was planning on travelling to England during the Easter break to stay with Archie and Bronagh, who were now living together in East London. How my dad agreed to this I will never know, but agree he did. I still hadn't forgiven Bronagh for my beating with the belt, but a trip out of this hellhole would be a welcome relief. At first my dad suggested that I stay behind to run the house in my mother's absence, but luckily she insisted on my company and within a few days the trip was booked and we were on our way.

It was early April as we set off for the airport and I could not have been more excited. This was only my second-ever flight, so my eyes were glued to my tiny window throughout and I marvelled at the sea of clouds below while chomping on tiny packs of salty peanuts. The flight was short and we were up and down so fast that practically the next time I looked up I was in a tube station.

I had missed London and all its quirks. The moment I set foot on the Underground it was not only as if I'd never left, it was as if I had travelled forward in time. The Piccadilly Line had been extended to the airport, so we could literally jump on the tube and travel all the way across London to my aunt and uncle's flat. It was, and still is, very impressive.

As we arrived on that bright sunny April day, it really did feel like a holiday. I was 500 miles away from my father and the chances of being beaten were almost zero, as my mum rarely initiated such things. I would get the odd clip around the head, but nothing on the scale of what I had become used to. It was heaven to be away from Ireland and all its horrors. I'm sure my mother was also enjoying her escape from the dark world of my father.

Archie and Bronagh were living on the upper floor of a tower block. It was my first experience of living in a high-rise and I liked it. I could see for miles around from up there. It was very different to my obstructed view of a concrete wall in Ireland. Bronagh had an Indian boyfriend who would bring home exotic treats like Gulab Jamun and Jalebi, which I found delicious, though insanely sweet. We would sit on the balcony consuming vast amounts of deep-fried delights in succession, without issue.

Archie was going bald. So, whenever he went out my mum and I would throw eggs at him, trying to hit his bald spot as he left. One morning we got the timing very wrong and hit some poor fellow with an uncanny resemblance instead. We only realised it wasn't him when Archie appeared next to the man, gazing upwards in confusion at our giggling faces.

Archie had a skill he wanted to pass on to me, one we would practise nightly until I had it mastered: lock-picking. I crouched quietly in the hallway as he taught me about levers and pins, guiding me until I could pick the lock to the flat armed only with a coat hanger. Eventually I was able to break into the flat with great ease. (Hang on a minute; now I think about it, perhaps that too was a squat?)

Whether it was her plan all along or not I will never know, but my mum contacted my nan and suggested that we meet. I thought this was both out of character and more than a little suspicious. She said it was only fair they see me, if only for a short while. Either my mother was secretly trying to protect me and get me as far away from my father as possible, or this was an epic lapse of prudence.

The chosen location was a small bakery café a few miles from my grandparents' house. Archie and Bronagh both urged my mum to cancel the meeting; they thought it way too risky. My mum, however, reiterated that her parents weren't the kind of people to do anything stupid. She still trusted them.

My grandparents were warned by my mother not to inform the police, as she would be watching beforehand. If there was suspicious activity of any kind she would abort the meeting and they would forfeit ever seeing me again.

If something were to go wrong, I was under instruction to make a run for it. My mum gave me all I needed: enough money to get back to Archie's, a tube map and a list of bus routes. Nobody knew about the flat, so it was effectively a safe house. If I did end up getting caught and sent back to my grandparents, I was to run away as soon as an opportunity presented itself. My mum would await my return at Archie's and we would flee to Ireland by any means. The only problem was, any faith I had in my dad's ability to change was waning and I wasn't wholly convinced that I would run back, given the choice.

As we approached the café my heart was in my mouth. I was looking forward to seeing my nan and granddad again, but I suspected they'd be upset with me for staying in Ireland against their wishes. Therefore, I felt as nervous as I was excited. We held back while my mum surveyed the area, but after seeing nothing untoward, we headed for the entrance, albeit with some trepidation.

Through the glass I immediately recognised my nan sitting alone at a table in the back. She had aged. She looked much more like an old lady.

My granddad was nowhere to be seen, which I thought a little odd. With a ding-a-ling-ling we entered the café.

My nan was overjoyed to see me and I received an enormous hug. It was so nice to feel her warmth and love. The only bodily contact I had really received since I last saw her had been at the hands of my father. I was not used to such physical affection and held on for dear life. In that instant I think I'd already made a decision to stay. My nan, unlike my mum, felt like home.

She then embraced my mother as if nothing bad had ever occurred between them; it was all quite peculiar. My nan seemed almost apologetic as she spoke. There was zero tension as they effortlessly engaged in conversation. It all felt very normal, perhaps a bit too normal.

My mum had her back to the door and so was unable to see what I could, and what I saw was in no way positive – at least for her. Four men, including two police officers, entered the premises, partially blocking out the sunlight as they walked towards us. My mum had no idea anything was happening until my nan suddenly held on to me and said 'I'm so sorry' to her daughter.

My mum's jaw dropped. She had been duped. I could not run as planned. The entrance was blocked, plus I didn't really want to. My mum was promptly arrested and taken into custody. As she was being dragged away she mouthed to me: 'You know what to do.' And then she was gone.

I felt instant loss. All I could think about was what my mum must have been going through. Regardless of all that had happened in Ireland, I still loved her and had an urge to protect her. This realisation manifested as a strong surge of anger towards my nan, who was still holding on to me. A plain-clothes officer then came over and escorted us to a waiting police car.

I was in safe hands and I should have been happy, but I no longer felt joy. That sense of feeling at home had lasted but a few moments.

I arrived at my grandparents' new house courtesy of the police. It was on the same street that we'd lived on when we first moved to East London, so everything felt familiar. For me, this day played out a bit like a movie; one minute I was in Archie's flat with my mum, and an hour or so later I was standing outside my grandparents' house in a completely different environment. It was very disconcerting. My granddad welcomed me at the front door with my second hug of the day. Although he'd avoided my capture, he had taken the day off work and was waiting anxiously at home for my triumphant return.

They were both so happy to see me. It was as if they had won the lottery. It was strange to see people excited by my mere presence. I was not used to it and therefore failed to comprehend it. Their affection, although well meant, was difficult to receive. My nan commented on how thin I had become. It was true; I was very slim. That was nice to hear instead of my mum's constant 'fat' jibes. Due to the torturous life in Ireland, I had lost around half my body weight.

Everything appeared brighter in London and way more modern than I remembered. It felt like a paradise of sorts; I just wasn't sure that it was one I particularly wanted. It had been drummed into me that in this situation all I had to do was run. The problem was I also wasn't sure if I wanted to run any more. I had finally escaped my dad's wrath and was not keen on putting myself in harm's way again.

My mum wasn't charged with anything substantial and was soon released. She returned to Archie's flat and waited for me to return. My nan allowed her to call me on the phone a couple of times, and each time my mum would ask me why I hadn't run away. I didn't really know what to say. I also knew my grandparents would be listening from the second phone in the hall and didn't want to give too much away. All I wanted was to have a private conversation with my mother. Unfortunately I was caught between two opposing worlds, so that was never going to happen.

After a few days I began to feel pretty comfortable. Life was good and there were no beatings, just love and affection. I was getting spoiled a little and I liked it. And why not? After that awful year in Ireland I deserved a little spoiling. I fell back into English life with ease and it soon became apparent that I would have been an imbecile to leave the safety of my grandparents' abode. So I stayed put.

My mum waited for me at the flat for over a week, but my decision was final. I did not want to go back. When I was younger I didn't have a clue how great life was in England, but now that I had lived with my parents in Ireland I could see the difference.

My mum kept calling, always with the same message. She even paid me a final visit to try to get me to change my mind, but eventually she had to face facts and went back to Ireland without me. God only knows what happened upon her return, but I assume my dad was anything but happy.

Once I knew she had left, I began to miss her terribly, just not enough to leave.

LONDON

1979–81

CHAPTER 15

CATERPILLARS

Adapting back into a life without violence was relatively easy due to the unrelenting love that I received from my grandparents. The nightmare of living with my father was now just a bad memory and I began to move on.

My grandparents' new house had just two bedrooms, and as Carol was still living at home, there was no way for me to have my own room. However, my nan came up with a nifty solution. She placed a single bed in the corner of her and my granddad's room, and as a result I became privy to their nocturnal activities.

My granddad had long since concluded that the toilet was too far away to visit during the wee hours (accidental pun alert). Therefore he acquired a piss pot. It wasn't necessarily the sound of him using this device that would wake me from my slumber; it was the accompanying vapour passing under my nose. As if this wasn't distracting enough, my nan was an Olympic-level snorer. Even her exhalations were akin to a hippo yawning. I could literally hear her lip quivering after each enormous wheeze. It was, however, still preferable to living in the horror house with my parents, so I tried to make the best of it. At least I had a corner to make my own, which I did by smothering the wall with posters and stickers of my favourite bands and television shows.

My newest interest was music, which I listened to avidly on a tiny portable radio. My uncle Tim got wind that I had become a fan of the radio station Capital Radio in London, and thus arranged a trip to their actual studios. This left me a little star-struck and I was given a bunch of free merchandise to take home: window stickers, cups and all kinds of tat. I can still smell the glue on the back of those stickers. No doubt it was some kind of liquidised horse.

Tim would often take me out for the day, no doubt giving my grandparents a much-needed break. Mostly we would travel around London, but occasionally we would trek as far as the east coast. I always wondered what he thought about the stories I drip-fed him about my time in Ireland; my mother was his sister, after all. Perhaps he simply blamed my father? Regardless, Tim always showed incredible generosity and kindness towards me. Apart from the excessive tickling, he was the epitome of a great uncle.

Now that I was back, I was also realising how odd my granddad could be. One day he arrived home in a decorating mood with bags containing empty egg boxes and rolls of what can only be described as bold-patterned wallpaper. I thought he'd gone a little doolally when he started sticking egg boxes to the alcove walls of the living room with Sellotape. He explained that he was fed up of hearing the neighbours through the walls and someone had told him that egg boxes provided a cheap alternative to expensive soundproofing. I decided to join him in this bizarre task and soon enough both alcoves were filled from top to bottom with empty polystyrene boxes. We were finished just in time for my nan to arrive home. She took one look at the wall and rolled her eyes.

It was around this time that my grandparents also fell in love with glass. Suddenly, our plates were made of glass and our cups became see-through. The door to the lounge was replaced with a heavy frosted glass portal and we began eating our meals at a glass table where you were subjected to a magnified view of everyone's thighs while trying to eat. The ugliness was transparent. Unfortunately, it was my granddad who found out that having all this glass around was not particularly safe.

One weekend, while hanging the unsightly wallpaper, he lost his footing and came crashing to the ground. I watched in horror as he fell backwards straight through a newly purchased glass coffee table. It smashed into hundreds of pieces instantly. He was stuck in the middle of the thing covered in glass, with blood pouring from God knows where. It was horrifying. Luckily, it looked much worse than it was and he escaped with just a few minor cuts.

My nan came running in and began removing shards of glass from his skin and hair as my granddad tried to compose himself. He looked vulnerable in that moment. I was so upset by his falling that it reinforced just how much I cared about him.

My granddad was a bus driver and made a crust working out of a garage a couple of miles away. I would often head to the edge of the park to meet him as he cycled home at the end of his shift. It was my favourite part of any given day. At first I went because he brought me humbugs, but after a while I started going just to spend time with him – plus I'd get a lift on his crossbar, which I enjoyed immensely. Those extra minutes together turned out to be precious.

On occasion, I was lucky enough to accompany my granddad on the buses. I would be so excited to see his grinning face pulling up at the bus stop. He'd usher me in without my having to pay and let me sit up front until we got to the terminus, where I would get to change the destination blind and help him reset. I also got to hang out at the bus garage during his breaks. The air was thick with oil and the smell of hot radiators as we tucked in to our lunch in the staff canteen. It all felt very VIP, even though all that was on offer were white crusty rolls containing either a fried egg or bacon with a dollop of brown sauce on top.

As a result of these visits I learned quite a lot about buses, probably too much. My granddad encouraged me to become a bus spotter. This newfound hobby took me all over London, visiting every bus garage I could find, just so I could write down the vehicle number of every bus that I saw. Alas, I soon became bored and threw in the towel. I realised I could never spot every bus in London; it seemed an impossible task, plus why on earth would I want to?

What I didn't know about riding the bus, at first, was that there was money to be made, knowledge my granddad would soon impart. Once the last passengers alighted, he would drive to the terminus and we would get to work. We'd work our way around the entire bus, lifting each seat looking for money that had rolled out of unsuspecting pockets. There was always plenty of coinage and I would find at least enough for some sweets on the way home. I felt privy to a secret. The beauty was there was no guilt to be had; it wasn't stealing, it was simply finders-keepers. I continued this practice until my early twenties on numerous buses, never finding more than a few pence at a time. Then it dawned on me. My granddad had clearly planted the coins himself. He had created a *de facto* treasure hunt for us to complete together, and I never even knew.

***

Door-to-door action was very much in vogue in 1979. We had a lot of people ringing the doorbell over the course of a week and it wasn't just milk and newspapers. There was a bread delivery, the window cleaner, the rag 'n' bone man, the pools collector and an insurance broker who would come fortnightly. My favourite doorstep visitor, however, was the Alpine lorry. Alpine was a soft drinks company and its lorries came around each week delivering fizzy drinks in reusable glass bottles. They would collect the empties and replace them with whatever my nan requested on a note she'd leave in the crate. It was magnificent to come home and find full bottles of cream soda, bitter lemon, and dandelion and burdock waiting for us on the doorstep.

My granddad was an avid player of the pools; it was very much the lottery of its day. The same man would swing by every Thursday to collect the pools forms that were conveniently left earlier that same week, plus the amount my granddad was willing to wager. Success hinged on him correctly guessing which football teams would win that coming Saturday, predicting their scores and such. I did not understand it one iota, but I knew to be quiet when the eventual scores were being read out on live TV. If one word left my gob I would receive a thwack from my granddad's readied newspaper. 'The Results', as they were known, were an important, albeit silent, weekly ritual in our household.

The pools were unlikely to make you a millionaire, but it was possible to pocket a few thousand pounds if you were lucky. Although we never hit the big time, my granddad would occasionally have a small win. The pools man would then deliver his winnings the following week, which my granddad invariably reinvested in the game.

One week I was surprised to learn that I'd had some success playing the pools myself, winning by way of the 'Spot the Ball' competition. I was astounded that I had won, mainly because I could not remember playing in the first place.

'Spot the Ball' was an extra game you could play along with the regular pools if you so desired. It contained a photo of two or more footballers in the middle of play with the ball removed. All you had to do was guess where the ball was and you would win. It always seemed obvious to me, but who knows how it worked. Was there really someone going through all those forms? Perhaps it was just a scam.

On this occasion, anyway, I was hastily summoned to the front door to collect my winnings. With my granddad beaming, the pools man handed me a small brown envelope with my name written formally upon it. I reached inside and pulled out a solitary crisp one-pound note. Clearly a nine-year-old indulging in a bit of gambling on the doorstep was perfectly acceptable in 1970s England.

Only later did I realise that, just like the coins on the bus, my granddad had probably made the whole thing up just to make me feel like a winner. It was a sweet gesture, but a risky business introducing a child to such things. Thankfully I never got a taste for it.

These doorstep interactions may seem terribly old-fashioned now, but I am glad to have witnessed such a period first-hand. And I am glad, particularly after the horrors of the previous year, that there was a father figure going to such efforts just to make me happy.

***

Something happened in 1979 that changed everything. I may not have understood the significance of general elections, but I was aware that public opinion was shifting. While I had been coping with life in Ireland, England was experiencing a winter of discontent, which paved the way for Britain's first female prime minister. One night in early May I heard my granddad say, 'She got in', without giving away his allegiance. That was the day that Margaret Thatcher was elected, of course, setting the land of my birth on a very different course, one that soon became seduced by the sexy legs of privatisation. It was the end of a Britain that at least pretended to care.

I knew only one thing about Thatcher: she stole our milk! Just before I had left for Ireland, my free school milk had come to an abrupt end courtesy of her tenure as education minister in the early 1970s. Up to the age of seven, we each received a third of a pint of milk and an accompanying break in which to consume it, but after that our supply was promptly cut off.

Talking of education, I was now attending the very same school that I had frequented when we first moved to the area, only this time I was at the junior school. This arrangement would prove to be temporary, as I wasn't fitting in particularly well. Most of the kids at these schools had grown up together and each time I joined a new class I would be made to feel like an intruder. This 'always being the new kid' mantle dogged my entire childhood and I learned to loathe it. I was sick of always having to prove myself to strangers and found fitting in nigh-on impossible.

***

As summer beckoned, the large tree in our front garden became infested with caterpillars. They were omnipresent. To avoid them dropping on my head, I would often run at speed up the garden path.

One day, however, I ran too fast on my lead-up to the front garden and failed to notice that the gate was still open, with the latch protruding. As I ran past the gate I was gripped by instant pain in my thigh. I looked down to see the latch embedded deep in my bloodied leg. I was literally attached to the gate. I winced as I pulled my leg away with a squelch. The rusty, blood-soaked latch popped out and I very nearly fainted. But did I go to hospital? No. Stitches? Nope. A tetanus shot perhaps? Nyet. Instead I fell to the ground squirming in agony, while my nan swiped at me from above with a rolled-up magazine shouting, 'Do you want a bloody thick ear?'

The caterpillars were becoming quite the nuisance and we were advised to have the tree felled in order to quell the infestation. Its roots were also heading towards the house, which was bad news for my grandparents. They were in the process of buying the house and were worried that once the tree got under the foundations it would render the property worthless.

Cut to a glorious summer afternoon whereby a bunch of tree fellers armed with blowtorches and saws set fire to the glorious old beast. This was the only sure method for killing the caterpillars, apparently.

I was playing in the upstairs bedroom when the first branch was ignited. The window immediately lit up as a ferocious wall of orange flames burned inches from the glass. I could feel the heat and became worried that the house might catch fire. The extermination was thankfully complete by evening, whereby there were no more caterpillars to be seen. Unless you count the thousands of dry-roasted ones lying on the front lawn.

***

Although I was not yet ten years old, I occasionally had moments of absolute clarity when I did not feel like a child at all. One of these moments occurred while strolling with my granddad in a nearby park. He began to open up in a way he never had, treating me as an equal. He was insightful, truthful and caring; warning me not to waste time and to do whatever I saw fit with my life, regardless of the opinion of others. He explained that, from his perspective, it was only five minutes ago that he was a young man in his twenties and yet here he was, suddenly sixty years old. That stuck with me. I asked him questions and he answered candidly, relaying stories about his time in India during the war and what he really thought about my dad. We pondered many topics during what became a very pleasant walk. Unfortunately it was to be an isolated incident and we never talked that openly again.

By the time September rolled around, it was time for yet another change of schools. I was now going to an establishment recommended by Carol's new boyfriend, Jeremiah, who was a former pupil. It was a bus-ride away, which made getting to school an adventure. It was one of the better schools I had attended and, for once, I made friends easily. I hadn't been back from Ireland very long and was still relatively thin, with longish, curly hair. I also wore quite a lot of denim. Both of these factors made me a hit with the girls, and for a limited time I became something of a novelty. Unfortunately my grandparents were slowly phasing out my cool clothes, replacing them with old-fashioned garments that I wanted to set alight at first sight. However, once I'd put on a little cake-weight, my nice threads became unwearable, making resistance futile. My mum continued to send trendy clothes from Ireland, but they were always too small as she was unaware that I was once again becoming what she would term 'a porker'.

At some point during that first term I was found to be 'of above average intelligence', not that you'd have known it from my behaviour. It transpired that the Irish education system was more advanced than England's at the time, so – despite my frequent absences from school in Ireland – I was now, apparently, ahead of the game. This was news to me. I didn't really take much interest in school, but perhaps the Christian Brothers' strict teaching methods had paid off? Who knew that being beaten over the head with a Bible could actually make you smarter?

I was taken aside and told that maths appeared to be my strong suit. It was then suggested that I join an advanced class in mathematics and computing. The teacher explained that computers were going to be shaping the future in every conceivable way, so if I wanted to get in on the ground floor, now was the time. He seemed passionate, so I thought, *why not?* The following week I would begin learning binary. It was ever so tedious, but at least it was a reprieve from being stuck in one classroom all day, being taught all the subjects on the curriculum by the same teacher.

It did not take me long to change my mind. Most of the boffins in the advanced class were a tad dull and I soon missed my 'normal' friends. I did not enjoy being separated and found the whole computer thing extremely boring. I preferred a bit more fun than they were offering. All I really wanted to do was play marbles on the manhole covers in the playground, or pretend I was looking at Australia by staring into glass particles on the concrete steps. I had spent way too much time in Ireland unable to enjoy my childhood and I wasn't about to let that happen again. Therefore, I decided to pack up my satchel and leave. Luckily the teacher allowed it, though he was clearly disappointed in my lack of interest.

I had many adventures at that school. My friends and I would concoct elaborate stories and investigate them. We looked for ghosts and killers, and imagined conspiracies involving teachers as suspects, which often resulted in us following them around searching for clues. I was also becoming something of a show-off and began performing in the playground to endear myself to the other kids. I did impressions and told jokes to my cohorts and anyone else who would listen. I learned quickly that if you could make someone laugh they were less likely to beat you up, and thus I avoided many possible scrapes. All in all I was having a grand old time with my new amigos, so much so that I could not believe I had left this all behind to live with my parents in Ireland. I felt confident that I would not let it happen twice.

***

This was the year that I first experienced the death of something I loved – not the loss of a relative per se, but definitely one of the family.

I was wandering the corridors at lunchtime when a teacher called over and escorted me to the headmistress's office. I assumed that I was in trouble, but couldn't remember doing anything to warrant my summoning.

Once inside, I was told that my granddad was coming to take me home. The headmistress then asked me to sit down; she had terrible news. Our dog Patch had died that morning.

I was aware that Patch had been unwell. The previous evening he'd appeared to be very docile indeed, but dead? Once the reality hit home I became upset and was grateful to have been pulled out of school. I could not comprehend that he was gone. Forever. Unlike the dogs we went through in Ireland, Patch had been around longer, in fact for most of my life.

In England, prior to my Irish misadventure, I had always had the company of our two lovely dogs. Pom, the older of the two, had died of cancer while I was in Ireland the previous year, so I never got to say goodbye to him. The fact that they were now both gone hit me unexpectedly hard. I cried for both of them well into the night: my little boy heart broken, with lungs wheezing in and out uncontrollably in the darkness.

The very next day I noticed that part of the paving in our back garden had suddenly become lumpy. It had clearly been dug up overnight and put back unevenly. I asked my granddad about it, and he explained that he'd had to rearrange the slabs due to a stray tree root. I knew very well that Patch was under those slabs, but we never discussed it, not once. He knew I knew, and I knew he knew I knew. That was enough. My cousins visited that weekend and asked about the lump while jumping up and down on it. Once I told them there was a dead dog under their feet, they soon stopped jumping.

The slabs were barely even by the time we found ourselves in Battersea Dogs Home looking for a replacement hound. My granddad took an instant shine to a German shepherd mix who was giving him the eye. He was young, although not quite a puppy. The relevant forms were soon filled in, and we were back on the tube in no time with one very active mutt. He was to be called Champ, an amalgam of Pom and Patch. I thought that was a nice touch.

Saying that, it felt odd having another pet so soon after Patch's demise. I looked over at our new house-wolf, hoping for a connection, but it was too soon. I felt nothing but resentment. What I saw, however, was something I would have to look away from regularly. He had his lipstick out.

CHAPTER 16

THE NAKED EYE

The postman brought me a present: a book of postcards from my mother. It was from a mystical land called Lanzarote, and contained photos of volcanoes and strange rocky moonscapes. I took them straight to school and showed them off to my friends, who seemed genuinely impressed. They had only ever seen me with my grandparents, so this sudden news of having a mother roaming the world was intriguing stuff. They asked many questions and I regaled them with a few choice stories, generally giving the impression that my mum was far cooler than she actually was. Suddenly I had gone from being a nan kid to being the cool kid with a hip, globe-trotting mother, and I liked it.

Accompanying the postcards was another gift, an actual piece of coral from Lanzarote. It was my prized possession for a few weeks, until I came home from school to find it in Champ's mouth. The dog was eating my coral and lumps of it were scattered throughout the house. I wondered if perhaps this new dog of ours might be an idiot.

Around this time, as we edged ever closer to puberty, a rumour began to circulate regarding certain magazines working their way around the school. I had never seen a naked woman before and became quite excited at the prospect. Upon investigation, a friend of a friend told us he had access to a dirty magazine and promised to bring it in the very next day. This aroused our interest and sent us home with Cheshire cat grins across our faces.

The next morning I wasn't the only one with a spring in my step. I met my friends at the bus stop and waited for the boy charged with getting the magazine to join us. He soon arrived, giving us the nod. He had it! We sneaked around the back of the shops and settled by the bins. This was it. It was time to delve inside its smutty pages for the big reveal. We all took a deep breath, looked at one another and opened up the magazine to reveal the naked centrefold.

Well, let's just say it was a little graphic for my tastes. We were all a bit confused about what we were looking at, turning the magazine upside down and so forth. I don't know what I thought was down there, but certainly not that! It wasn't what any of us were expecting and we trotted off to school more confused than ever before.

***

Thatcher's election seemed to generate numerous strikes, which continued throughout the summer and long into winter. It became so bad that one of our three television channels went off-air completely. ITV was now just a dead button on a rented television set.

As well as ITV being on strike, there were regular power cuts through-out the year and we always had to have candles to hand. We would sit for hours without television or lights and just hang out. It was actually quite nice, it felt a bit like camping. However, the first time it happened I became a little scared. I was certain it was a nuclear strike. I had recently seen a programme where the narrator mentioned that in order to launch a nuclear warhead they would need to access all available power, which would result in dips in the nation's power supply or even a total blackout. Even now, whenever I see lights dim, a small part of me gets the willies.

The strikes ended and ITV came back on air just three days before my tenth birthday, along with the same old programming: *George and Mildred*, a silly comedy series I happened to like, followed by *Coronation Street*, which I did not.

Unfortunately, by the time my birthday rolled round I was rather unwell and spent the entire day being sick into an orange bucket while watching cartoons. However, it turned out to be quite a memorable birthday, not only for my being ill, but for what my dad considered an appropriate gift for this milestone.

My nan and granddad didn't vet presents in the same way my parents did, so all sorts of oddities found their way to me unchecked. That morning I began opening my presents, starting with the ones sent from Ireland. I ripped into the paper to reveal four large white cards containing etchings. As I turned them upside down, not yet comprehending the images, they were snatched from my hands and immediately confiscated. I was told that they were graphic images painted by J. B. Priestley; sexually explicit images, no less. They were definitely not suitable for a ten-year-old boy. My dad would later contest that these were original pictures that he found in a skip and that, by throwing them away, my granddad was destroying something that could be of value to me later in life, my birthright if you will. I had heard some bullshit from my dad, but this took the biscuit. His track record suggests that if in fact they were of any value, he would have definitely sold them and kept the proceeds, no question. (Incidentally, I can find no record whatsoever of J. B. Priestley ever painting such things.)

I opened the second gift, which turned out to be even kookier than the first. The 'Priestley' prints were images of individually naked people and could technically be described as art. This second present was rather more pornographic. As I opened up the heavy atlas-sized book I was greeted with Salvador Dali-esque images of individuals engaging in various sexual acts. The image that has stuck with me was that of a woman giving oral pleasure to a moustached man in the back of a stretch limo. It stayed with me for many reasons, most notably because of how insanely psychedelic it looked. This was of course also ripped from my grasp and immediately destroyed, or so I was told. However, unlike the prints, the big book of porn survived and ended up stashed at the back of a cupboard, where I stumbled upon it months later. Perhaps my granddad was a fan after all?

So. Two gifts, both of which were grossly inappropriate. Although they were in another country separated by water, I felt like my parents were still messing with me. To this day I cannot fathom why they would send such things to their own child.

**

My partially blind eye was deteriorating. After a visual test at school, it became apparent that it was time to see a specialist. Prior to this, I had often been told that I might lose the sight in my one good eye due to strain. I found that prospect too terrifying to contemplate and thus avoided thinking about it altogether. I was used to my broken eye letting in vast amounts of bright light, making me feel light-headed, but being summoned to the hospital made me realise just how serious this eye lark actually was.

My nan accompanied me to Borough Eye Hospital in South London, where a number of tests were carried out. All I could see with my right eye by this point were outlines, my brain apparently filling in the gaps, giving the impression of partial sight. As it was too late to repair that particular optic mess, they suggested saving my good eye by relieving some of the stress on it. It was suggested that I try a new invention that was bringing some patients success. They were called contact lenses.

They fitted me with various models over the coming months and all of them hurt to some degree. The first lenses were huge and latched onto my eyeballs – they felt akin to blades trapped beneath my eyelids. Next were contacts that felt even harder in my eye than the first: I might as well have been blinking with LEGO blocks in my eyes. Finally I received a softer pair that more closely resembled today's variety and these were the ones deemed suitable for purchase.

The optician suggested we procure two pairs, as they would need swapping out halfway through each day. The NHS would provide the first pair for free, but my grandparents would have to cough up the moolah for the second set. My nan made no attempt to hide the fact that this was an expensive experiment, and made me promise to look after them. She explained that this was a one-off; if I lost them, that was it. There was no way they could afford to replace them.

I was sure I could look after a couple of plastic lenses. I mean, how hard could it be? As well as not misplacing them, however, I had to learn how to clean and care for my tiny see-through optics, and that's where it got fiddly.

A week or so later at school, while applying the cleaning solution, I accidentally dropped one of my transparent discs down the sink. It flew right down the plughole and disappeared into the Victorian pipework. I stood there, gutted. My grandparents were bound to be upset. As it was an accident I hoped they would be forgiving, but within hours I would manage to lose yet another one of those little blighters.

My granddad was relaxing in the sitting room when I began annoying him with my voice. To shut me up, he grabbed a magazine and threw it in my direction. It caught me square in the eye, flicking the contact lens I was wearing straight onto the overly patterned carpet. It was a disaster. I could not find the bloody thing and my granddad refused to believe me. He was convinced that I'd lost both lenses beforehand and was using his outburst to shift blame. Within hours lens number three vanished without a trace, and with it my foray into the world of contact-lens wearing.

***

I'm not sure if it was the busy carpet or the insane 1970s wallpaper that was sending me cuckoo, but a few days before Christmas I heard something very strange in the lounge. My granddad had just popped in to throw a turkey head into the fireplace, which began to melt before my very eyes. Once he got back to the kitchen he called on me to help him, but I was way too comfy to bother and refused to shift. It was then that I heard it.

'Go on then,' came a voice in a northern English accent from behind my head.

I looked back, but there was only wall. The voice was crystal clear and I became spooked. For reasons I can't explain, I had a notion that it was my granddad's mother. That alone was strange, given that I had never met her or, to my knowledge, even seen a photo of the woman.

When I told my granddad what I'd heard, and who I thought the culprit might be, he seemed unsurprised. He stated nonchalantly that it probably *was* his mother. He made the whole thing seem natural and in no way spooky. He was a firm believer in psychic phenomena and was no stranger to odd things happening around him, often being quite open about his experiences.

My granddad was something of a devotee and often took me to spiritual meetings so I could see these apparent miracles first-hand. He wanted me to believe, but I could never quite accept that I was witnessing anything other than flannel. The few times I did attend, my grandparents seemed to be really taken in by it all. We would visit semi-religious halls and watch mediums ask vague questions. They might as well have asked if anyone knew a man or a woman whose name started with a letter of the alphabet. It was quite ridiculous.

Over the years I have grown to despise these kinds of money-grabbing parasites. I realise it is important to remain open and be able to change your opinion, but I find the way that these people prey on the weak and vulnerable utterly unforgivable.

Something I am sure the psychics could not have foreseen was who was coming to Christmas dinner that year. My mother arrived just in time to celebrate the Yuletide season and for reasons unbeknownst to me, she was allowed to join us for the duration. Just as I was about to hug her, she commented on how fat I had become. Well, that soured the occasion. From that moment on I saw her as nothing more than a gatecrasher.

This was my first Christmas with my grandparents since escaping my parents' clutches and I didn't particularly want her around spying on my every move. She was a constant reminder of all things past, and whenever we happened to be alone, she continually asked me why I hadn't run away earlier that same year. I did not want to feel guilty about that any more; all I wanted to do was be a kid and play with my Etch-a-Sketch and stare at my new Timex watch. I wished, on more than one occasion, that she would just fuck off back to Ireland and leave me be.

I also thought it was more than a little odd that she was staying with us at the end of the year in which my nan orchestrated my recapture. There may have been bad blood between them, but she was their daughter after all, and perhaps in some way they didn't blame her for what happened? However, they made no attempt to hide their distaste of my father. My granddad would often call me over whenever a Monster Munch advert or something ugly came on television and tell me that my dad was on TV. I laughed with him, although secretly felt like only I should be able to say things of that nature. It was a constant reminder that my life was anything but the norm.

CHAPTER 17

WEB-TINTED SPECTACLES

Going to the shops was a very different affair when I was ten. We had yet to build giant supermarkets in the UK and goods were still purchased locally from the relevant retailer. My nan and I would go shopping for essentials at a local parade of shops nearby that included a baker, a newsagent, a greengrocer, a fishmonger, a butcher, a chemist, a post office and a small Co-op supermarket. The fishmonger could be the scene of particularly gross imagery, especially the day a woman ahead of us ordered eels. The monger threw the poor souls into a tray, pulled out a cleaver and started chopping them up into tiny pieces, all while still alive. There was blood everywhere. The woman, however, left happy with her purchase and I never attempted to eat eels, ever.

The Co-op was where we bought cereals, tins and dairy items. I guess they were ahead of their time, as they had a *de facto* loyalty card system – only it was not on futuristic plastic, but consisted solely of stamps. They would hand out empty books, which, once filled with the free stamps you accumulated with every purchase, could be used as currency to buy groceries. This was akin to getting free money, which is why I ended up stealing an entire reel of stamps worth many pounds. My nan found out about my indiscretion, but instead of getting upset, she offered to buy them from me at a discounted rate of fifty per cent of their worth.

Over the coming weeks my nan collected a stamp book each time she visited the supermarket. Once home, we would fill the book with our stolen money stickers. On the back of each book you had to add a name and address, so, in order not to arouse suspicion, we used a few fake names. No one ever checked, it was simply a precaution. We got a lot of free groceries courtesy of those books, but we never once told my granddad. It was our little secret. To her dying day my nan swore she'd never stolen a thing in her life. Well, I beg to differ, dear girl.

***

Coal was delivered weekly to our house and there was always a mountain of it piled high in the back yard. Whenever it was needed for the fire, which was mostly at night, one of us would have to don a pair of dirty slippers and head out into the pitch black with the scuttle to retrieve the much-needed fossil fuel.

I detested going out there for one reason and one reason alone: spiders. They were attracted to the dark crevices created by the coal and on more than one occasion I came across some seriously large arachnids.

Unfortunately my encounters with spiders were set to continue. While I was walking through the local park one afternoon, a group of kids from a rival school began pelting me with stones. One of the rocks hit me slap bang in the forehead and it stung. As blood trickled down my noggin, I looked for a way to escape their catapults. I headed for the trusty bent railing at the edge of the park that acted as a shortcut to the shops, but – just my luck – it had been repaired and I was now cornered. Knowing that the kids would catch up with me at any moment, I then spotted a row of unkempt hedges and decided that it was the perfect hiding place. I ran with a sprinter's pace, pushing my way through the foliage before coming to a stop in a tiny clearing. It was then that I felt something.

I looked down and saw that my arms were covered in spiders. I froze to the spot, terrified. There were a number of bushes encircling me, all of them covered in webs; even the gaps between the bushes were blocked by heavy webbing full of crawling beasts. Whichever direction I looked in, all I could see was spiders. I had no idea how I even got in there, but I needed to find a way out. My only option was to go back the way I came, as I had already broken through an enormous cobweb upon entry. I bolted, screaming. I ran home with a bloodied head, brushing off spiders as I went. It was all very unpleasant. This incident stuck with me for some time and gave me some serious nightmares to boot.

***

It was around this time that I realised I could beatbox. I was suddenly able to create a drum sound with accompanying melodies using only my tongue and teeth. I would make up all manner of melodies and perform these mouth extravaganzas on the way to school. One day, however, this newfound 'skill' led me into the path of some bullies.

Three older boys heard me making strange noises and started to tease me while trying to steal my school bag. My contact lenses were long gone, so I was now wearing a pair of embarrassing national-health glasses, which I was also getting grief for.

At one point one of the boys tried to snatch them from my face and I became enraged. I felt threatened and could see no positive outcome. Mad with anger, I decided to switch on my crazy. I ripped the glasses from my own face, scrunched them up in my hands and threw them on the ground, stomping on them until they were completely destroyed. I picked up bits of the broken plastic and threw these at them while asking them if that's what they'd wanted. They called me a nutter and ran off confused. I shouted after them, promising to enact revenge upon them. And I did.

I went straight home and told my nan that three boys had attacked me and had broken my glasses. She was furious. So much so that she called the police. Shit. I instantly wondered if perhaps I'd taken it too far, but I couldn't exactly back down.

I stayed home for the rest of the school day until my granddad got home. It was then that the police arrived. The cops offered to drive us around the local area in order to search for my attackers. We knew the route they'd taken to school, so we knew exactly where to find them on their way home. We drove around with me procrastinating in the back while my granddad got ready to pounce. I had no intention of actually pointing them out; I knew if I did I'd be rumbled. Unfortunately I had given the cops too accurate a description and it wasn't long before we found three boys walking home together who fitted the description.

When they saw me in the police van they looked horrified. The police jumped out and asked the boys if they recognised me. They admitted that they had an altercation with me that morning; however, their story did not reflect my own. It wasn't long before the truth seeped out, albeit slowly. It was painful to watch. All the while I could tell that my granddad was starting to doubt my story and so were the police.

I regretted blaming them. They were little bastards, but I was trying to get them into a lot more trouble than they probably deserved. So I decided to come clean while in the van by telling my granddad the truth. I admitted to making up the part about the boys breaking my glasses, but insisted they provoked me. The policeman rolled his eyes and let the three boys go. I was then reprimanded for wasting police time and told to better defend myself in future. The police dropped us back at the house, whereby my granddad forced me upstairs and told me to stay put. He was furious. He had defended me, and for what? I could see the disappointment in his eyes and I felt terrible for letting him down. The whole episode was a catastrophe.

***

My troublesome streak continued a while longer thanks to a little blue book. Through the letterbox one morning came a most curious article indeed; a pamphlet of international dialling codes. Apparently you could now call anybody, anywhere in the world directly from your own landline. This was a revelation. I was both intrigued and keen to see how it worked. Without any regard for the monetary costs, I began to call the entire planet, just for fun. My inquisitive nature had struck again and was about to get me into a whole world of trouble, quite literally.

I started with the As and worked my way through the book until someone picked up. I would dial the country code, then the city code and add something similar to our number. I figured seven digits must be the norm. Most of the time it didn't work, but on the few occasions it did I would hear a voice from the other side of the earth. It was magical.

I was fascinated with geography as a child and spent a great deal of time both studying and drawing maps. I would trace the shape of each country until I could draw it freehand from memory. I loved nothing more than learning the names of countries and their respective capital cities, Montevideo being a particular favourite. These phone calls connected me directly to the very places I was studying. I chatted to a man in New York, who I clearly annoyed, a woman in Australia, as well as a few people in Europe who didn't understand a word I was saying. I made most of my calls before school, after my granddad had left for work. These were treasured moments indeed, but inevitably they would end up costing me dearly.

Next to the phone was a coin box. If relatives or friends came around and used the phone, it was the done thing to put the relevant cost of the call into the box. We even did it. That way, once the bill came, all my grandparents had to do was empty the box. They would usually have enough money to pay the bill plus a little left over. In my infinite wisdom I decided to borrow from this box. It was one of the most stupid decisions of my young life. Not only was I running up huge costs by phoning foreign countries, I was now technically stealing money from the phone bill.

I only took two pounds and had every intention of putting it back once

I received my pocket money. It should have all been fine. But of course it didn't turn out that way.

I planned a fun day at school with the money I'd borrowed. So, once off the bus, I went straight to the shops in search of goodies. I thought it might be amusing to buy a bunch of joke items and trick my friends throughout the course of the day. It seemed like a great idea at the time. I bought a whoopie cushion, fake-blood capsules, chewing gum that would snap your finger if you tried to pull a stick out, and sneezing powder, which I am sure was just pepper. I played tons of pranks that day and had loads of fun in the process. It was a great day and I skipped home happier than Larry.

Once I'd closed the front door it was obvious that something was very wrong. My nan looked worried. My granddad appeared with an expression on his face that I had never seen before, not on him anyway. He looked mad, really mad. The phone bill for my overseas calls had arrived, but that was not all. They had looked in the phone box and seen that I had stolen from that as well. My nan had deliberately put four fifty pence pieces in the box that very morning and now they were gone. All fingers pointed to little old me. I tried to explain that I had every intention of putting the money back, but it was too late.

Suddenly I bore witness to my grandfather's dark side. His ferocious temper was unleashed and he came at me with a foaming mouth and a wooden broom handle. He hit me with it hard a number of times as I tried to get away. Alas, I could not escape and he chased me halfway up the stairs trying to hit me with the pole while my nan screamed at him to stop. It was very short-lived, and impulsive on his part, unlike the premeditated attacks from my father. I could see that I had made a grave error and my granddad was clearly upset that he'd been forced to resort to such methods.

In addition to my bad telephone manners, I also used to engage in some rather nifty food reallocation around this time. My granddad loved his chocolate and was particularly partial to a Cadbury's Flake, which he stored in large boxes in the freezer. I wasn't allowed to eat his chocolate, but my lack of willpower left me little choice. I would take out the box and carefully remove just one flake from the back. Then I would slide the box back into the freezer so that it still looked full from the front. I knew it would be a while until I was caught, so I didn't think about the consequences, preferring to worry about it later.

It was a similar situation with fizzy drinks. When it was noticed that I was guzzling too much dandelion and burdock, pen marks started appearing. My nan would draw a very distinct line on the side of each bottle to dissuade me from drinking any more. The way around this was easy enough: I would simply pour myself a glass of whatever I fancied when they weren't looking, then fill the bottle back up to the line with water, give it a quick shake and put it back in the fridge. I did this all the time and no one ever seemed to notice.

My confused relationship with food was not helped by the fact that my nan kept a stash of cakes and sweets for her and me to consume in secret. She would bring out the naughty food whenever my granddad either went to work or took the dog for a walk, allowing me to scoff my greedy little face to my heart's content.

I don't mean to blame my grandmother for this ill-advised act, but it was hardly the greatest of ideas. She may have done it out of love, but it definitely further complicated a relationship with food that was already anything but positive.

CHAPTER 18

BENT OUT OF SHAPE

In early 1980 my parents moved back to England. My dad had broken into a squat and made it their home. I had no concept of where it was in relation to where I lived, I only knew that it was in deepest South London. I'm pretty sure my grandparents were unaware that they were squatting, as it was somehow agreed that I could visit my parents over the Easter break.

The flat was actually quite pleasant. It was in a lovely, post-war, red-brick building that sat opposite a high street. My dad had done an amazing job in transforming it from a squalid flat into a desirable abode; it was actually nicer than my grandparents' house. My room, however, lay opposite a graveyard, which I found unsettling; the last thing I would see before hitting the light switch were the skulls that adorned the graveyard entrance.

There were no beatings or any indication of violence whatsoever during my stay. My parents were clearly on their best behaviour, no doubt doing the hard sell in order to persuade me to return when the time was right.

In my absence, my mum had found another boy to mother. His name was Luke and he was older than me. He lived a couple of doors down and was clearly very streetwise. He also seemed to get on with my mother far better than I did. She showed him a lot of affection, which of course made me jealous. However, Luke had a problem; he liked to sniff glue. I didn't know that kids did such things until I saw him huffing a small brown bag in the car park.

On the second night, we returned to the flat to find the locks had been changed. The council had apparently swung by while we were out. This was no problem for my dad. Without batting an eyelid he simply produced a clothes iron out of thin air and launched it through one of the small panes of glass that made up the front door. He reached through, opened the lock from the inside and we were back in. It was as if he'd been expecting this outcome all along. Where the clothes iron came from I have no idea; I suspect it might've been hidden behind a plant pot or some such, but from my perspective it was akin to a magic trick.

I became very excited the following morning when I was told that I might get to meet the stars of my favourite TV show, *George and Mildred*, as they were opening a new section of a football stadium nearby. My dad promised to get me close enough to meet them and he did not disappoint.

After making our way through the crowd, shoving as we went, I saw them. Right before me stood the first famous people I had ever seen in real life. They were coming my way, so I pushed forward so I could talk to them. I managed to get their autographs and have the briefest of chats, mainly with Yootha Joyce (Mildred). I was elated. I was so impressed that I'd met them, even for a couple of minutes. I walked away on a high, with no idea that the woman I had just met was a raging alcoholic who would be dead within a few months.

At the stadium there was an accompanying Sunday market, which pleased my parents no end. They loved any kind of market or car boot sale.

My dad had seen something he fancied, signalled by a single, muted 'Jesus'. He'd spotted a wristwatch that was on offer for a mere two pounds. It was void of numbers, containing just two gold hands on a black face. It was a very stark design and I kind of wanted it too. He bought it, popped it on his wrist, then began telling me how great it would look on me, mentioning that the bulky one I was wearing seemed unsightly by comparison. It was obvious that he was trying to persuade me to swap my watch for his piece of market tat. I loved my Timex; it had been the main present from my grandparents the previous Christmas, the very one my mother had gatecrashed. I have to assume that she told my dad about it, as he attempted to pry it from my wrist the entire afternoon.

Eventually his jibber-jabber paid off and I reluctantly agreed to the swap. It was the line about it being 'more of a man's watch' that finally convinced me. I put it on, admiring its simplicity. My dad then popped my Timex in his pocket and promptly changed the subject.

Predictably, once I returned home, my granddad saw that I was wearing a different timepiece and asked where my Timex was. I told him about the trade and he immediately began to turn red. Clearly he could tell my 'man's watch' was a piece of tosh compared to the costly watch they had bought me. He ordered my mother to return my watch, but she simply brushed it off. Regardless of my granddad's insistence, I never saw my watch again.

***

In August Carol married her fiancé, Jeremiah. Having a new uncle had its advantages. Not only did Jeremiah have the obligatory Ford Escort in which to whizz us around, he had his one true love: football. He was an avid fan of Tottenham Hotspur, which led him to help me overcome one of my biggest childhood obstacles, namely my unorthodox dislike of the beautiful game.

Every boy in the playground followed one team or another in an almost fanatical manner, except me. It was always over my head. I could not understand the appeal. 'Why on earth would I want to watch twenty-two grown men kick a bag of wind between two sticks?' I wondered. When asked the constant infernal question, 'Which team do you support?', I would always reply with a joke, hoping nobody would find out that I was, in fact, a footie atheist. I had even tried collecting Panini football stickers for a while to garner some interest, but gave up after being subjected to more perms than a boy could handle.

The only elements that appealed to me were the colour combinations and logos of each team. I had a propensity towards yellow and black, which

I attribute solely to my preference for Irish road signs. This alone had me leaning towards Wolverhampton Wanderers. Jeremiah, it turned out, had other ideas.

He had generously bought a selection of gifts to set me up for the new school year. I received an official Tottenham Hotspur bag, along with a bobble hat and scarf, all in the team colours of blue and white. I was convinced that my new apparel would help me fit in with the sportier kids, as I now had a team to support, albeit by default. However, I knew merchandise alone would not suffice. Therefore, I decided to learn all the players' names in order to partake in the conversations that were bound to arise. I was ready.

For once I felt like a real boy as I walked through the school gates proudly kitted out in my new football gear. However, my classmates remained unimpressed. As soon as I set foot on school grounds I began to get grief. The day was spoiled further when I received a thorough kicking at break time, simply for supporting Spurs. It transpired that the team West Ham had dominance in the local area and wearing any other colours than theirs was seen as an act of disrespect. Everyone at my school supported them. And I mean everyone, even the teachers. This accidental act of defiance had turned me into an outsider yet again and I was royally miffed. *Fuck this*, I thought, as I threw my hat and scarf in the bin. I kept the bag, though, making sure to carry it with the logo facing inwards so as to avoid unwanted hassle.

And that, folks, was my brief foray into the world of football, unless of course you count the time when I managed an own goal during my one and only attempt at playing the actual game. I scored rather proudly, then looked up for support, only to see heads in hands. Football and I were never destined to be good bedfellows.

***

My granddad occasionally collected me from school on his bicycle, giving me a lift home on his crossbar. I loved it when he turned up, as it was almost always unexpected. Even though it was both dangerous and a little scary, I enjoyed being a passenger on his bike. On one such day, he arrived at the gates beaming. He had big news.

In previous years, there had been some issue with their guardianship, none of it made easier by my disappearance to Ireland. But at long last they were now officially my full legal guardians, a ruling that could not be overturned. My granddad then uttered something that seriously, if unintentionally, ruffled my feathers: 'You're ours now.'

He was very proud of his statement as we cycled home, his arms encircling me as we rode. This was normally a feeling of protection that I would welcome, but on this day it felt sinister. The significance of his statement seemed so final that I began to have pangs of guilt about returning to them. My mother was sure to be upset by such news and although she had been annoying me of late, I still found myself contemplating her possible sadness as we rode home. Once I'd received what felt like an ownership hug from my nan, she suggested I change my surname to theirs, rather than my father's. I hated it when they did that! They were always trying to get me to alter my name; presumptuous letters would constantly arrive with my surname changed and it used to annoy the life out of me.

***

My eleventh birthday soon rolled around, and with it my hope of getting a new bicycle. I was in luck, or was I?

My granddad trundled my new two-wheeler around the side of the house and waited for my reaction. Without trying to sound ungrateful, I definitely had to fake it. Any happiness on my part was purely an act. It was not quite the model I'd hoped for and it was anything but modern. He had purchased what could only be described as an old man's bicycle. It had long metal mudguards and a full chain cover. The frame was so tall that I could barely mount it. Still, I thanked him and tried to remain optimistic. I am pretty sure he could sense my disappointment, which of course was not fair on him.

My uncle Tim was visiting and tried to put a positive spin on things by suggesting I take it out for an inaugural ride. He was craving fizzy liquid and asked me to pop to the shops in order to get him some Tizer. I was keen to at least have a go on the thing, so off I trotted.

What that bicycle lacked in cool factor it made up for in weight. As I began pedalling it became abundantly clear that this was one heavy beast. I got a few choice looks from the other kids, who were all out and about on their choppers, racers and other trendier bikes of the day. Alas, just like the clothes they were dressing me in, this was a very unfashionable item indeed.

In order to get to the supermarket I had to ride on a very busy road, if only for a few minutes, before crossing to the other side. As I came upon the parade of shops, I looked right (with my partially blind eye), saw that the coast was clear and turned.

THWACK!

I travelled through the air for a nice little while before landing with a thud on the pavement. I had somehow traversed the entire width of the road and was now on the opposite side of the street. My bike was a contorted mess, as was I. Apparently I had been hit by a car, although I saw and felt nothing. The irony of this incident is that I was run over by a driving instructor.

The instructor had recently dropped off his last student and was heading home when he slammed into me. He maintained that I turned without looking, which was totally untrue. I did look. It was just that I couldn't see properly.

My nan opened the door to a frazzled boy with a bicycle bent out of all proportion. My granddad then came to the door, took one look at the state of the bike and lost his rag. He accused me of destroying it on purpose, saying I neither appreciated his efforts, nor realised how lucky I was to receive such an expensive present.

He was clearly upset and insisted I was lying as usual. Did he really think I would let myself get hit by a car just because I didn't like the style of my bike?

***

As Christmas approached, we got some shocking news via the radio. My granddad was tinkering about recklessly with the cooker switch when a news bulletin came on the radio: John Lennon had been murdered.

Suddenly there was a flash of green light and the radio exploded. Now, I'm not sure if it was the news itself or my granddad's dodgy electrics that burned these few moments into my memory, but knowing that my mum was a fan, I knew this news would hit her pretty hard. Although I was young, I understood the significance of his death, and the fact that there would be no more John Lennon songs felt particularly disheartening.

A few weeks later, with New Year's Eve upon us, my granddad prepared to perform one of his yearly rituals. This consisted of him going out shortly before midnight with a piece of bread, a lump of coal and legal tender. Once the clocks struck midnight, he would wait briefly before coming back in, the theory being that by bringing those items through the door in the first moments of the year he was ensuring the well-being of all who lived in the house. The coal represented the heat needed to stay warm, the bread signified food, and the money was to ensure prosperity. It was a lovely way to start the year. However, these old-fashioned traditions did nothing to ensure our well-being, as the coming year would attest.

CHAPTER 19

WAITING FOR THE BUS

It was early morning in mid July 1981 when the phone rang. I was downstairs, about to leave the house, when I heard it. I was heading for the door with my coat on, but as no one else was around, I decided to pick it up. Strangely enough the person on the other end of the line was my mother.

I called to my granddad, assuming that she would want to speak to him, but he didn't hear me. She then explained that she was calling from Ireland and couldn't speak for long. Also, she only wanted to talk to me. I was confused by that statement and told her I was about to leave for school and didn't have a lot of time either. She said she wouldn't keep me long, so I agreed to the briefest of chats. She began by asking me a series of odd questions about my day; like what I would be up to and when. She was also making small talk regarding the forthcoming royal wedding between Diana and Charles. I told her it would be better if she rang back later, as I really had to go or I'd miss my bus. She reluctantly agreed and hung up. It was all quite bizarre. I don't recall saying goodbye to anyone as I left that morning. If I'd known how the day was going to pan out, perhaps I would have made more of an effort.

I walked briskly towards the stop where I caught the bus to school, beatboxing as I went. I had taken to adding complex melodies, which gave the impression from afar that I might be speaking. I boarded the bus, making my way to school as if it were any other dull London day.

The subjects that morning were the usual forgettable mix of everything, sending me into a hard stare. I was brought back to life by the ringing of a loud bell, signifying the first break of the day. As I headed towards the playground in search of entertainment, a boy I barely knew came up and told me that there was a woman at the school gates asking for me. I looked over, perturbed, and saw a hunched figure hiding behind the gatepost. On closer inspection I could see that it was my mother.

I was flabbergasted. That very morning she had claimed to be calling from Ireland. What in the Sam Hill was going on here? I trotted cautiously over to the gate, trying not to arouse the suspicion of the teachers in the playground. My friends looked on inquisitively as I stepped outside the school gates for a brief moment. My mum was grinning wildly. She told me she had a question for me. She leaned in and asked excitedly, 'Do you want to go to Africa?'

Africa? What was she going on about? I thought my mother had finally lost the plot. She then told me that if I did, in fact, want to accompany her and my father to the wilds of the aforementioned continent, we would first have to travel to Ireland, where we would wait until the time was right. There was to be a European leg en route to Africa too, so a good time was guaranteed for all. She assured me that both her and my father were keen for me to join them on this great adventure. However, if I did want to go, we would have to leave immediately. The decision had to be made right there and then, apparently, at the school gates at half past ten.

I could not believe that I was being offered this amazing chance to see the world, and became quite excited at the prospect. I had always wanted to travel and, instead of simply looking at maps and calling people on the landline, I would now get to experience these places first-hand. All thoughts of previous violent episodes in Ireland had long since faded and life in London had become tedious enough to make me want to jump at the opportunity. Just like the last time, my mother persuaded me to leave my grandparents behind and follow her into the unknown.

Obviously I did not consider the pain I would be causing my

grandparents. It didn't even enter my eleven-year-old mind in those moments. The closest I came was to worry that the dog might miss me. 'What about Champ?' I asked.

Just to be clear, my mother asked me one more time if I was certain that I wanted to leave with her. It was as if the decision would rest on my shoulders alone.

'Yes,' I said, purposefully.

My mother then took me by the hand and we vanished into the back streets. I could hear my friends calling me as I walked away from them without so much as a wave.

We jumped on the first bus and headed straight for the National Westminster Bank. Somehow my mother was aware that I held a savings account in that particular branch and she had taken me there to empty its funds. She even had the identification necessary to make the withdrawal, meaning I was soon on the pavement outside with twenty-seven pounds that my grandparents had deposited for my future in my tiny hands. She hailed a black cab and we jumped inside our *de facto* getaway car.

My mum directed the driver to the Strand in London's West End. Once we pulled up at the kerb, to my dismay, she asked me to pay the fare. I did not take kindly to this; was she taking the piss? I was then installed in a greasy café on Aldwych and told to wait while she allegedly went off to buy tickets. She took a fairly long time and I became suspicious of her activities, especially considering how close we were to the law courts. I always wondered if perhaps she was trying to take me back using legal means. Either way she returned looking stressed, telling me that it was time to go. She grabbed my things and rushed me out of the café. We were on our way to Africa.

The fact that we had to stop off in Ireland first and pick up my dad should have set alarm bells ringing, but it didn't. I trusted her. She was my mum. I had missed her and they had both been good to me for a couple of years now, albeit from afar. Things had changed for the better, I felt, and I was looking forward to cultivating a new kind of relationship with my parents.

My mum was keen to escape London as soon as possible; therefore, we climbed aboard the first available bus bound for Birmingham, which in itself was exciting. I had seen so little of England that even the idea of the West Midlands seemed exotic.

Once in Birmingham we had a three-hour layover until our next bus, which would be heading further north. To kill time we went shopping in the old Bull Ring, where my mum bought me a new jacket. It was mid length, with a red tartan lining, and instantly became my favourite ever piece of clothing. I adored it. We were having such a great evening that I almost forgot I was a runaway. For me, at least, it was a very special time and one of the few times that I can honestly say I enjoyed my mother's company.

***

Of course I had no idea what was really going on. Although I possessed a good understanding of geography, I seemed oblivious to the long-way-round route we were embarking upon. It later transpired that my mum had deliberately pre-booked two flights in her name from Heathrow to Ireland purely as a decoy. The flights were for early the following morning, giving us plenty of time to leave the UK by other means. We were travelling north to Scotland, where we would be taking an early morning boat to Northern Ireland. We would make landfall around the same time as our missed flights, giving the police the royal runaround. By the time they realised we weren't on the plane, we would already be long gone. It was a masterstroke. It must have been very costly for my parents to enact their plan, so when I eventually learned of this, I assumed they must have really wanted me after all, regardless of how they were treating me.

Their plan worked a treat. The only issue was that I often suffered from terrible bouts of travel sickness and the bus we were on was extremely bumpy, especially once we'd left England. I had never been to Scotland before and my very first view of it was through a rain-soaked windscreen. The July sun eventually rose to reveal a stunning, if damp, landscape. After many twists and turns of both the road and my stomach, we arrived in the port of Stranraer, where we boarded the ferry and sailed across the Irish Sea. The crossing was pretty smooth and relatively fast, but I still felt a little queasy.

I was concerned about travelling through Northern Ireland, as 'The Troubles' were in full flow at the time and the news was awash with stories of murders, car bombs and general scariness. We arrived in the port of Larne and caught a bus into Belfast. My initial visuals were of rubble and derelict buildings. The parts that weren't bombed to shit looked incredibly run-down. The murals on the walls, although artistically mesmerising, were scary to my young eyes. Imagery of republican and loyalist fighters in balaclavas holding machine guns and surrounded by skulls, coffins and flags did not sit easy. I was, however, hopeful that we would pass through Northern Ireland unscathed and get to the relative safety of the South without incident.

My mum's plan was to keep moving, so we never stopped anywhere for too long. Once in Belfast, we headed directly to the train station and climbed aboard the first locomotive to Dublin. I was so happy to be getting out of Northern Ireland; rightly or wrongly, it made me nervous.

Once we were out of Belfast and into the countryside I felt relief, at least until I noticed crowds of people gathered in the fields up ahead from my window seat. As we passed by they began throwing eggs at the train windows. My mum explained that they were all nuts and were objecting because our train was heading south. I didn't really understand why that was a problem, but she told me not to worry, so I didn't.

Apart from an eggy window, all seemed fine until about ten minutes later, when, out of nowhere, there was an unholy screeching sound as the train came to a violent halt, throwing everyone forward in the process.

We reversed a little before coming to a complete stop. 'What now?' I wondered. Suddenly over the speaker system came an announcement telling us to disembark from the train immediately.

There were no proper roads to speak of next to the train line, just fields and rolling hills. I didn't understand where we were going exactly, but my mum grabbed me by the hand and I followed her and everyone else up a steep bank to a nearby gravel path, where we were told to wait.

Eventually a pair of ancient buses from God knows where arrived and we boarded them. Everyone was keen to get out of the area as fast as possible and these old buses were our Lord and Saviour. Once aboard we were told rather candidly that there had been a device on the tracks ahead and luckily for us it was spotted by the attentive train driver.

'A device?' I asked my mother.

'A bomb,' came her matter-of-fact reply.

Are you kidding me? I thought. *The one time I come to Northern Ireland and there's a bomb on the line. What are the chances?*

The new plan was to take the buses slowly through Portadown and Newry, which were apparently two of the most dangerous towns in the province at the time. The roads were notorious for being littered with incendiary devices and the driver understandably took his sweet time, looking ahead the entire way for suspicious activity. I was not used to being so close to the action, and although scary, it was also kind of exciting. We had to go the long way round to avoid a couple of roadside bombs that the police had found near the border, meaning there were going to be hills to climb.

Although everything that was happening seemed pretty dangerous, I had other concerns. On the train I had been fine, but now that we were back on buses, travelling on bendy roads and up and down hills, I became violently ill once again. It was the worst bout of travel sickness I have ever experienced. It was so extreme that I spent the rest of the journey in and out of consciousness, though this was probably for the best.

By the time we arrived in Dublin I was exhausted. I had been awake the entire night and was now drained from constantly throwing up. This was a level of travelling I was not used to. In Dublin we caught yet another train, and I sat back in my seat, desperate for slumber. The journey took the rest of the day, due to the painfully slow trains operating in Ireland at the time. I thought it odd that just twenty-four hours earlier I had no idea I would even be back in Ireland so soon. It was thrilling to be on the run, and although I now realised that I would be causing my family in England a fair amount of grief, in that moment I didn't care. I was with my mum and it felt right.

My mother had a question for me regarding the previous day's events. 'Who were you talking to at the bus stop yesterday?'

'No one,' I replied. 'Hang on, what do you mean?' I asked with some confusion.

It transpired that my mother had been hiding quite close to the bus stop the previous morning and saw my lips moving from afar. She was convinced that I had told my granddad about the phone call, which would have made him suspicious. Therefore, she assumed that he'd followed me to the bus stop and was hiding on the other side of the wall, ready to pounce. I told her she was mistaken. All I was doing was my usual singing and beatboxing. She told me in that case I should stop doing such things as it made me look like a fool.

Her original plan had been to take me from the bus stop, not from school, as that had been deemed too risky. However, my mouth-antics had deterred her, forcing her to adopt plan B.

Again I thought of my grandparents. My nan and granddad must have been worried sick by my disappearance. Perhaps at first they didn't even think to suspect my mother. There had been a lot of kids disappearing around that time, so maybe they thought I'd been kidnapped, or worse. It was a very selfish move on my part and I'm sure in some way they never quite forgave me for running away with my mother for what was technically a second time.

When I saw my father again he was back in his hometown. Their new abode was a mere stone's throw from the cul-de-sac that housed most of his family. He was sitting upright in an armchair, watching a programme about the royal wedding. As we entered he jumped up, seemingly happy to see me, saying something along the lines of 'There's the young fella!'

I was back with my parents at long last and I was content. For once, being in Ireland felt good and I was looking forward to a new start. I was older now and things were different, plus my parents had a plan. Africa beckoned.

The next morning the mood was positive as we tucked into our first family breakfast in years. A brand new life was unfolding and I was all smiles. Later that same day my dad suggested we go for a drive to the beach in one of the two Morris Minors my parents now seemed to own. I sat on the back seat, excited to be going to the seaside.

It was during this bumpy ride that my dad uttered a series of words to my mother that sent a chill down my spine. 'So what is his punishment going to be?' he said while giving me a glance in the mirror.

Shit, I thought. *Are they being serious?*

I was sure they were just messing around. My dad was even smiling. *Yeah, it was probably a joke*, I thought. *Phew!*

My mum then turned around stern-faced and looked me square in the eye. She said she wasn't sure, but something had to be done about my disobedient behaviour.

My dad informed me that it could be weeks until I was punished, but once he and my mother had decided on the relevant method, he would enforce it. I had caused her much suffering by not running away two years previously and now some of that suffering would be handed back to me.

I immediately spoke up. I was no longer a little kid they could just push around. I told them straight that I had done nothing wrong and objected to receiving any kind of chastisement whatsoever. My dad then turned to me and spoke very slowly. He told me that I had shown incredible disloyalty to my mother when I refused to rejoin her at Archie's flat. He then said, 'You *will* be punished, believe me.'

Were they kidding? This was ancient news. Then it dawned on me that I might have been lured back to Ireland under false pretences, so I piped up and asked about the time frame for our trip to Africa. My mum then turned to me and, without any shame whatsoever, told me that it might not happen due to money worries, but if it did it would be at least a year away. What the hell?

I sat in the back of that old banger, painfully aware that I had been duped yet again. I had returned to the very same nightmare from which I had escaped. How could I have been so stupid?

IRELAND

1981–82

CHAPTER 20

THIS TOWN IS NOT MY HOME

Eventually my punishment was decided upon. I was to receive a mild beating from my father at a time of his choosing, and such a moment soon presented itself. My dad came home from work caked in the usual cement dust and when my mum suddenly made herself scarce, I knew this was going to be it: the moment of retribution. *Okay, brace yourself,* I thought.

My dad had acquired a new twist to his beating technique. He now applied a verbal caveat that shifted the blame away from the oppressor and onto the victim. The first time I heard these words my bladder emptied itself on the spot without consent. From now on any kind of beating would be preceded by his newfound mantra: 'This is going to hurt me a lot more than it is going to hurt you.' Then there was that smile, which made my heart descend into my stomach. I wasn't quite sure when I was younger, but I now knew that he enjoyed inflicting pain on me. I could see it in his beady little eyes.

Once the beating was over, I was sent to my room to think about what I had done. *Really?* I thought. What I'd done was so long ago that it was in a previous decade.

I had a small cassette player in my room, the rectangular type with the buttons on top with a tiny speaker at the back. This, along with my mum's Bryan Ferry cassettes, got me through some particularly dark times. I knew I'd made a terrible mistake in coming back, but I had no way of returning to England. I had burned my last bridge and was now stuck in the smallest of Irish towns with no obvious way out. I was trapped.

It was decided by my parents that I had two major flaws that needed to be addressed. Apparently I walked duck-footed and slouched too much – bad habits I had supposedly picked up living in England.

The slouching was to be cured first. My parents devised a new kind of torture by insisting I stand with my back against the living-room door for a selected number of hours each evening. It doesn't sound that bad, but over time I would become quite sore. It would usually begin after dinner, whereby I would be made to stand flat against the door until I was instructed otherwise, sometimes for entire evenings. If I moved I would be reprimanded or given a slap. My parents would watch television, which was just out of view, while I simply stood there as stiff as a board. It was a new type of abuse. I was as bored as an underpaid security guard.

The duck-footedness was to be dealt with by forcing me to accompany my parents on long walks. My mother would observe my technique from behind and guide me in order for me to lose my abhorrent habit. These walks would take place on Sundays and we would walk an average of ten miles each time. It was worse than the forced running, not due to the distance, but because every time they thought I wasn't walking properly I would receive a clout around the head. These almost always came from my mum and, as she was behind me the entire time, I had no clue when the slaps were coming. She was obsessed with me walking with my feet pointed straight ahead. It felt completely unnatural and was impossible to maintain.

**

I began attending another school, the only secondary school in my father's hometown. I now sounded completely English and this proved to be a thorn in my side once again. Most of the kids came from homes that supported Sinn Féin, the political wing of the IRA, so I was not the most popular boy. I did sometimes try to disguise my accent, but it was a pointless task as everyone knew where I was from.

However, I soon developed a knack for mimicking accents while never allowing my own to change. I had always been surprised by how much my mum's accent wavered between English and Irish depending on where she lived. I didn't want to be like her. I wanted to retain my voice even if it did occasionally cause me strife. Instead, I practised the local accent on walks to and from school for my own personal use. A time would soon arise whereby this newfound skill would come in very handy indeed.

Once I'd accepted my fate, I settled back into Irish life and tried to forget about my family and friends in England. Compared to London, there was nothing at all to do in this sleepy town, yet I had to somehow amuse myself daily. It was also imperative that I devise ways to make a buck, as my parents refused to give me a cent. Luckily I was often left to my own devices and I soon came up with a cunning plan to reverse the old empty-pocket syndrome.

While down by the river, I noticed that the back yard of the main hotel in town was completely exposed; there wasn't a fence or a gate to be seen along the whole stony bank. Best of all, the yard appeared to be piled high with full crates of empty soda pop bottles. I knew that each receptacle was worth two pence once returned, as we would take our own bottles back to the shops often. It was then the penny dropped or, in my case, two pennies.

I decided to clamber up the bank with full crates I'd taken from the yard, walk straight into reception and sell them back to whoever was on duty. I performed this trick many times and it worked without fail. It was a simple idea and I did it often, but not enough to arouse suspicion. Once I received my cash I would usually hang around the hotel chatting to guests, cause a little mischief, steal some cutlery, that sort of thing.

On one such scam-filled morning, I was bringing a crateful of bottles from around the back of the hotel up towards the town square when a lorry pulled up abruptly in front of me. The canvas sides lifted to reveal around twenty men in full paramilitary uniform, wearing balaclavas and holding rifles. I very nearly shat myself.

A coffin was then lowered onto a stand accompanied by much shouting. The only thought in my mind was: *Don't say a word.* I did not want these guys hearing an English accent. One of the paramilitaries asked me to move out of the way and I responded by putting on my strongest Irish accent: 'Ah, sure, no problem, you're fine.' I was terrified and using far too many words, but it worked. There I was, an eleven-year-old English boy with a crate full of stolen bottles, doing a bad impersonation in the middle of what appeared to be some sort of IRA funeral ceremony.

They pointed their rifles towards the sky and let off a few rounds of gunfire. The coffin was then hoisted back onto the lorry as the paramilitaries packed up their kit with gusto, and within seconds they were all driving away at speed. The whole thing lasted but a few minutes. It was quite surreal.

Such open shows of Republican Army support were frowned upon at the time, but I noticed many familiar faces blend in and out of the crowd during this odd, sudden ceremony. As soon as the masked men were gone I took my bottles into the hotel, got my money and went and chomped down on a big bag of monkey nuts.

Stealing bottles wasn't quite doing it for me, however, so it wasn't very long before my thieving antics began to spiral. It all started when my mum insisted on sending me to school with nothing but half a sandwich; again, it was all about me being too fat. She decided that, in order to lose weight, I now had to live on this meagre amount of food for the entire school day.

I wasn't too worried. I don't think I even ate her stupid half sandwich. Instead I stole food from around town. Mostly I would consume fig rolls, a packet of which I could easily devour in one sitting.

The shop from whence the stolen biscuits came was very old-fashioned, which made it easy to pilfer. Although it kept most of its stock in the back, there were no mirrors to speak of and security was non-existent. I would often buy a couple of penny sweets to show good faith, but I took something from that shop almost every day. It's a wonder I was never caught, especially as one fateful morning I decided to take my crookedness to a new and unforgivable level, most notably to the first floor.

With a packet of biscuits already stashed, I noticed a door at the back slightly ajar. I was intrigued. I decided to explore by pushing it wide open, creating a loud creak that stopped me in my tracks. I looked towards the counter, but the shopkeeper hadn't noticed. The first thing I saw was a set of narrow steps, and before I could decide whether or not it was a good idea, I was already climbing them.

At the top were three doors. I pushed open the first one to reveal an old man lying on a bed; he was clearly very ill. He was sleepy but awake. On the far side of his bed was a collection of dusty brown coins, which immediately caught my eye. I walked slowly around the bed with his eyes burning into me. I swept up the coins and stuffed them in my jeans pocket. It couldn't have been more than a few pence. I gave the old man a look as if to say, 'Sorry mate', and ran down the stairs and out of the shop.

I wish I could say I felt bad at the time, but I didn't. That came later. In fact, I got such a thrill from that single event that I went looking for even bigger kicks.

There was a bed and breakfast hotel in town, quite close to my school. It was just the right distance away for me to be able to sneak in and out during my lunch breaks, and I broke in often, looking for treasure. I would go into each room, opening drawers as I went, always on the lookout for that elusive stash of cash, though making sure to take only small amounts each time. This pastime was to be short-lived, however, as clearly they had received complaints and were on the lookout.

And so, one fateful afternoon, while escaping with my booty, I saw a guard running towards me at high speed. I legged it as fast as I could, desperate to get away. However, I could not outrun him, how could I? He knew the geography of the town far better than I did. Plus, it was a tiny place. Eventually I could take no more and gave up rather unceremoniously. I was then handcuffed and marched off towards the station.

The guard already knew my name and took down my details. He informed me that he would be accompanying me home to inform my father of my wrongdoings. I began pleading with him. I promised that I wouldn't do anything of the like again, if only he'd just let me go. He remained unconvinced. It was only when I started panic-crying, fearful of what my dad might do, that he realised something was amiss. He sat me down, gave me a glass of water and told me to calm down. I probably shouldn't have, but I ended up telling him all the nasty things my dad was capable of. I begged him to let me off with a caution, promising to return the money I'd stolen and apologise to the hotel owners. I would do anything as long as they didn't tell my dad.

Another guard entered the room and the two men began a brief conversation regarding my family. Our clan was well known in the town, some more than others. Although there were members of the family who were nice enough, some were also known for being particularly unpleasant and violent. The guard decided that I was probably telling the truth and that throwing me to the wolves wasn't going to help anyone. I could not believe my luck! They unlocked the handcuffs and let me off with a warning. I was reminded that under no circumstances would I get a second chance. As I ran off one of them told me to 'not be such a blaggard'. *What a funny word*, I thought.

I stopped all my shenanigans around town that very afternoon. I would not put myself in that position again. It was a ridiculous thing to have done and a pretty shitty one at that. Those two guards were so kind and I never forgot their generosity and understanding. They certainly did not fit the mould of 'pigs', the term my dad used when describing any member of the police force, whether in England or Ireland. Since then I have never been able to agree with his assertion that 'all police are bastards'. I knew better now, although I could never reveal to my father how I gained such knowledge.

CHAPTER 21

BOILING POINT

Although I had ceased all thieving, I did end up hanging out with a small group of kids who would tear around town getting up to no good, but it was pretty innocent compared to my own misdeeds.

We would often hang out at the church on the town square, invariably getting thrown out by the priests. The reasons were varied: gambling in the pews, making too much noise, or simply lighting all the votive candles at once. One day, however, I had an experience that would end my church frolicking days rather abruptly. I will have to put it down to a lack of iron, B12 or maybe even vertigo, but what happened to me in that church seemed as real as anything else I had experienced up to that point.

All that hanging around the Lord's house meant that I often got to sample those 'body of Christ' wafers they gave out during Mass. So, of course, I got a taste for them. I would go up for second or even third helpings. I figured I didn't necessarily have to believe in God to sample his sacramental snacks.

After one such service I decided it would be fun to play a little hide and seek with my compadres. My hiding place was to be one of the confessionals. I thought it would be amusing to hide in there, especially should a priest enter the central chamber. But as soon as I set foot inside I got the fright of my young life. The booth seemed to descend hundreds of metres instantly. It felt like a lift dropping. I was pinned to the floor, terrified.

Once the sensation stopped, I swung the door open and got the hell out of there. All was quiet in the town square and I wondered if I was perhaps losing my marbles.

I was not the only scoundrel in town. Our neighbours, who were an Irish traveller family, were always trying to steal from us, and one fateful day they almost outdid themselves by trying to appropriate my mother's car.

I arrived home from school one evening to see my mother leaning on one of the two Morris Minors we owned. She appeared to be arguing with the next-door neighbours, and it was becoming heated. The players included two rather large women, some skanky kids and a couple of dodgy-looking young fellas. The women were threatening my mother and becoming increasingly aggressive. As I approached I could just make out the basics of their conversation.

Our shifty neighbours were acting delusional, claiming that my mother's car was in fact theirs. They accused her of obtaining the motor by devious means and said they could prove it, if only she'd show them the logbook. The truth of the matter was that my dad had been given the car as an alternative form of payment for building work he'd completed. The owner couldn't pay, so my dad simply took the car instead. He did things like this often, to my mother's eternal disdain. My father was, rather ironically, considered generous and good-natured by all those who didn't really know him.

My mum and the neighbours had a very long and pointless slagging match in the street before my mum eventually gave in. 'Fine,' she said, 'I'll show you the fucking logbook.'

With that the two women nudged each other like a couple of pantomime dames and proceeded to follow my mother into our house. As soon as they were in the sitting room their mood changed, appearing more civil. They began admiring the furnishings and attempted to make small talk. I recognised this as a distraction technique and therefore watched them like a hawk. I was convinced that they were up to something. 'Why are they being so nice now?' I wondered.

My mum went to retrieve the logbook and upon her return the women seemed almost uninterested in the argument they had been so passionate about only moments earlier. They took one look at it and conceded that they had made an honest mistake. After apologising they suddenly changed tack. They started talking about town gossip, the price of food, anything to put my mum off the scent. Then I saw it; one of the women snuck the logbook into her pocket mid conversation, before giving the other a second nudge to say she had it. Both women then got up to leave. I was trying to get my mum's attention, but she was shooing me away, telling me not to get involved. However, once the front door was closed, I shouted, 'Mum, they took your logbook.'

I explained to her that I had seen one of the women put the logbook in her pocket. Not missing a beat, she threw open the front door and stormed over to the two women, who were now back on shared pavement. She grabbed hold of both of them, looked at me for an indication as to which of them had taken it and, once I'd given her the nod, punched the guilty woman hard in the face.

This was not like the sucker punch she had given Carol years earlier; this was a full-on boxer's right hook. I was oddly proud. She grabbed the logbook from the woman's pocket and told them both to 'Fuck off', at which point they ran back into their house. From that day forth we never had any further confrontation with these neighbours; in fact, they became firm friends, purely out of respect.

I thought my mum kicked ass that day. She could really handle herself and it was impressive. I only wondered why she never stood up to my dad like that. Unfortunately it was not long before an opportunity to defend herself against him arrived, but, alas, once again she did not take it.

My mum and I were playing board games late one night when my dad suddenly awoke from his slumber. We were alerted to this fact by the usual thud on the ceiling followed by his stomping feet on the staircase. We were back in the loop. I realised in those few moments before all hell broke loose that it could easily have been three years earlier in that town twenty miles south. It bore an uncanny resemblance to the night he allegedly killed the dog, or when he smashed my *Star Trek* toy at Christmas.

The next few minutes were horrific and I remained frozen to the spot throughout. My dad entered the room like a man possessed. He told my mum that he'd given her plenty of forewarning about making noise late at night and it was time for her to learn a lesson. She was begging him not to hit her, when he spotted a saucepan on the stovetop. My mum was in the process of making herself a hot chocolate, but this particular pan of water was no longer heading for her Cadbury's mug. My dad grabbed the saucepan and proceeded to pour the boiling hot liquid down my mum's neck, that same sadistic smile I knew so well lighting up his face as he did so. She let out a high-pitched shriek as the water charred her skin, forming an almost instant scab along her neck and shoulders. She fell to the ground, screaming in agony. I wanted to kill the bastard, though of course I did not.

Soon after, my mum accidentally inflicted some burns of her own, and unfortunately they were to my pale buttocks. She lifted me up and placed me atop the range to dry off after a shower, courtesy of the twin tub (more on that shortly). What she forgot, however, was that one of the burners was still on, so my skin was instantly scorched. Not content with experiencing that dose of pain, I ended up burning my lips a few days later by kissing a boiling kettle, all in the name of curiosity, of course.

As if things couldn't get any worse, soon after this my father came up with a new set of rules for me to abide by, a set of commandments that were hereby etched in stone. The first being that, from that day forth, I was to no longer refer to my father as 'Dad'. Well, this was a pretty confusing concept. What was I supposed to call him exactly? I had a few choice words of my own, of course. It's not like I said the word 'Dad' that much anyway, but this new rule led to me having to slide up to him and enter conversations mid sentence. It was all very awkward.

Over the course of the next few months 'he who shan't be named' added many new decrees to his list of dos and don'ts, all of them equally ludicrous as the no-dad rule. All sneezing, sniffing and coughing was now banned in his presence, especially in the car. Who was he, the Queen? If I so much as sniffed I would get hit. It was an impossible rule to maintain and although I nearly passed out trying, I did of course sniff, cough and sneeze before year's end. Each violation of the rules led to a few slaps in return.

***

It was September when my mum came up with the bright idea to make some extra money selling pies. She decided it would be lucrative for us to make and sell them at a forthcoming public event. My mum would bake a selection of pies and flapjacks and we would then offload them from the back of my dad's work van at the venue, making a tidy profit in return. Apparently we didn't even need a licence.

I had a feeling my dad was in agreement. How? Because when I came home the sofa had been replaced by a giant chest freezer. We now had a place for our pies, though nowhere to sit. Brilliant. I found it odd that buying a gigantic freezer was a priority, especially as we didn't even own an electric kettle or have a proper way of cleaning ourselves, as we were 'showering' using a washing machine, for goodness sake.

I should probably explain.

To give us some form of bathing apparatus, my dad had combined a slab of concrete with a twin-tub washing machine to create a *de facto* shower. Stay with me, it gets better. Firstly he fashioned the standing area out of stolen cement, which he positioned at an angle to allow the excess water to run off into the freezing yard. Secondly he worked out that if he put the washing machine on a quick wash, it would heat up just the right amount of water in which to shower. We would have to keep an eye on its progress, as it was only during the drain and spin cycle that the hot water was expelled, by which point we would have to be in position. We would then have to hold the low-pressure extraction pipe high above our heads in order to wash ourselves. It was all very cumbersome. My dad never once thought to attach a showerhead, so it was akin to washing oneself with a garden hose. I should mention that if you missed the point in the cycle where the water was discharged, you would have to start again from scratch, which could be tedious, especially if you were standing butt naked in sub-zero temperatures.

Coincidentally, my dad would often stand there, stark-bollock naked at the edge of the kitchen, hosing himself down while simultaneously telling me it was okay to come in and make myself a jam sandwich. It was all quite peculiar.

The toilet was also, of course, outside and contained the coldest lavatory seat in the known universe. I wasn't sure if I was living in 1981 or 1891. It was bloody difficult to tell.

Anyway, now that my mum had a huge freezer to fill, she began the pie-making process. She made a whole lot of everything. There were boiled bacon pies, mutton pies, beef and cabbage pies and various fruit-filled variants including blackberries, which I would collect from the stream opposite, having to reach through spider webs to obtain my spoils.

Making pies was actually fun and for once the atmosphere in the house was good, possibly because we were all on a sugar high. We used an awful lot of golden syrup in those flapjacks.

Once the event was up and running, we set off to sell our wares. Within the hour we were nicely situated in the middle of the wet car park, ready to get cracking. We took a fair amount of stock with us, but were worried that we might run out by lunchtime. No need to concern ourselves there. By mid afternoon all we'd sold was one measly flapjack. It was desperate. We tried our best to engage with the public, but nobody seemed interested. If anything, they appeared to be puzzled by our existence. Did my mother simply pull this idea out of thin air? Was this not a thing? I guess the fact that there were no other caterers in the entire car park should have been a clue. We gave it another shot the following day, but my mum soon got the message and pulled the plug by mid morning. It had been a misguided enterprise from the outset.

My mum later explained that our failure to sell didn't matter. She had a back-up plan.

'Great, are we going to sell them somewhere else?' I wondered.

'We're going to eat them ourselves,' she said with a straight face.

Apparently, in the long run, we would actually save money on groceries if all we ate were pies. Now I don't mind a pie, but come on. You can't eat them every day, right? Well, let me tell you, you can, and we did. I was so sick of pies by Christmas that I'm surprised I ever ate another one of my own volition. For nearly three months all of our meals were pie-based. Only my dad seemed to embrace it without issue, giving an answer to the age-old adage of 'who ate all the pies?'

***

Once the pie-making fiasco was over, I took to visiting the river once more, whereby I stumbled upon a game that I subsequently became somewhat addicted to. There were many cattle down by the river and a series of electric fences had been installed to keep them from falling into the water. I accidentally brushed past a strand of this powered string one evening and received quite the jolt for my sins. I grabbed it again to see if it was indeed the fence; it was.

Over time I devised a little game for myself: to hold onto the wired lightning as long as possible without blacking out. I could handle quite a few shocks, but I would always lose after a second or two and wake up on the grass. It may not have been the cleverest of ideas on my part, but I guess at least I felt like I was in control of my own pain for a change.

It was around this time that my mother pretended to be a teacher again. Instead of attending the secondary school full-time, I would once again receive life instruction from her. She had been homeschooling me throughout the summer and had decided to continue this practice into the new school term. Although she had no formal tutoring skills to speak of, my mother thought it paramount that I learn about life, the universe and everything directly from her. However, the lesson structure was identical to the one she set out for me three years earlier and appeared to cover just two subjects: geography and very long words.

My mother's insistence that I be locked away studying all the livelong day was having a particularly adverse effect on my relationship with my new best friend: my dog Benjy.

A few weeks earlier I had been roaming the streets of the town when a little brown dog appeared by my side and started following me. I just couldn't give him the slip. He was dirty and didn't have a collar, a sure sign that he was a stray. He followed me home that afternoon and I ended up feeding him. This routine continued for a couple of days; every afternoon he would somehow find me in town and follow me home. My dad, of all people, saw a connection and asked if I wanted to keep him. My mum wasn't sold on the idea. Still, my dad said as long as I understood that the dog would be my sole responsibility, technically he didn't have a problem with it. I would, however, have to find work to pay for dog food. I agreed to his terms on the spot and headed out to buy a collar for my little tail-wagger.

I found honest work in the form of a job loading heavy crates onto lorries at weekends. Most of the boxes contained temptation in the form of sweets and snacks. And although I pilfered the odd item, I never took enough to cause suspicion. It was technically my first job and it was backbreaking work, but I certainly didn't resent having to work to provide food for my new dependant. My dad continued to show his softer side by helping to build a kennel in the back garden. He seemed genuinely supportive of me having that dog. I could never quite understand it.

A few weeks into studying my mum's bizarre curriculum, I heard a violent crashing sound outside in the street, followed by a squeal. It sounded a lot like a dog and I suspected it was poor Benjy. Panicked, I relayed my suspicions to my mother, who in turn retorted with her usual soothing dialogue of 'Don't be so fucking stupid.' Even though she could see that I was clearly perturbed, she insisted I carry on spelling words like 'lackadaisical' while reminding her where Ulaanbaatar was.

All afternoon I could hear a constant whimpering coming from outside and I just couldn't shake off the feeling that something was terribly wrong.

Later that afternoon my dad came bounding up the stairs to tell us that Benjy was indeed in the neighbour's garden and was in a bad way; he'd been hit by a car and needed to be taken to the vet immediately. It was out of character, but I could tell that my dad was annoyed at my mother for not showing compassion. I think he found it embarrassing more than anything. My mum, as she so often did, continued to convey only nonchalance.

My dad scooped up my mangled pooch from the adjoining garden and placed him carefully onto the floor of his work van. We then sped off to the nearest veterinary hospital, which happened to be in our old haunt twenty miles south. Benjy was whimpering the entire way and I had the distinct feeling my stray pup wouldn't make it through the night.

Later the vet gave us the inevitable bad news. To survive, Benjy would need to have metal plates inserted into his legs and a wooden cot built around him, in which he would have to live for up to nine months. It would be costly and he would be in severe pain throughout. The vet suggested that it might be more humane to simply put him to sleep. My parents also had tentative plans to bring their African adventure back in from the cold during this period, and this scenario did not fit with their schedule. Subsequently my scruffy little street mutt was put down that very evening. Just a few weeks after our chance meeting, he was dead.

There were a lot of dogs around in Ireland while I was growing up. Almost every year we seemed to go through at least one unlucky hound. There were far too many to mention, but one dog stands out. Zoe was a black Labrador and the only female dog we ever had. Unfortunately she was killed by the guards, the poor bitch.

On a surprisingly sunny day we decided to go for a drive to the beach, forgetting to ensure that the dog was properly secured in the back garden. She was a bit of a barker, but in no way dangerous; she was actually quite a loving and placid animal. However, once we'd left she apparently started barking avidly, before jumping the fence and making her way down the street to the local newsagent. It was there that she spent several hours barking at all the customers who came and went, becoming quite the nuisance. The owner became so aggravated that he called the guards for assistance. Once they were on the scene, they decided the best course of action was to shoot her. Yes, you read that right. They decided the best way to stop a barking dog was to fire a bullet into her head. And so that is exactly what they did. They pointed a loaded gun at Zoe, right there in the middle of town, and then she was gone.

As we arrived home a neighbour relayed the tragic news to us through a hastily rolled-down window. I was mortified. It seemed like such a barbarous and unnecessary act. Those were different times, I suppose, and not necessarily good ones.

***

Shortly after Zoe was killed, my mother once again became bored with the status quo. I returned to school and she got a job at the local supermarket in town. It gave her the opportunity to steal both money and food. In fact, once she started working there we never wanted for anything. One evening she even had the audacity to walk through the door with an enormous frozen chicken, which she proceeded to cook in the range. I only remember this because the next day I was given half a sandwich made from the leftovers to take to school and it didn't go down well. Literally.

My mum always insisted that I only eat the food she provided and not the free slop supplied by the state. However, I would sometimes become quite hungry, especially after, say, playing Gaelic football in the freezing Irish mud. Nice segue, I think you'll agree.

This particular day, I had been allocated the role of goalie, which I assumed would result in me becoming slightly less muddy than the other lads, but for some reason my clothes ended up being caked in just as much filth as everyone else's. After the game all the kids were given a large scone and a tin mug containing milk. My mum had previously told me that the scones contained actual snot from the catering staff's noses. I was sure she was making it up and on this fateful day chose to eat a whole one, regardless of her outrageous claims. It was delicious, though I did keep an eye out for green bits.

God only knows what happened to that chicken overnight, but upon eating my sandwich I became violently ill. I was writhing around in a corridor covered in my own vomit by the time a teacher found me.

I was promptly driven home by one of the staff, who suggested that I go directly to hospital. My mother, however, seemed unconcerned, and instead sent me to my room for a lie-down. She was confident that I was exaggerating my symptoms and therefore paid me no attention. It was only when my dad arrived home that he realised the severity of my condition. He saw that I was turning green and in and out of consciousness, and instantly took charge. The next thing I knew I was in the back of the van heading to the hospital, watching the trees pass by at speed.

It was like a scene-for-scene action replay of what happened to my dog, except I was now the one on the floor of the van being rushed to get medical attention. My mum kept the déjà vu going by moaning the whole way, claiming I was putting it on. My dad was arguing with her throughout, at one point saying, 'Jesus, can you not see that he's sick?'

He suspected that something was very wrong and he was right. It turned out that the chicken my mother had stolen contained salmonella. I had to have my stomach pumped. So much for stolen bird meat.

My mum would often flip flop between giving a shit and not. However, I found it far weirder that my dad would sometimes care for my well-being more than her, while at other times showing me no mercy whatsoever. It really was like living with a couple of psychopaths.

CHAPTER 22

THE FISH FACE INCIDENT

My twelfth birthday soon rolled around. It was to be a momentous year: easily the most interesting of my young life, but it had a pretty shitty start. One of the Brothers at school decided to throw me in detention for the duration of the lunch break, the reason being incredibly minor. I had simply failed a test that morning, but my lack of studying was deemed disrespectful. My incarceration was made all the worse by the knowledge that my mum had prepared a special birthday meal at home. It was extremely frustrating sitting there writing lines in a damp, grey prefab with the Brother's biblical eyes burning into my neck, knowing I could be at home eating birthday cake.

In England my birthday always fell within half-term; a week off in the middle of term. In Ireland, however, things were different. Half-term did not exist, so instead I spent my birthday learning about the Italian automotive industry. I must say that learning what FIAT stood for has held me in good stead over the years; I cannot tell you how often I have needed to convey the words *Fabbrica Italiana Automobili di Torino*.

It was a very cold winter that year and it snowed like it does in black and white movies. The hills and fields were covered by many inches of fresh snow daily and every morning my feet would produce a crunching sound as they made the first impressions of the day. It was wonderful. I had never seen snow of that magnitude before. In London it would turn into a thick black sludge within minutes and become hazardous for vehicles and pedestrians alike. In Ireland it was lush and deep, the only danger being if you accidentally kicked a frozen cowpat.

At weekends it was as if the whole town headed to the hills, grabbing whatever they could fashion into a sled so they could speed down the surrounding hills. My parents and I boarded what can only be described as a car bonnet and set off down the hillside. That thing spun like a motherfucker as it made its terrifying plunge. More perilous still was the long sheet of corrugated iron some of my younger relatives and I clambered upon. We'd bored two makeshift holes in the front and attached a piece of tatty rope for the lucky one at the front to grasp onto. It couldn't be steered as such, but it gave us a false sense of control. We would begin our descent slowly, but the sheet metal would accelerate quickly. The hill was steep and contained a small precipice at the bottom from which we would become airborne. We would fly through the air for several seconds before crashing onto a bed of flat grass close to the main road. The thud would throw us from our giant razor blade, scattering us in the deep snow. It was great craic, though in hindsight it's clear we could easily have been cut to shreds.

My parents were on the resin one evening shortly before Christmas when my mother suggested we call my nan. It was to be a prank call. Life in Ireland was easier to endure when my parents were high. They were more fun to be around and they would often behave like teenagers, which I found refreshing. So off we trotted to the only phone box in town from which you could make an international call, and lined up the coins in the dispenser. Once connected, the coins would fall in one by one. The longer the call, the more coins a person would need to juggle in order to avoid a series of loud distracting beeps. It was very much the epitome of pre-cellphone multi-tasking.

The plan was that my mum would talk first, before telling my nan that I had something I wanted to say. It was then that I was supposed to come on the line and call her a 'fish face'. For some reason this was of great amusement to my parents. I was desperate to appear cool, so I agreed to do it, regardless of the repercussions. Sure, I felt guilty, but in some way I think I wanted to do it.

Unfortunately my mother ended up having a blazing row with my nan shortly before handing me the phone. This was no longer the lighthearted jape we had planned; it was a full-blown argument. I picked up the phone and heard my nan on the other end of the line, clearly upset. Instead of feeling sorry for her, though, I became angry towards her for upsetting my mother. I told her I was never coming back to England while delivering my 'fish face' line with venom instead of whimsy.

I fully intended to keep that promise and remain with my parents no matter how terrible our home life became. I had decided to ride it out, hopeful of eventual change. Regardless, I could not imagine returning to my grandparents after all we'd been through, not now. Calling my nan that silly name was the final nail in the coffin.

My parents were cracking up as I put down the receiver. They may have been in hysterics, but I was doubting whether or not I'd done the right thing. It was awful to think that I'd upset my grandparents just before Christmas. They were, after all, the only people to have shown me unconditional love and here I was being an asshole.

My mum and dad ran through town that evening throwing snowballs at each other while I tried to keep up. My mum was being so playful that at one point she opened the door to a busy pub and threw a massive snowball at the barkeep. He in turn ducked, sending the ice sphere into a line of bottles behind the bar, which then fell to the ground with a crash. The three of us legged it, laughing as we ran.

Except for the insensitive phone call, that night was the most fun I'd ever had with my parents. It was a welcome relief.

After the 'fish face' incident things became more serious. Relations with my grandparents soured to an all-time low and the animosity between our two camps escalated rapidly. My grandparents decided enough was enough; they were my legal guardians and they wanted me back, end of story.

A court case was hastily put together to enact their wishes and we were summoned to court so that my parents could have an opportunity to fight for my custody. However, if they lost, the Irish courts had been instructed to hand me over to the UK authorities. They in turn would deliver me back to my nan and granddad and that would be that. Job done.

Unlike in our previous town, there weren't any guards trying to catch me and drag me off to England. They simply came around and told my parents that they were aware of the situation. They added that if the time ever came when I had to be returned to London, they would come and remove me – with force, if necessary. Until that time I could stay with my parents; however, we were instructed not to leave town, except for our court visits.

This was a terrible time for us all. The tension surrounding the court case caused my parents to consider that I might not be worth the trouble. Although they were fighting to keep me in Ireland, I had a hunch that they were actually ready to wash their hands of me and perhaps just hand me back.

We took many overnight trips to Dublin during this period, and always in my dad's cold-ass van. Night after night I lay freezing on the floor in bad need of a pee, listening to their derogatory comments about me and my grandparents, never daring to suggest a toilet break. I always pretended to be asleep, but it was never the case. I heard every cruel word.

I soon realised that they had no intention of handing me back, regardless of what they actually thought of me. I was too useful, a plaything in the war between themselves and my grandparents. I was merely a pawn in their twisted little game.

***

As I was now twelve years old and legally allowed to have a say in my own future, it was decided that I could testify before a judge. This meant I was swiftly coerced into making legal statements to help my parents win the case. My mother became my confidante, advising me to retract anything I may have said to my grandparents regarding my previous experiences in Ireland, especially if it referred to my dad's violent ways. I was not comfortable lying about such things, as I felt it let him off, but what else could I do? I did not want to be sent back to England. I had picked a side and I had to run with the lies, even if it meant committing perjury.

It all got out of hand pretty quickly and aspersions began to be cast from both camps. At one juncture it was even suggested that my mother had threatened my grandparents and Carol with the IRA. What nonsense. As if we had any connection to the actual Irish Republican Army. The whole episode was farcical.

Around this time, my mother got her dog back. Wolf was an enormous German Shepherd that she'd befriended while I was in England. Since my return he had been living in another town with friends. However, their situation had since changed and, regardless of how up in the air our own lives were, we had to take him back. My mother was delighted, but I thought it odd to have such a big dog roaming around the house during this tumultuous time.

As the case was drawing to a close it became clear that we were going to lose. My mum informed me that it was only a matter of time before the guards came to the door and took me back to England. She may have given up, but my dad had other ideas. He came up with a different plan entirely.

My dad hated the guards, so the idea of losing me to them was unthinkable. He therefore decided that if we did, in fact, lose the case, my mother and I would go into hiding. While we laid low, he would dispose of the house and all our worldly possessions. We would then regroup and travel through Europe to Africa, as previously planned. However, there was no mention of what we were going to do with Wolf. 'Where is he going?' I wondered.

Once my dad had showed his hand, I was bundled into town to have some photos taken. My mother then applied for an Irish passport on my behalf, which she had processed at lightning speed for a sky-high fee. Once it arrived we were ready to bolt if we had to.

In my mind the outcome of the case created an odd sort of Catch-22. If we lost, we would run away to Europe. But if we won, we would stay put in Ireland. My mum had persuaded me to return on the promise of adventure; therefore, in my view, it would be far better for us to lose.

It was around this stressful time that I began to experience some pretty severe night terrors. As well as my waking up with a fast heartbeat on a sodden sheet, there was some other odd behaviour creeping in. I would often wake in the middle of the night due to the moon reflecting on my gold-coloured wallpaper, but occasionally I would also creep downstairs to the lounge where I would stand by the door as stiff as a board, no doubt emulating my parents' cruel posture-improving technique. I wasn't sleepwalking as such, but I wasn't fully awake either. I felt numb.

As I stood there I would begin to hear voices, and although they were speaking within me, they were loud enough for me to hear them in the room. The weirdest part was they spoke at the slowest possible speed, like a tape recording slowed down. It freaked me out, but no matter how hard I tried, I could not block out the voices. It only happened a handful of times and always in the dead of night. It was quite worrying for a while and I had to consider that I might well be going slightly mad.

***

On a rainy January afternoon, in the brand new year of 1982, we got the news. I returned home from school to find my dad packing boxes and my mum crying in the corner. I ran over to console her and received a mouthful of abuse for my sins. 'This is all your fucking fault,' she screamed.

My dad wasn't interested in arguing. He just wanted to pack up and get us away as quickly as possible. We were going into hiding, as planned.

'Where's Wolf?' I asked. My mum cried harder still. I then realised what had happened.

My dad had gotten wind that we'd lost the case and, without even asking, had taken my mum's dog away, likely to the pound. She didn't even get to say goodbye and was therefore very upset. I think she thought we would leave him with a relative, then come and get him later in the year, but now he was gone and my dad refused to tell her where. She made it known to me for many months afterwards that she would've much rather kept the dog and gotten rid of me. 'Why didn't you then?' I often wondered.

We were bundled into my dad's van and driven to our new temporary home, a caravan park near the coast. It may not have been a million miles away, but it was just far enough for the guards to be unsure as to our whereabouts.

My dad planned to tell any visiting guards that my mother had run off to England, taking me with her. They had conspired to write a letter from her to make it all the more convincing. He played the jilted husband well and simply waited for the heat to die down before making his next move. He even carried on going to work as normal.

While we waited, my dad informed us that under no circumstances were we to leave the caravan park. He would swing by with supplies every few days, although only after driving miles out of his way to guarantee he wasn't being followed.

So there I was, seated in a small caravan, with my mother sobbing at the loss of her dog and blaming me for all her woes. It was not an ideal situation and I had no idea how to resolve it.

I had my cassette player with me, so, to change the vibe, I decided to put on some music. I had asked for Pink Floyd's *The Wall* for Christmas, but had instead received a compilation album of cover artists singing various chart hits. I inserted the cassette and a generic version of 'Another Brick in the Wall' began to play. I had rather hoped that the music might lighten the mood, but on hearing the song my mum barked, 'Turn that shit off.' The next few days continued in much the same vein. It was one tense caravan.

My dad started to get rid of all our belongings and even claimed that he had managed to sell the house – and not to one person, but two. He had apparently conned two folk into believing they were buying the same house and he was very pleased with himself. I thought it was a bit short-sighted. Was he planning on never returning to his hometown? Looking back, I'm not quite sure I believe him, as I could have sworn my mum told me that the rent was ten pounds a week when we were living there. And if it was indeed rented, then how could he have sold it? It was all very suspicious.

My mother and I continued to hide out at the campsite for two whole weeks and it was our very own version of hell. I was bored senseless and she was the worst possible company. She missed the dog terribly and cried every night. It was an awful experience and I couldn't wait for it to be over.

On the last day of January we finally left. My dad came and picked us up in the wee hours, allowing us to skip out on part of the bill for the caravan. (If there's a way to not pay, my parents will find it.) We tiptoed over to the van, crept inside and fled under cover of night. The vehicle swung around a few roundabouts on the edge of town before getting onto the main road and picking up speed. The lights of the town began to fade behind us and we were soon surrounded by nothingness.

During the overnight drive my dad told us of his new plan. Once in Dublin we would find a flat and lay low for a couple of months. He mentioned that various relatives had been instructed to tell the guards that my mum had phoned from England. That way they would give up looking for us altogether. My parents would then get jobs and earn enough money to fund our forthcoming trip. It was simple and sounded feasible. It was certainly more feasible – I hoped – than the next sentence that came out of my mum's mouth: 'Oh and by the way, when we get to Kenya, we're leaving you there.'

CHAPTER 23

TROPHIES

So had my parents finally shown their hand? Was the whole premise behind going to Africa to leave me behind? According to my dad, if we ever got to Kenya I was to be left with a suitable family who would raise me as 'a real man'. This was the only sure way to cure me of my spoiled ways, apparently. Once I heard this nonsense, I thought, *Fuck that*, and wondered if it might be better to run away, return to London, go anywhere really; there was no way I was going to be left in bloody Africa. Were they unhinged? But these thoughts soon dissipated.

We arrived in Dublin with a van full of gear and nowhere to go. Initially we went to a B&B and my dad then went off in search of a suitable abode. He'd stuffed his coat pockets with large rolls of cash held together with thick elastic bands, which I assumed were the proceeds from selling the house we didn't own. He arrived back at the B&B that first evening with good news; he had found a place for us to live and had already paid two months' rent upfront. We would be moving in the following morning. It was also apparently within easy walking distance of the city centre.

When I first saw our flat, I asked my dad about the ominous grey building in the distance. 'What's that?' I enquired. 'Oh, that's a prison,' he said.

That's a bit too close for comfort, I thought. *Let's hope none of us ends up in there, eh?*

The ground-floor flat was made up of a large sitting room, a small kitchen and one solitary double bedroom. Before I could ask about my own sleeping quarters, my dad volunteered that I would, in fact, be catching my zs in a separate bedroom upstairs, far away from theirs. *Sweet*, I thought.

While unpacking I began to wonder if I'd be in Dublin long enough to attend school. It was then that my dad entered the room with an answer to that very question.

'You'll be needing a job,' he said loudly, before morphing seamlessly into a cop-show police chief: 'You've got twenty-four hours!' He went on to explain that if I did not find gainful employment the following day, he'd throw me out.

'Hang on, is this another joke?' I wondered.

He reiterated his stance as he descended the stairs: 'Don't bother coming home without one. Jesus.'

This seemed a little preposterous, considering we were in this mess due to their refusal to return me to my grandparents. Why on earth had they gone to so much trouble if they planned to leave me to my own devices in Dublin? As usual, it made absolutely no sense whatsoever.

The next day I arose early and was soon wandering the streets in search of work. My mum and dad were also looking for jobs, so, after a quick breakfast at home, we split up and went our separate ways. Surprisingly, for me, it turned out to be relatively effortless.

I was pounding the pavement near St Stephen's Green when I noticed a job recruitment centre, so in I popped. They asked for my age and I immediately claimed to be sixteen. Although I was only twelve, I looked much older, thanks to a recent growth spurt. I was acutely aware that I would have to be liberal with the truth in order to gain steady employment, as no one was going to hire someone my age. Weirdly, I was never asked for any form of identification; all that was required was the filling in of a few basic forms and I was on their books. Easy. After a brief chat I was told of a possible opportunity close to where I lived. It was then that I attended my very first job interview.

I made my way to a sculptures company and was surprised to see quite how close it was to our flat. It was literally over the road. If I got the job I could simply roll out of bed and into work. It was perfect. The pay was terrible, of course, just twenty pounds per week, even though it was full-time work. I was promptly shown around and luckily nobody questioned my age.

The job on offer was as a *de facto* helper in the workshop, assisting in the making of sports trophies. This particular company utilised Connemara marble and there were huge slabs of the stuff in all directions. My duties would entail cutting said marble, polishing it, then adding felt to the underside using hazardous scalpel blades and poisonous glue. If I wanted, I could also learn how to engrave. I made sure to be courteous throughout and at the end of the interview I was told the job was mine if I fancied it. I took it, jumping at the chance to prove my father wrong, as I knew he didn't believe I could find a job in the space of a day.

I arrived home pretty chuffed with myself. My dad, however, showed no signs of being pleased whatsoever. He was of the opinion that I should have got a job anyway, so what was the big deal? My mum showed zero emotion either, simply enquiring about my wage. I should have lied but decided to tell the truth. 'Twenty pounds,' I volunteered. She immediately told me they would need fifteen pounds from me each week in order to save for Africa; I could keep the remaining five pounds, but that was all. I therefore decided to use that five pounds very wisely.

On Saturday mornings I attended a weekly karate class. I enjoyed learning to defend myself and fantasised that one day I would be able to fend off my dad's violent behaviour with a powerful jab to the throat. I took to it quickly and became rather good, so much so that I was asked if I could perhaps accompany the other kids to a tournament in Scotland. Of course I knew I couldn't go; I was presumed missing and couldn't exactly travel to the UK to compete in a karate bout: that would be ridiculous.

Still, I decided to ask my parents anyway. It was nice to be good at something legal and perhaps there was an outside chance that I could somehow attend. There wasn't. I parted company with karate a short time afterwards, mainly due to an embarrassing fainting fit. When I came around, the instructor asked if I was eating enough, though due to my parents' strict rules on nutrition, I most definitely was not.

The rest of my kept earnings allowed for a much chillier pastime altogether. Shortly after my arrival in Dublin I fell head over heels in love with ice-skating, finding it to be a tremendous escape. I also stumbled upon it quite by accident.

After attempting to stay upright while roller-skating with my parents some weeks earlier, I'd noticed an adjacent ice rink and wondered if it might be more conducive to my needs. At my earliest opportunity I returned in order to find out.

The rink was a long way from home, located in the south of the city. Therefore, I had to use nearly half my money just to get there. Still, it was worth it. I wasn't particularly competent, but it didn't matter. I treasured my time on the ice regardless. The simplicity of skating in circles to whatever music happened to be playing was of enormous appeal. By far my favourite tune to skate to was Kraftwerk's *The Model*; whenever I heard the opening riff to that song I would spring to life and be in my element.

Everyone was a stranger on the ice, giving me an anonymity I found to be of great value. It was easily the most enjoyable part of any given week and I went every Saturday without fail.

My mum had suffered with epilepsy for most of her adult life and, while living in Dublin, she began having severe episodes once again. Often my dad was at work when they struck, but luckily he had given me specific instructions on what to do should the situation arise in his absence. Mostly it consisted of stopping my mother swallowing her own tongue, something that up until that point I didn't even know could happen. It was often pretty difficult to get her to sit still, let alone do anything else. It was not unlike being in the company of a complete drunkard. Her eyes would glaze over and she would disappear for a while, often talking to me as if I were someone else entirely. Mostly her episodes were manageable, but occasionally they could be quite worrying, ending up with her convulsing on a Dublin pavement, for instance. Once the seizure had passed, she would lie down for a few hours, only to emerge looking drowsy and slurring her words. However, by the next day she was usually back to normal.

Regardless of these episodes, my mother somehow managed to secure herself a job in a fancy cake shop. My dad has always denied having a love of cake, but during this period all he did was shovel pastries into what could quite rightly be described as his cake-hole. My mum would bring home a shocking amount of cakes and pastries, and my dad would eat them all with much gusto, his favourite being the rum babas. He ate them daily, yet he didn't seem to gain a pound, mostly due to his obsession with running. Perhaps he ran for the sole purpose of being able to eat baked goods? As I was still considered the fat one, I was generally denied such delicacies, but on occasion my mum's resolve would falter and I would be allowed a custard slice. They were astoundingly rich but oh so very delicious.

Not content with free cakes, my mum engineered a way of making some extra dough on the side. I was subsequently instructed to frequent the cake shop with a five-pound note in hand. The plan was simple. I would enter the shop and wait for my mum to be available; I was to ignore all other servers. I would then order the cheapest thing in the shop and hand over the fiver. My mum would then return from the register with change of a twenty-pound note instead. I was convinced it wouldn't work, as I looked just like my mother. I was sure that her work colleagues would see the resemblance and we'd be rumbled, but somehow they never did. This scam went on for weeks. How she explained the constant missing funds is beyond me. Each time we did this I was walking out with almost as much as my weekly wage. 'Why on earth am I even bothering going to work?' I wondered.

When my mum finally left the job, I was sent to pick up a wristwatch that she'd accidentally left behind. As soon as I entered it was obvious her co-workers recognised me as the customer who always waited for my mum, but surprisingly no one said a word. They just handed me the watch and I left.

The reason my mother had decided to quit her job was due to her and my dad hatching a new plan. A plan to make a lot more money than the odd cake-shop scam could provide. It was time to do things the old-fashioned way.

***

My parents reckoned they could make a lot of cash quickly if they reverted to their old ways: robbing post offices. A soupçon of worry collected on my brow. That was exactly how my dad ended up incarcerated a decade earlier. I had visions of them being arrested and banged up in the prison I'd spotted in the distance. What would happen to me if they were caught? I imagined I would be on my own, homeless in Dublin. That didn't sound too appealing. Before I could think about such things, my dad handed me a pile of prize-draw scratch cards. He had found them in a skip on the way home and had decided to use them as a way of retraining himself. The date of the draw had passed some six months earlier, but as the cards were unscratched, they appeared to be new.

My dad's forgery skills were magnificent. He took each card and changed the date of the draw from October 1981 to October 1982. The numbers were tiny, but once complete, it was impossible to tell that they had been tampered with, even up close. He then revealed his technique.

Firstly he would scrape the original ink from around the date using a razor blade. He would then meticulously imitate the background hue using colouring pencils, before carefully constructing the desired number dot by dot. It was painstaking work and I watched in admiration as he demonstrated a skill I hadn't known he possessed. I was unaware that he could be so patient and gentle; it was a side to my father I had not seen before. Before the week's end, he was teaching me how to do the very same thing and I felt like I was learning from a veritable master.

We were only supposed to be changing the dates on the cards as practice, but before long my dad had a light-bulb moment. He suggested that I go door to door with the freshly forged cards and sell them for fifty pence each; half of face value. I was bound to get some takers. Most people assumed they weren't going to win, so technically no one would ever find out. I thought it was a clever ploy but wasn't sure I possessed quite enough moxie to pull it off. However, I was desperate to impress my father and this was a perfect opportunity to show him what I was made of. I therefore agreed, grabbed a fistful of scratch cards and set off around the back streets of Dublin in search of gullible souls.

My subterfuge began by striking up a little conversation on the door-step before getting down to the nitty-gritty. I then asked almost reluctantly if they perhaps wanted to enter a prize draw, while at the same time assuming they didn't and half walking away. Every person without fail would then usher me back. I was surprised at how easy it was to part people from their hard-earned cash. I sold every single card I took out that night and returned home with my booty, feeling pleased with myself. The draw was actually for a charity, so if there is a hell I undoubtedly have a nice warm room waiting for me down there. I continued to sell as many cards as my dad could forge, making a nice wad of cash towards our trip.

I had obviously impressed my father and I soon graduated to the next level of trustworthiness. He revealed the methods being considered for their up-and-coming attempt to defraud the post office. I therefore gained an intimate knowledge of what it was they were about to do, and wondered what, if any, my part in it would be. Work was rather dull, so I was up for a little excitement.

***

I never told my parents, but I had recently had a bit of a dodgy experience with one of my co-workers. I didn't know him very well, but one afternoon, while I was walking in the centre of Dublin, he approached me in his car. He rolled down his window and asked me if I wanted a lift home as he was going my way. I declined. Firstly I liked walking, and secondly I hardly knew the guy, plus I had seen more than my fair share of adverts in England attesting to the dangers of strangers. Somehow, though, he managed to persuade me, mostly by joking that of course he wasn't going to kidnap me, he was merely offering me a friendly ride home.

I got in and we began chatting. I soon noticed, however, that we were going in a completely different direction and became concerned. He told me not to worry, and said he was simply taking the long way around due to traffic. My suspicions were aroused further when we entered a section of secluded parkland. That was all the proof I needed that something was awry. I demanded that he stop the car and let me out, but he insisted it was simply a shortcut. I was no fool. I had excellent location skills and knew damn well that we were nowhere near my flat. I shouted at him again to stop the car and let me 'the fuck out'.

The vehicle came to a sudden halt. He then turned to me and said rather brazenly, 'I'll let you out, but only if you answer my question.' By this time I was pulling on the handle, expecting the worst. 'Do you want to earn five pounds?' he added in a casual manner.

'What?' I said, perturbed. Upon realising the level of danger I found myself in, I began to scream with increasing volume until he gave in and reluctantly unlocked the door.

As I ran, I heard him shouting about how he knew plenty of young boys who would love to earn five pounds. *What a bloody pervert*, I thought. I felt extremely lucky to have escaped unscathed. I never did see him again, thankfully – though mostly that was because I was subsequently sacked.

I used to mess around quite a lot at work, as did my workmates. They would play pranks by sending me out to pick up various non-existent items such as glass hammers, a ladder for climbing up skirting boards and that old chestnut, 'a long weight'. While trying to get my own back one afternoon, I invariably became unstuck. My spatial awareness failed miserably when, while larking about in the workshop, I accidentally knocked over the biggest tub of glue imaginable, right onto the wooden floor. It went everywhere. Every nook and cranny was full to the brim with rubbery glue. It also stank. I was immediately summoned to the main office and dismissed on the spot. The official reason was my immature behaviour (if only they knew!).

What on earth was I going to tell my parents? They were bound to be furious and a beating was sure to ensue. It was then that I had an idea, a plan that might just save my bacon.

I arrived home in time to hear an inane conversation between my father and the landlord comprising mostly of the words 'Jesus' and 'quare hawk'. As I brushed past, I gave my dad a strong look as if to say, 'I have something I need to tell you.' I had something to tell him all right, and it was either going to result in him considering my idea or me receiving a good hiding for merely suggesting it. I weighed up my options and decided it was a gamble worth taking.

Once my dad came into the flat, I blurted out 'I got fired', my words accompanied by an open-arm animation that suggested 'shit happens'.

'Jesus,' came his reply.

My mum was on her way home, so I knew I didn't have much time. She was sure to shoot me down, but my dad might just go for it, especially considering all the pointers he had given me of late. I explained that there could be an upside to my getting sacked and that he should hear me out. He stared at me, his eyes getting smaller by the millisecond. 'Jesus,' he exclaimed again. From what I could tell, he didn't seem angry at all, so, while I had him to myself, I spat out my idea.

'What if I help you and mum rob post offices?'

'Jesus,' he repeated, while looking for something to hold onto. 'Your mother will have none of that,' he replied.

I told him I was serious and that, with his help, I could convince her. I was good at scamming and stealing, and I knew exactly how to distract people at the right moment. Thanks to him I even knew how to forge a little and could perhaps help in that department. He thought for a moment, rubbing his chin and pulling at his beard, deep in thought. Another 'Jesus' and we were there. 'Fine, I'll talk to your mother.' He was sure that my mum would be against my involvement but agreed in principle that it was an interesting idea, though essentially a bad one.

I was excited at the prospect of helping them. I wanted my parents to see that I wasn't just some little kid. I had my own skills, some of which they knew nothing about.

Once my mum got home she could sense something was afoot and immediately asked what was going on. I told her I got fired. 'For fuck sake, go to your room,' she barked. I tried to explain that it was a blessing in disguise, but she was too irritated to listen.

As I left I could hear my dad fighting my corner for once. I eavesdropped on their conversation and heard my dad suggest that maybe all three of us could 'do the business'.

My mum said, 'No fucking way, have you gone nuts? He's twelve!'

Over the coming days there was much discussion to be had, eventually resulting in my being seated in the living room awaiting some sort of announcement. A decision had been made. One that I was convinced included a decreed punishment for getting sacked.

Suddenly my mum let loose a grin. 'Okay, you can do it,' she said.

I could not believe what I was hearing; I never thought she'd actually go for it.

'Really?' I stuttered.

They explained that I would have to adhere to everything they taught me, to the letter, or I was out. I hastily agreed, before bounding upstairs to my room. I was so excited for what was to come that I could barely sleep that night. I felt as if I were part of the Bonnie and Clyde gang. It never once occurred to me that we might actually get caught. I also felt no signs of guilt whatsoever for what we were about to do. It was only money, right? Obviously it was absurd to be looking up to criminals, but despite everything they had put me through, from my perspective my parents were rock stars.

CHAPTER 24

LIKE IN FILMS

I began my training in earnest, eager to learn exactly how we would be removing funds from the Irish postal system. My dad mentioned that, with the right focus and dedication to detail, we could easily make around 3,000 pounds in a single month; that was all we would need, apparently. Four weeks and we'd be done. We already had a chunk of money saved from our jobs, so it appeared relatively realistic.

The plan was simple. We would spend a week or more casing many of Dublin's post offices to see which ones were more and less secure. We would ideally select branches with weaker employees who were unlikely to give chase, old ladies and so forth. Once we had chosen our favourite locations, we would monitor staff movements in order to learn who took lunch when, keeping an eye out for any suspicious activity. In addition to these stakeouts, we were also on the lookout for the best place in town to acquire the rubber stamp. It was the one essential element, containing the official franking seal. Without it we would have nothing.

Unbeknownst to me, it was decided that it would be my job to obtain this particular item. According to my parents, a child would arouse less suspicion and would therefore be more likely to get away with such an audacious move.

Still, at this early stage I remained somewhat confused as to how we planned to make our money. So, after checking out what seemed like every post office in Dublin, I asked my dad to explain exactly how we were going to enact our plan. It turned out that the method they had settled upon was quite straightforward.

My mother and I would open post office accounts all over the city using fake identification that my dad would have forged earlier at home. The names would be unisex, monikers like Leslie, Leigh or Ashley. At the time of opening each account we would deposit just five pounds and be on our merry way. Each time a new account was created the teller would give us a brand new post office book containing the deposit, all stamped and signed for. For the first couple of weeks this was all we would be doing, opening accounts and sitting back.

Once we'd acquired the much-needed rubber stamp from the chosen post office, my dad would be able to 'deposit' extra funds into each account with ease. This was achieved in the very simplest of ways. He would first add an amount, say fifty pounds, into the deposit column. Next he would stamp it with the official seal and sign it with a banker's squiggle. That was it.

He would have to change the date on the stamp daily using tiny rubber inserts, which was a bit fiddly, but as soon as the ink hit the paper, all that was needed was a fake signature to make it seem like the monies had been collected by an official teller. It was genius. We would therefore be withdrawing money that was never deposited in the first place.

My dad of course had to do this many times, forging a vast number of signatures in the process. Sometimes we would just make them up, but in order to be convincing, we had to use lots of different handwriting styles, so both my mum and I helped him with his task. I enjoyed coming up with different variations of handwriting. We would use different-coloured pens, different widths of nib, lean one way or another. I also learned the differences between spiky male handwriting and the loopier female script. It was thoroughly interesting.

Once we had 3,000 pounds 'deposited' into our dodgy accounts, it would be time to start the withdrawal process. We were to take out just thirty pounds at a time, which meant we had to attempt 100 withdrawals.

Between my mother and I that would be fifty withdrawals each. My dad did not seem overly concerned about this and reckoned we could complete the task in just under two weeks. Such small amounts rarely raised an eyebrow and did not require identification; all that was required was the account book and a smile. I felt like this was exactly the kind of thing I could do and was eager to get started. But first we needed that pesky stamp.

***

My dad had selected the perfect location for my caper, a small sub-post office in the northern outskirts of Dublin. I was told that the much-needed stamp lay just behind a security window. All I had to do was reach my small hand up and under the glass and I would be able to grab it with ease.

This particular branch kept much of their stock along the back wall, including airmail stickers. Therefore, the plan was for me to buy letter stamps for England, then, at the last minute, ask for a couple of airmail stickers. The teller was bound to head to the back wall, giving me ample time to grab the stamp and get out before anyone was any the wiser. This was the plan and it seemed relatively simple. I was convinced I could do it.

My parents reiterated the serious nature of what we were about to do and began drumming our back-up plan into my subconscious. If anything was to go wrong during our escapades, I was to run, but under no circumstances was I to return to the flat. Even if I saw them in the street afterwards, I was to keep my distance; they would find a way to contact me when the coast was clear. All I had to do was wait for them at our secret meeting place: Bewley's Tea House.

'Got it,' I said, and off we trotted.

I was very nervous as we drove north and noticed that my hands had become clammy. I tried to remain focused as we approached the area in which I was to do the dirty deed. My dad went over the plan again and again. All I had to do was swipe the stamp, run the length of the back alley and jump into 'The Blue Avenger' – our newly acquired getaway car. My dad would be waiting with the engine running. He told me not to worry and reassured me that this would be the scariest part of the entire process. After this, all I would have to do was a bit of acting while withdrawing money. He asked one last time if I was sure I wanted to do it. I swallowed hard and said yes, while trying to convey an air of calm that I did not possess.

A few minutes later, we were there. The post office was tiny, one of only four buildings in a small parade of shops built onto the side of an ugly concrete block. My dad pulled up nearby and ushered me out, wishing me luck as he hit the gas, vanishing into the misty distance.

I was on my own and it was time.

I walked into the post office and a small bell rung above my head. A woman in her fifties smiled in my direction and asked what she could do for me. I immediately eyeballed the stamp on the counter. It looked ever so slightly out of reach. She was beaming at me, so I knew the moment had come to give it a try.

'Hello there, two first-class stamps please,' I said in my best Irish accent, 'for letters to England,' I added, nearly forgetting.

She had begun to tear the stamps out of a large book on the counter when I pulled out my distraction, 'Do you have any airmail stickers to go with those?'

She nodded, got up and walked towards the back wall where they were stacked. I immediately shoved my arm beneath the window, through the tiny metal tray and behind the glass, grabbing the stamp with force. To my amazement it was in my hand. The very thing we needed right there in my sweaty little palm.

It was then that time started to slow right down. I turned on my heels and headed towards the door in a cumbersome sort of canter, not running, but not walking either. Right then I heard a second ring of the doorbell. And who should walk in? Only a real, life-size, 3D guard! I nearly shat myself on the spot. What were the chances? Luckily I was on autopilot and kept walking towards the door. The fear I felt in that moment consumed my very being. It was a similar feeling, I imagined, to being in a car shortly before it crashes, that moment when you brace yourself for impact.

As the guard entered, we sort of circled each other in a 'Shall we dance' fashion, all the time with the stamp hidden in my palm. I apologised to him in a bad accent and exited the post office as fast as I could without being obvious. He was calm and didn't seem suspicious of me at all; in fact he even held the door open, which was helpful.

As soon as I felt fresh air, I heard the lady say something to him. Whether he chased me or not I will never know. Something clicked within which allowed me to run extra fast. I doubt anyone could have caught me that day.

As I ran, the lane behind the post office seemed to become longer the more ground I covered. I turned left halfway down and saw the wheels of my dad's car burning rubber on the asphalt. He had spotted me and the engine was revving in anticipation. I ran towards that car with all my might. Getting caught was not an option.

As I got closer, the back door of the car swung open, but I could tell that my dad was already pulling away. I dived into the already moving vehicle. The tyres were screeching as we hit the road at a speed not dissimilar to a rocket launch. I was pinned to the back seat without the need of a seat belt and could barely lean forward.

With one hand on the wheel my dad turned to me, grinning. 'Did you get it?' he asked.

It was then that I produced the stamp, holding it high. I watched as my dad's face filled with pride. I had never seen him look at me that way before. He said something along the lines of 'That's my boy' and I felt a twinge in my gut.

As we fled the scene in that getaway car, I felt as if I were on television. It was, in that moment, I thought, just like in films.

CHAPTER 25

THE GPO

I'm now going to tell you the story of how I technically robbed the renowned General Post Office in the centre of Dublin. Whenever I return to the fair city I always think back to that event. Rightly or wrongly, I am still proud of my twelve-year-old self for having the balls to rob such a prestigious money house. In some ways I was fearless as a kid. Of course it was foolhardy and dangerous too, but to know that you have fraudulently removed cash from the biggest post office in Ireland before you were a teenager is something that makes a smile form on your face, whether you want it to or not.

I was getting on better with my parents than ever before. The criminal element to our relationship had formed a temporary bond between us. I did not receive a single slap or beating throughout our Dublin exploits; I was simply one of the gang. At the time I had no interest in contemplating the ethics of what we were doing, I just wanted to have some much-needed fun with my parents.

The withdrawal process was in full swing when it was decided that we would return to a number of branches we had previously visited to take out further funds. This made me nervous. I disliked visiting the same place twice; to me it was a definite no-no. To make us feel better, my dad promised he would be standing by with his foot on the gas just in case. It was reassuring to know we had our very own getaway driver waiting in the wings, but I was still apprehensive.

I soon realised while working with my mum that often the tellers would figure out that we were related. Our facial features were just too similar. In those instances the person who was yet to make a withdrawal would stand down and go over to the other to make conversation, just in case it looked like we were avoiding each other. After a while it became obvious that we could only comfortably do two separate withdrawals at bigger branches with more than one counter. Even then it was preferable that we were far apart.

With that in mind my dad suggested that we take on the biggest post office of them all: the GPO in O'Connell Street. It was, and still is, a vast building with many tellers and is always extremely busy. We would also up the stakes by taking out more than usual. My dad would forge the required paperwork for the larger withdrawal overnight, so we could be ready to hit the GPO the next morning. To say I was hesitant would be an understatement.

***

'Hello,' I said with a huge smile across my face. I was standing before a rather stout lady, who seemed, at first, to not engage with me at all; in fact, she barely looked up. I almost always went up to female tellers. They were more likely to make conversation, which in turn made it easier to distract them. The men were usually more robotic and less likely to ask questions; this made transactions all the more awkward. When being served by men I had the constant feeling that I was about to be collared at the door. With women I rarely felt this way. It was just a more relaxing way to commit fraud.

I was taking out 100 pounds that weren't actually there, a huge amount at the time. As this was a withdrawal that could easily raise red flags, I began chatting to the teller, hopeful that she would engage in conversation. At the exact moment she began to process my transaction, I told her it was my birthday. She did not respond. I then told her that I was thirteen. I was not. Still nothing. Why wasn't this woman speaking to me? How was I going to work my magic if she didn't …

'There you go,' she said, handing me the most money I had ever handled.

For some reason, instead of making my escape I continued the conversation, even though I was the only one talking. I figured if I didn't skedaddle immediately I would appear more legit; I mean, who in their right mind would hang around after having committed such an act?

She finally warmed to me and asked what I was intending to do with the money. I told her I was buying a bicycle. She then asked if I lived in Dublin and I told her that I did. It was then that I started to wonder if maybe she was the one playing me. Perhaps she was trying to keep me there? I decided to make haste. As I said my goodbyes, she called after me, warning me to ride safely. Holy shit, this was it, the moment where I got caught and sent to juvenile detention. I could see my mum out of the corner of my eye, but I didn't dare look at her. She had waited until I was finished before approaching her own counter and was mid withdrawal. I tried not to panic, or at least to not let it show. I was painfully aware that I could be pulled to one side at any given moment, sending my young life hurtling towards a very dark tangent.

I was scared but kept on walking regardless. Then, just before the door, I stopped, again to show that I wasn't in a hurry. I thought it was a great little move, my move. I checked my pockets, counted my money and only then did I leave. Once the sun hit my face, I knew I had gotten away with it. I walked tall and even tipped my invisible hat to the security guard as he passed me.

I continued to withdraw monies all over Dublin over that fortnight, but nothing matched the excitement of robbing the GPO.

CHAPTER 26

THE PURSE CRASH

Please forgive my direct authorial interjection at this point, but I shall be brief. As you can no doubt tell we are all caught up. But as we approach the third act I want to clear up any confusion regarding the timeline. The following chapter occurs directly after the prologue.

Time had run out. Almost being caught left us feeling flustered, and it was paramount that we leave Dublin immediately. Hence, on one crisp April morn we found ourselves carefully manoeuvring our heavily laden bicycles along the hallway. We were trying our best to be quiet, under strict orders from my dad, who was desperate to avoid the landlord, after hearing his voice just moments earlier as he left via the front door. Our trepidation was born from the fact that we were skipping out on the rent.

My dad was the first to enter daylight, breaking into a sort of semi-jog with his bike until he reached the end of our street. I watched as he peered around the crumbling brickwork, spying on the bus stop opposite to make sure the landlord boarded his regular bus into the city.

We soon received our signal. The coast was clear. My dad mounted his bike and my mum signalled for me to do the same. I found it a tad cumbersome, at first, and a real task to stay upright. This was mainly due to the ridiculous amount of gear we were carrying.

As I glanced back at the flat, it struck me that I was a very different boy to the one who'd arrived here some months earlier; I was wiser and more street-smart. A veil had lifted while living in Dublin and certain knowledge had been imparted to me. I was one of the gang and it felt good.

We were off.

We had three bicycles, all of them stolen. My parents, of course, had already equipped themselves for a trip without me, so I was the only one who still needed kitting out. Prior to our leaving, we'd returned to the very same rental shop they had frequented just days earlier, so we could 'rent' a third bicycle. I was surprised that the guy who ran the place wasn't suspicious. Surely it was odd that they would need another bike at such short notice. It must have appeared as if they had somehow forgotten they had a son in the first place. Regardless, I was soon set up with a children's model that bore a striking resemblance to my dad's bike, only smaller. The words 'Le Jeune' were emblazoned along the crossbar, giving the bike a continental feel.

Europe was getting ever closer and I could barely contain myself. I did, however, have to wonder why we couldn't simply buy some bicycles like regular people; after all we had the money. My parents, it seemed, were always scamming in some form or another, even when they didn't have to.

Once in France, the plan was to cycle through the entirety of Western Europe, arriving in North Africa by summer's end. And the first stop on this epic journey was to be Paris. My parents had visited the city of romance a decade earlier and were showing signs of nostalgia at the prospect of returning. They clearly shared fond memories and those recollections were bringing out a softer side that I hadn't previously witnessed. They were acting as if they were any other young couple in love; it was odd.

**

As our trip drew closer, my excitement grew. I had yet to visit Europe and was keen to explore this uncharted continent. However, I was once again getting the distinct impression that my parents would rather do this trip without me. My mum was being particularly vocal, dropping less-than-subtle hints. She kept mentioning how she regretted coming back to check on my whereabouts that fateful night. That it had been such an easy decision for her to leave me alone in Dublin still troubled me greatly.

During those final days they began to treat me differently. Without warning, we had somehow gone back to square one. I wasn't getting hit, but they began talking to me as if I was a piece of shit on their shoe and I did not appreciate it one iota. After all, had I not recently helped them amass 3,000 stolen pounds? That fact now seemed to be conveniently forgotten. To them it was as if I were now an anomaly that didn't quite fit in with their plans.

On the day of our departure, as we cycled towards Connolly train station, both my rucksack and saddlebags were heaving, making my bike extremely difficult to control. I was not used to such a heavy load and struggled to keep my balance as I rode along the bumpy Dublin streets. My dad was way out in front, my mum second, and trailing behind was little old me.

Although the ride was a bit tricky, everything else appeared to be going swimmingly. I was excited. The adventure was finally beginning and I felt like a mini explorer. I became so lost in thought that I didn't see what came next. There was an almighty thud and when I next looked ahead of me my mum and dad were in the middle of the road atop a pile of bicycles, rucksacks and saddlebags.

It transpired that my dad had hit his brakes rather suddenly, causing my mum to plough straight into him at speed, landing on top of him and badly buckling her front wheel in the process. Once they had brushed themselves down, it was blame time and my dad insisted the fault lay squarely with my mother; she had failed to brake adequately. He was an innocent man, even though he'd stopped suddenly in front of her without warning. I have no doubt this deflection was born out of the embarrassing situation he found himself in. Unfortunately, as he dragged their bikes and bags out of the busy road, the anger kicked in. He soon began hurling obscenities towards my mother, most of them beginning with C.

Once their belongings were safely on the pavement, he briefly stepped back out into the road, this time reaching down towards the gutter to pick up a small black item, which he subsequently popped into his jeans pocket, hoping neither of us would spot his sleight of hand.

'What was that?' my mum asked.

'Nothing. Jesus,' he said as he attempted to shove whatever it was even deeper into his back pocket.

'Show me,' she demanded. The little boy inside my dad begrudgingly reached back into his pocket and pulled out the suspicious item. 'A purse! Are you fucking kidding me?' she snapped. My dad became further embarrassed. My mum was laughing, and it was most definitely 'at' him, which was never a good thing.

They pushed their mangled bicycles towards the train station, chaperoned by a wall of bickering. My mum was convinced that my dad had seen the purse and applied his brakes in response, which in turn had caused her to crash into him. He, on the other hand, still blamed her for not responding to his actions in time. It was all quite ridiculous and I tried to stay on the outskirts of the conversation so as to not get drawn into their argument.

We clambered up several flights of stairs with our bikes and bags until we reached the correct platform. It was all so awkward, and we hadn't even left Dublin yet. My dad was convinced that he could repair my mum's bike before our train departed and set about removing her front wheel. In an attempt to straighten out the buckle, he found a suitable bench and shoved the wheel between the slats until it was wedged tight. He then applied pressure in the opposite direction, hoping to resolve the damage. Of course, it did not work; if anything, it made things worse. This didn't stop my mum and the commuters on the opposite platform from enjoying the show, much to my dad's annoyance.

Soon we were on-board the train, heading south, our bikes set aside for the time being. Though my parents' argument was still in full flow, of course. As the carriages shunted their way through the suburbs of Dublin, I was spared my parents' unpleasantries thanks to a recent purchase by my father. He had acquired a new invention from Japan for our trip and it was called a Sony Walkman. He'd purchased the best one available and it sounded fantastic. At first I couldn't understand why he was so excited about buying a small cassette deck with orange headphones, but the moment I got to plonk those tiny foam bad boys onto my earlobes, my life changed forever. Music became my escape. I no longer had to focus on the nonsense going on around me. Although I didn't always have access to my dad's new toy, I savoured the moments when I did, disappearing into a world where my own thoughts were king. Life now came with a soundtrack.

***

Shortly after lunchtime, the train creaked into the port of Rosslare, where I immediately spotted a number of large foreign ships. I was in awe. I couldn't quite believe that I was going to board a ferry to France that very evening. I would soon see Europe with my own eyes. This excitement was dulled ever so slightly by my dad's next great idea.

We had a few hours to kill before boarding the boat, so he suggested that we ride into the nearby town of Wexford and get my mum's wheel fixed before we left. The town was relatively big and was sure to have a bike shop, and as it was only ten miles away we'd be back in no time. *Ten miles!* I thought. *What the hell?* Then of course it dawned on me that it would actually be twenty miles, there and back, and my heart dropped even more.

An hour of pedalling later and Wexford was still nowhere in sight. My mum's warped bicycle was definitely slowing us down, but she didn't seem too bothered by it. That was because I was the one riding the fucking thing.

Although I was the only person not to crash their bike that day, I was given the task of cycling my mother's distorted clown bike across the brutal Irish landscape. Apparently it was causing too much resistance for my poor mum to handle, so she enjoyed a nice smooth ride on my bike while I struggled with hers. At one juncture she even had the audacity to demand that I keep up with her, to which I responded in my head, 'Die bitch!'

We cycled for so long that it gave me plenty of time to ponder. If this was what Europe was going to be like, then I wasn't so sure it was my cup of tea after all. I had always enjoyed cycling and therefore assumed this trip would be right up my alley, but perhaps I had been mistaken.

We finally rolled into Wexford late that afternoon and found a bike shop without much effort. The bike mechanic in residence took one look at the twisted rim and shook his head in bewilderment. He wasn't convinced it was worth fixing such a contorted mess, and suggested that we simply buy a new wheel instead. My dad informed him that the bike was a rental and that we had no choice but to fix the original wheel or we'd be liable for a huge fine upon its return (as if that was ever going to happen). After some debate he agreed to give it a go, asking us to come back in an hour or so.

While awaiting the repair, we went in search of nutrition. The food on the boat did not come with the greatest of reputations; therefore a hearty meal in town was sought out. I cannot recall what we ate, but I am 100 per cent certain that it contained potatoes.

We returned to the bike shop to find the wheel ready and waiting. The man had done an excellent job: the only marks that remained were the ones that had been inflicted by my father on the railway bench that morning. He'd reattached the wheel, and even checked the front brakes.

We were good to go. I was so relieved that he managed to fix that stupid wheel. I would now get my own bike back, which made for a much easier ride back to Rosslare.

'Five pounds, please,' said the man.

'Jesus,' came my dad's near automatic response. He was just about to unzip his money belt when he remembered the item that had caused this entire episode in the first place. He reached into his back pocket and pulled out the dirty street purse. His fingers delved into its slimy gutter folds in hope of gold. I watched with bated breath as his fingers grasped one solitary note. Would it be a twenty, a fifty perhaps?

The loudest of guffaws from my mother pierced the silence, ending the suspense. She had spotted the reveal before any of us. The five-pound note dangling from my dad's fingers made her laugh so hard that she had to leave the shop. The fact that the cause of this whole debacle contained the exact cost of the repair was just too much.

The sun was setting behind the cliff top at Rosslare by the time we were pushing our bikes up the stony slipway onto the ferry. We'd just made it back in time. Before stepping onto the ramp I bent down and picked up a solitary pebble, placing it in my jeans pocket. I wanted a little bit of Ireland to take with me; it would be a constant reminder of the adventures I'd had in the old country, especially as I now felt more connected to my Irish roots. Up until this point I had always considered myself completely English, but now I wasn't so sure. I stood for a brief second, drinking in the moment. I made a vow to return, only the next time I set foot upon these shores I would no longer be a boy, I would return a man.

EUROPE

SUMMER 1982

CHAPTER 27

GOING SOUTH

The combined weight of my rucksack and two overfilled saddlebags glued my bicycle to the road, but I didn't care. I was in France. Proper Europe. It was a moment I had contemplated for some time, and now that I was finally here, breathing in French air, it was marvellous. We had escaped our transgressions in Dublin and were free, about to start yet another adventure. In a few days we would be in Paris, a place I had only seen on television. I was so excited. I mounted my bicycle and pushed off, following my parents. 'Hang on. Why are we on the wrong side of the road?' I pondered.

The first day was slow going; we barely managed twenty-five miles, a lot less than expected. After a lunch of baguette and Laughing Cow cheese, we pushed on into the hills of northern France. The incline came as a terrible shock to my young legs and I became convinced that my bones were about to exit via my kneecaps at any given moment. It was made all the harder by the stupid amount of gear we were carrying. I also had my suspicions that my bicycle might well be the heaviest, given that my parents seemed to be having an easier time of it.

As if it wasn't an already difficult ordeal, it then began to rain – a lot. This put my dad in a dreadful mood, so, to appease him, it was decided that we would stop earlier than planned. We called it a day at a clearing just outside the tiny hamlet of Lillebonne. The fields were drenched from the storm, making it difficult to find a suitable spot to set up camp.

My parents were squabbling about the best way to erect their quarters. I had removed my tent from its bag and was staring at the contents blankly.

I didn't recognise a single object. I had never slept in a tent before, much less put one together. It was an alien concept. I concluded that the best way forward was to copy my parents. They appeared to be banging tent pegs into the ground with a discarded brick, so I began to do the same. Unfortunately my tent was nothing like theirs. My dad, spotting this schoolboy error, came over to help, or so I thought. He pulled one of my poles from the ground and began hitting me with it.

Holy shit, I thought, *he's back!*

I recognised the look in his eye and knew I was in for a very bad time. He continued to beat me, calling me a 'stupid little cunt' in between thwacks. The pole was made of a heavier metal than the types used today, so it felt like I was being hit with a piece of thin scaffolding. My mum eventually intervened, telling him to 'calm the fuck down', but as they were already in the midst of a bickering match, he simply turned his anger towards her instead.

Once the drama was over, my dad explained my mistake. I was informed that my tent poles had thinner poles contained within, which had to be pulled out and locked into position. It was on these thinner internal poles that my tent was supposed to be secured in order to keep its shape. However, because I had banged my poles into the ground with a rock, these thinner extensions were now firmly wedged deep inside the now-bent main rods, so my tent would sag in the middle and be about half its original height.

My mum added that because I had, in effect, 'broken' my tent, I would be going to bed without dinner as further punishment. *Really?* I thought. *The beating wasn't enough?*

I was at a loss. She blamed me for upsetting my dad and felt that I should be punished for it. I was about to remind her that they were squabbling long before Lillebonne but thought better of it. Instead I crawled into my body bag of a tent and got settled in for the night.

The ground was incredibly uneven and I could feel many stones assaulting my fragile spine. The tent was cold and I struggled to keep warm in my moist sleeping bag. Outside, I could hear the clanging of metal and assumed my parents were cooking dinner. I was hungry from our ride but dared not ask them to reconsider; instead I forced myself to go to sleep regardless of my gurgling belly.

As I drifted off I thought about what had happened. I could not believe my dad had hit me like that again. I had assumed the age of beatings was over, replaced by an era of respect gained in Dublin. Clearly I had been mistaken. Now, instead of pride, my dad seemed to feel only irritation when in my presence. My last thoughts that night were along the lines of: *What a pair of ungrateful bastards.*

***

I awoke the next morning to a face full of stalactites, pointing down at me from inside my frozen wigwam. The night had been extremely uncomfortable and I'd barely slept. The ground felt even rougher during the night; add to that plummeting temperatures and a thin sleeping bag that didn't quite cut it, and you had the perfect ingredients for misery.

As I unzipped my sagging canvas, I wondered what kind of mood my parents would be in. Luckily they seemed jollier than usual. My dad was busy packing up our belongings while my mum made warm drinks on the tiny gas stove. The field was crisp and cold, the morning dew already frozen. My mum asked how I'd slept and I told her. 'Terrible,' I said. She told me I would get used to it, though I wasn't so sure.

We didn't have any food, so breakfast was a croissant en route. The roads were very slippery that morning, especially on the hills. The second day's objective was to get to the city of Rouen, thirty-five miles south. It was pretty hard work, but after a lunch of bread and cheese, already a staple, we were well on our way. The last few miles were a joy due to a long, steep hill that took us all the way into the city. We flew down that thing at a dangerously high speed. It was scary but in a good way – thrilling. I should probably point out that we were not wearing helmets; they were not yet the norm and usually only reserved for Tour de France riders and the like, which we most definitely were not.

The only part of Rouen I saw was the campsite. We arrived under cover of night and left before breakfast the following day. My mum was keen to push on to Paris. She had worked out a schedule and it was imperative we keep to it. I couldn't understand why we were in such a rush.

The third day was tough going and my legs were starting to seize up. I was not used to this level of cycling and, come to think of it, neither were they. My dad was a keen runner and relatively fit; my mum, however, did not partake in any exercise and had only recently given up smoking, so she must also have been finding it a struggle. I began to doubt that the three of us could realistically pedal all the way to Africa.

***

We arrived in Paris two days later. My dad was now fuelled solely by cake, his nose for locating *patisseries* along the way refined to the point whereby he would stop and consume multiple pastries without breathing. As we entered Paris, his oversized nose was on the lookout for more French Fancies and before long we were by the roadside refuelling my father.

I knew we were in central Paris when the road beneath me changed radically. Without warning I was cycling on cobblestones, which made my bike rattle violently. It was hard to stay vertical with the weight I was pushing through those old Parisian streets. My mum had hinted that because we were staying a few days, it might be a good idea to decant our rucksacks and lose some of the stuff we didn't need. *Praise be!* I thought.

As we cycled further into the city I became enthralled by the architec- ture. I had never seen such beauty. Once I finally uncoupled myself from my Le Jeune, I was thrilled in the knowledge that I would not be living in that saddle for a while. My arse needed a well-earned break.

My time out of the saddle proved to be short-lived, however. We remained in Paris for just a couple of nights; due to a constant rainy spell my parents were keen to push on towards Marseilles. It was nearly 500 miles to the south coast and, in my opinion, the trip was turning into a bit of a nightmare. My luck was in, however, as my parents were no longer keen on cycling that far either. My mum suggested we take the train to Marseilles instead and continue by bicycle from there. It was cheating a little, but we would still be doing plenty of pedalling down south, plus the weather would be far more conducive to our bike-based antics.

It took some arm-twisting, but I managed to secure one full day of sightseeing for myself before we left for Marseilles. I was taken on a speedy tour of all the major sights: Place de la Concorde, the Louvre, L'Arc de Triomphe and, of course, the Eiffel Tower. My parents seemed thoroughly bored throughout and by the time we got to the world's most famous edifice they'd had enough. I was keen to ascend the nineteenth-century structure and begged my mum until she gave in. I was told to be quick and to not go all the way to the top. My parents wanted to get back to the campsite so they could pack for the train. I had forty-five minutes tops. I agreed to their terms and scurried off, beaming as I went. I climbed into the elevator and waved to my nonchalant folks below, who were planning to wait for me at the base.

As it climbed the leg, the elevator sort of leaned forward, which caught me by surprise. I had yet to be at such an angle and I got quite the view. Considering I'd arrived at the first level pretty fast, I decided to follow some of the other tourists into the adjoining elevator up to the second level, which turned out to be very cramped and nothing like the first. It seemed to creep slowly upwards at about one mile an hour while swinging from side to side, which I did not enjoy. Eventually it arrived at the second level and I stepped out to a tremendous view of Paris. I had never been up so high or seen a panorama like it. I was aware that I couldn't stay long, but I tried to enjoy the short time I had nonetheless. I knew I couldn't go up any further as I'd get into trouble; therefore, after just a few minutes, I decided to head back down.

I turned the corner and saw the mother of all queues. I immediately knew this was going to cause me grief. By the time I squeezed myself into the lift I had used up most of my allotted time. I was wishing for it to go faster, but it was travelling at a snail's pace. I was sure my parents would now be furious. Once I disembarked at the first level there was yet another long queue for the final elevator. I gave in to the fact that I was going to be late; there was nothing I could do about it. When I eventually boarded the elevator, instead of thinking about the amazing experience I'd just had, all I could think about was the awful predicament I now found myself in.

As soon as I stepped onto the tarmac I could see my dad hiding in the bushes. *That's odd*, I thought. My mum then appeared alongside and dragged me off towards him while hitting me around the head. She asked me why I had taken so long. They were convinced I had disobeyed them and gone to the very top. I told her I really hadn't, but she wouldn't believe me. 'You were up there for an hour and a half!' she screamed.

I couldn't quite believe her. 'Was I really gone that long?'

My dad grabbed my arm with a policeman's grip and marched me off towards the back of one of the famous tower's legs. He then threw me down into some nearby shrubbery and made me wait. Once he was sure nobody was watching, he bent down and began serving me a series of fist punches while telling me that I deserved it with each blow. I buckled over, putting my hands up for mercy. Instead of showing leniency, he inflicted further jabs. I could see that he was smiling as he walked away. I found that particularly repugnant.

The next day I was aboard the fastest train in the world: the TGV.

From my seat the French countryside was merely a series of coloured lines moving at ridiculous speed. The TGV was incredibly fast and until that point I had no idea that trains could travel at such velocity without flying off the rails, something I then began to concern myself with. We were heading to Lyon, where we had to change trains in order to get to Marseilles. My parents were being particularly nasty that day. As well as a few smacks around the head, I was the butt of some nasty jibes and it was starting to piss me right off. So much so, that when we changed trains I went and sat in a different carriage altogether. *Fuck them,* I thought.

CHAPTER 28

PARDON COMPLET

Once we arrived in Marseilles I was informed that we would once again be pushing on. Of course we were! We would have just one full day in the city before heading off on our bikes towards Cannes. We would see Marseilles on the way back, before heading to Spain. For now, it was merely a stopover.

Due to the fact that my relationship with my parents was deteriorating rapidly, the following day was to set a precedent. They clearly wanted to be alone and so, to engineer this, my dad began offering advice. 'Jesus, I don't know why any young fella would want to spend the whole day with his parents. He should be off on his own,' he stated rather transparently. My mother was in firm agreement, suggesting that I spend less time hanging around them for the rest of our travels.

Fine by me, I thought; it wasn't as if I was enjoying their company either. I'd just assumed that most twelve-year-olds didn't stray too far from their parents while travelling around continental Europe.

The following morning I mounted my bicycle without a word and rode out of the campsite, spending the entire day alone. At first it was out of spite, but after a while I understood the value of being on my own, and in the coming weeks this would become the norm.

Marseilles was a tricky city to navigate and I got turned around a couple of times while trying to find the centre. Finally I came across a large shopping area and spotted an intriguing-looking mall. I parked my bike, locked it as per my dad's instructions, and went inside in search of amusement. There were more shops in one place than I had ever seen.

The first establishment I passed was a stationery store, which is always a dangerous place for me. There on the shelf was one of the nicest journals I had ever laid eyes on. I wanted it. No, needed it. However, I didn't have enough money, so I decided instead to try to steal it. Clearly I was not nearly as street-smart as I thought I was. This was not some tiny Irish town without cameras, this was a bustling French shopping mall equipped with modern security systems. If I'd had the funds I would have happily bought it, but I was only ever given a few francs at a time, so instead I picked it up, perused it thoroughly, then began my little ruse.

The storefront was made of glass, through which I began motioning to a fictitious person outside, who in my mind was my mother. I held up the journal as if to show it to her while mouthing a few random words, all the time getting closer to the exit. I reckoned if I kept on walking nobody would stop me and, even if they did, they would think it was an innocent mistake; after all I was only trying to show it to my mother to get her approval. The fact that there was nobody there didn't really concern me, I believed in the lie. Why I thought this would work is anyone's guess – it was a pretty stupid plan.

As soon as I took my first step outside I began to levitate. My feet left the ground like those of a fraudulent American magician and I began to float backwards into the store. My own act must have lacked conviction because I now found myself being escorted 'backstage' by two burly store detectives. They were shouting at me aggressively in French and I, of course, had no idea what they were saying, which was a scary situation in itself. They dragged me along a corridor to a bleak-looking office and sat me down forcefully. One guy perched next to me while the other leaned on an overflowing desk in front of me. They were both smoking.

It was a comically stereotypical interrogation. The room was dim and windowless, the only light source being a single desk lamp and the sliver of daylight that managed to fight its way through the false ceiling. It was kind of funny, but this was no time for humour. I was in deep shit once again and I knew it.

The only way out of this predicament that I could fathom was to stick to my guns and try to lie my way out. If I could convince them I was innocent then maybe they would let me go; otherwise it was bye-bye Birdie. If I brought the police back to the campsite my dad would kill me, I was certain of that. I guess I could always tell them I was a missing child, in the hope that they'd send me back to England. But I was getting ahead of myself. It hadn't come to that quite yet; I still had a chance. I therefore decided to stick to my story, knowing that any CCTV footage was bound to back me up. The camera doesn't lie, regardless of whether I do.

I had a theory when it came to security cameras. I figured as long as everything looked above board once the footage was played back, all would be well. I never acted suspiciously or did anything to bring added attention to myself – being a kid on his own in a shop brought enough attention as it was. If I did get up to no good, I always did it in a way that looked legit on camera. I had quick hands and if, for instance, I was changing a price tag to a more affordable price, I would do it at a speed that could not be detected by CCTV. I was always aware of security cameras and would give a little performance each time, usually to cement my innocence. In this case, even though my mother wasn't actually outside, the tape would make it seem like she was.

In the early 1980s stores rarely had more than one camera, and the one they did have would be pointed inside the store, typically near the exit. Should a store have two cameras, the second lens would generally be pointed in the direction of the cash register, in order to spot employee-related pilfering. Therefore, unless they had a third camera filming outside, which I was confident they did not, it would be impossible to prove that my mother wasn't outside, regardless of what the store detectives thought. This information alone gave me some hope.

'Mama, outside,' I stated, over and over. They didn't seem to understand and kept shouting at me, so close that at times I felt their spittle hit my own lips. I stood up and tried to convince them further by performing the actions. I explained that my mother was outside and I was merely showing her the journal, I wasn't stealing it. I kept saying, 'No stealing, only showing', but they continued to bellow at me, becoming increasingly frustrated with the language barrier. The fact that no 'mama' had followed me into the store once I'd been apprehended did not deter me. I just kept reiterating my deceit.

Without warning one of the men grabbed me by the shoulders and bundled me out of the room and back down the corridor, shouting at me throughout. He shoved me against the breeze-blocked wall and motioned for me to shut up. I became quite scared by this. I couldn't believe the mess I had gotten myself into, and for what? A bloody book! I was prepared for the worst when my eyes were suddenly blinded by sunlight. A door had been flung open and I felt myself being pushed through. As my eyes adjusted I could see that I was in a delivery bay surrounded by cardboard boxes. The guy who released me conveyed a gesture I interpreted as 'now fuck off' and slammed the door. I was free.

Wow, that was way too close, I thought. I'm not sure if they believed my story, or if my not being French meant their interrogation was just too much hassle. Who knows? I had a word with myself after that. If I wanted something I couldn't afford, I would have to be smarter from now on. Stealing was for idiots.

Incidentally, although I have never seen the proof, I would later be told that my face had allegedly been on an Interpol list of wanted and missing children in Europe that summer, so it was a good job that I was keeping my head down, eh?

The stress of the situation left me perplexed for the rest of the day, so when it came to making my way back to the campsite that evening I just couldn't find it. I rode around for ages looking for a familiar marker, but I couldn't find a single landmark. Over time I became quite worried, as I was getting light-headed and disorientated. I was also hungry and had hardly any cash on me. Then I recalled that the campsite was near the sea, so I took out my phrasebook of European languages and began to ask the locals for help. 'La mer?' I asked. Most ignored me, but one older gentleman came to my aid and thankfully pointed me in the right direction. Finally I saw some buildings I recognised and felt instant relief.

It was almost dark when I arrived back at the campsite, just in time for dinner. On tonight's menu: tinned beef ravioli. It looked disgusting and tasted like it sounds. I could not understand why we were eating such utter shit when we had 3,000 pounds. It was so much money, yet we were still living as if we were penniless. Technically a third of that money was mine and I seriously thought about asking for it. If I had, I certainly wouldn't have been eating what looked like dog food out of a tin can, I can assure you of that. My mother saw my reaction to the slop on my plate and told me that I should be grateful and not pull faces.

After the horse meat, it was straight to bed. The following morning we would be resuming our cycling duties, so a good night's sleep was in order. *No chance of that*, I thought as I looked down at the hardened ground. Just as I was zipping up the tent, my mum came back over. She had some news: 'Oh yeah, I forgot to tell you, tomorrow the first ten miles is going to be hills.'

Oh goody.

***

Once we were out of Marseilles and into the foothills it became obvious that our plan to get to Cannes in one day wasn't going to work. Our bikes were still way too heavy and the gradient was too steep for even my dad to attempt, so all three of us spent the entire morning pushing our bikes up into the hills. It was exhausting.

Eventually the road evened out a little, but the ups and downs were still commonplace and there was plenty of getting off and pushing. Our revised itinerary meant it would now take two days to get to Cannes. I was looking forward to Cannes for two reasons: firstly, we would be there in time for the world-famous film festival, and secondly, topless beaches. That certainly gave me the extra zest needed to push on when my energy was waning.

The hills in the south were even harder to traverse than those in the north, but at least it wasn't raining. On the second day we came rolling down into flatter pastures and I started to see signs for St Tropez. My spirits rose; surely it wasn't much further now? I was looking forward to seeing the Côte d'Azur, as I had recently read that it was one of the most beautiful stretches of beach in all of Europe. I figured it would therefore start to feel more like a proper holiday once we got there; I mean, it had to be better than the slog we were –

THA DUMP KLIMBLE KLUMBLE …

Suddenly I was on the ground. My dad had yet again applied his brakes without warning. This time I was unfortunate enough to be the one directly behind him and ploughed straight into his bike and him. We both went down pretty hard. Why he stopped this time was never revealed. Another purse, perhaps?

I was sprawled out on the concrete entangled between both bicycles and their respective saddlebags, but my dad was somehow already upright and swearing at me. Of course this was my fault. It couldn't possibly be his, how could it? Just as in Dublin when he blamed my mother, he told me that I should have been able to react in time.

Well, excuse me, how was I to know you were going to slam on your fucking brakes, you complete and utter twat, I thought, or words to that effect.

I was now covered in what looked like blood but was actually my dad's raspberry jam, which he had insisted I carry for him. He reached down to me, which I first assumed was to help me up, but then I spotted he was making a fist with his other hand, and so I braced myself for pain. But it never came. Instead I heard a commotion in the distance and it was getting closer.

The crash had happened as we were coming into the town of Fréjus and some of the townspeople had seen the accident and came running. They brought with them a first-aid kit, iodine and drinking water. They were all very sweet and kind, plus they had foiled my dad's plans to give me a good thrashing, that fact alone winding him up something rotten. It was funny to me at the time. He wanted to hit me so badly, but he couldn't, not in front of the locals. He gave me a look as if to say, 'Don't worry, I'll get you for this later.' And I gave him my own look in return that said, 'Yeah I'm sure you will, you fucking coward.'

My mum put the blame for the crash squarely at his feet, no question. She backed me completely and told him to leave me alone and to stop being such a bully. He then turned his sights on her and began calling her various distasteful names instead. He was just as angry with her as he was with me, as he'd seen her laughing at him while the locals were helping us. He hated being helped and desperately wanted to escape the situation, and she knew it. This made her laugh even more, which in turn propelled him to a new level of internalised rage.

Once we were all fixed up and ready to push off again, it was apparent that my dad was still in a shockingly poor mood. Again this was probably just embarrassment, but he didn't know how to express that, so instead we were subjected to violent outbursts. If only the man could say sorry like a normal person, it could have all been avoided. But he didn't say sorry. Instead he continued to argue with my mum in the street. She decided enough was enough and told him to go fuck himself.

While mounting her bike she told him she was cycling ahead and then turned to me and asked if I wanted to join her. Well, I wasn't going to stay with him, was I?

So we left him there, swearing his head off in Fréjus. As we rode off, even though he was being a complete arsehole, I kind of felt sorry for him. Don't ask me why.

***

We cycled for miles without looking back, but eventually resentment turned to worry and we both started to check if he was perhaps cycling behind us. He was not. After a time my mum remembered that my dad was wearing the money belt containing all our cash and passports, so she realised that she had to go back and find him. Also, I think she genuinely wanted to see if he was okay. Regardless of the terrible things they said and did to each other, it was obvious that they were still in love, albeit a strange version thereof.

When my mum told me that she was going back to look for him, I thought she was nuts. We had just ascended the mother of all hills and now she wanted to go all the way back down to find that moody bastard. It seemed like a giant waste of effort on her part, but she was adamant. I was told to stay put and to not cycle on any further, as she would be back soon enough. I told her I was hungry and reminded her that we'd missed lunch due to the crash. She told me I would just have to wait until we got to the campsite, as there were no eateries en route anyway. Cannes was only a few miles ahead, making her decision all the more infuriating.

'Look, we'll have dinner together later, okay? I just want to fix things with your father first,' she said, before riding off down the hill. I took a seat by the side of the road and prepared for the long haul.

Two hours passed and there was still no sign of them. I was incredibly unimpressed. I was also famished. I'd cycled fifty kilometres on nothing but a Laughing Cow baguette. I also could not believe that my mum had left me stranded without money or supplies. Where the hell were they, anyway? I had many thoughts while I waited by the roadside and some of them were pretty dark. At one point I even mounted my bike and seriously considered cycling into Cannes without them.

However, once the sun began to set, I heard them. They were pushing their bikes up the hill and I swear I heard laughing. As they got closer I could tell they were getting on better. I was relieved that the row between them was over and hoped that my dad would be in a good enough mood not to attempt a deferred beating for the crash. If anything, I expected some sort of apology from them for taking so long. Instead of a sorry, all I received was abuse.

'What's wrong with you, are you some kind of moron? Why didn't you come and look for us?' and that was just my mother.

She always had a tendency of switching sides on a sixpence. One minute she was defending me, the next she'd be taking the piss to appease my father. It was all very vexing. She always had a talent for making me feel shitty about myself.

I snapped back and reminded her of the explicit instructions she gave me to stay put. In her opinion, however, I should have realised something was up and gone down the hill to look for them. In her mind I was a complete idiot for waiting two full hours by the roadside. However, I suspect that had I disobeyed her and gone searching, she would have reprimanded me for that also. This was a common tactic and in no way a winnable situation.

I was so hungry by this point that my stomach was cramping and I could not wait to get to Cannes and have some much-needed supper. My mum, however, had some surprising information on that very subject. 'Oh by the way, we're not stopping for dinner any more; me and your father have already eaten.'

I did not think she was being serious, but she clarified by telling me that, shortly after their reconciliation, they'd stumbled across a restaurant and decided to pop in for a steak dinner. That's why they had taken so long.

Now, I don't recall my exact words, but they must have been along the lines of 'What the living fuck?' I was starving and these clowns went for a meal without me? Leaving me atop a hill while they did so. I was livid. So much so that I didn't even enjoy the first sight of boobs as we rode into Cannes. Well, maybe a little.

CHAPTER 29

EVERY TRICK IN THE BOOK

I was sleeping on the beach. Not on the sand, but in a dilapidated beach hut my dad had somehow secured for the night. We had arrived into Cannes quite late and failed to find our campsite, so we were attempting slumber by the sea. We weren't staying in Cannes itself; instead we were in Golfe-Juan, a small town a few miles further along the coast. From here we could easily explore the surrounding areas. As we were planning to stay for a couple of weeks there would be no long-distance cycling for a while. I was happy with this information.

Shortly before bed my parents started arguing again, and while they were trading insults I had something of a revelation. I concluded that the constant tension being caused was coming from one source: me. I decided in that moment to run away and leave them to it. We would all be better off.

Admittedly I was still pissed off that they had gone for a meal without me, but it was more than that. At the beginning of our European adventure, I had wrongly assumed that we were in the midst of a new level of respect and understanding due to our joint exploits in Dublin. Now I was truly back at square one, even after such a monumental shared experience. Also, it was obvious that they would rather be alone; they made no secret of that. But, regardless of their feelings towards me, I actually wanted my mum and dad to be happy together. I was therefore convinced that if I were to flee the scene, it would be significantly easier for them to be content with one another.

So I made a tentative plan. Once they were asleep, I would sneak out and vanish into thin air. Somehow I would make my way back to London; that's where they had wanted me to go, anyway, so it seemed like the logical answer. I didn't have any money or a clue how to get there, but I didn't care. All I wanted was to be away from the messed-up situation I now found myself in. I did not want to hang around and watch it deteriorate further. I knew the pattern well and sooner or later severe beatings were bound to return, and then it would be too late. It was better to get out now.

We were all pretty tired from the day's cycling, so it wasn't long before my parents had bickered themselves to sleep. As I lay there, I became fixated on a strange noise, consisting of mild thuds and a muted clicking, coming from the roof; it was a bit freaky. I thought there was someone up there for a while, but in retrospect I think it was probably just an animal trying to get settled.

I waited a long time before eventually crawling down from my bed. It felt like the middle of the night, but it was probably only eleven o'clock. I gathered my things quietly. My rucksack was massive, I had no intention of taking such a thing with me, so instead I simply grabbed a few essentials and quietly crept out of the hut with just the clothes on my back. Taking my Le Jeune was not an option, as all three bikes were intertwined with multiple locks. Any decoupling on my part would undoubtedly have woken my parents and I'd have been for the high jump.

I was amazed that I'd managed to sneak out undetected, and continued walking along the beach for a few minutes before bothering to look back at the hut. I felt bad about what I was doing, but it seemed like the right thing to do. I walked off with every intention of making my way back to England. I clambered up to the main road in the town and pondered my next move. The last train to Cannes had been and gone, but I figured I could perhaps hitchhike or take a bus into the city, and from there I could probably sneak on a train back to Marseilles and then on to Paris.

As I walked towards the edge of town I noticed a crowd of rowdy tourists coming back from a night out in the city and decided to approach them. I planned to ask them for a little money, just enough to get into Cannes.

Once they got close, one of the guys asked me why I was out so late. My reply was quite surprising, not just because of the words that came out of my mouth, but also for the way in which they emerged. An unplanned pan-euro accent had taken over without my permission.

'Le autobus?' it said. It was a mixture of French and Italian but sounded like neither. 'Do yoo eh know le autobooos iz tymez?'

They looked at me confused. 'I think he wants the bus,' said one of the women.

I replied, 'Oui.'

She then asked if I was staying in Cannes, to which I replied, 'Si', clearly hopping between two languages. They told me I would have to take a taxi as the last bus had already left. One of the guys asked if I had enough money to get there and I shook my head. Unbelievably they all chipped in and handed me enough cash to get into the city. They smiled, told me to take care and walked off into the night. I was stunned. Their generosity touched me, but it also switched on my fraudster's light bulb.

A few minutes earlier I had every intention of travelling into Cannes, but now I had a better idea. If I asked more people for money and everyone gave me a small amount, I would soon have enough to get all the way back to England. With the film festival coming up there were bound to be hundreds of people around and ample opportunities to make money. I spotted more tourists walking towards me and decided to try the act again just to be sure it wasn't a one-off. This time I added waterworks to the mix for increased effect. Again they handed over money. It was all the proof I needed.

I had a plan. I would save money to run away. It wasn't very ethical, but it was practical – at least for my purposes. I would, however, need somewhere to stash my accumulated monies. If my parents found a large amount of cash upon my person, I was sure to receive a good thrashing, and that was something I was dearly trying to avoid.

I went for a walk in search of a suitable location and found the perfect spot under a bridge. I spotted a pile of large rocks on the bank of the river, which looked ideal. I rolled up my newly acquired notes and shoved them, along with a handful of coins, into a small discarded plastic bag and hid it beneath the rocks. I was worried it would get found, but I had little choice; there was no way I could keep it on me. This was to become a safety deposit box of sorts. My private riverside bank was now open for business.

I headed down to the beach and crept carefully back into the hut. My parents were restless in their bed, but not enough to wake. I climbed up onto my mattress, closed my eyes and thought about my discovery. I enjoyed the fact that I had technically run away yet my parents had no inkling. I still planned to escape. I had simply postponed it until the trip was better funded.

***

The following day we moved to the campsite. It was in a particularly noisy spot behind a bottling plant. As we pitched our tents, the other residents came over to introduce themselves. There was a blonde woman who took an instant liking to my father. It was fascinating to see how my parents were perceived by strangers. The blonde lady clearly thought my dad was someone he was not. She flirted with him, mentioning how she thought he was a big softy who wouldn't hurt a fly. How wrong she was.

In the evenings they would all sit together and chat, a beer in one hand and a cigarette in the other. My parents were beginning to take the piss out of me again, and this time in public. I was the butt of many jokes and I appreciated it about as much as I usually did. My mum had come up with an extraordinary way of embarrassing me even further. She would demand that I strip naked and shower me with a garden hose right in front of the other campers while calling me 'a dirty bastard'. She was certain that I didn't wash properly and this was her way of making sure I was clean. I occasionally saw the other residents laughing wildly at my predicament.

She was now as horrible to be around as my dad was. Therefore, when they suggested, as they did in Marseilles, that I should go off on my own for the day, I did not need convincing.

My parents were extremely tight with our money and only ever gave me minimal currency to play with, which I found particularly annoying, considering the money we had was as much mine as theirs. We never seemed to spend any of our spoils; it was quite ridiculous. Why did we accumulate all that cash in Dublin if we were going to live like bloody paupers throughout Europe? Therefore, when they insisted that I cycle everywhere along the Côte d'Azur to save money, I resisted. I had cycled quite enough, thank you very much.

Once I had picked up the francs from my 'safety deposit box', I would take my very distinct bicycle and lock it in a well-hidden spot behind the train station. I had to park it in a place where my parents would never see it, so as to not arouse suspicion. If they thought for a moment that I could afford the train, they would suspect I had my own money and would demand to know where it came from. The irony is that not once did I have to buy a ticket into Cannes. It was easy to evade the inspectors and there were no barriers at either end. I would travel this way daily without spending a centime.

***

I loved Cannes. There was such an incredible buzz around every corner. The film festival was in full swing and the atmosphere was carnivalesque. My youth made me a ghost. I managed to sneak into all kinds of events without so much as a word. Sometimes I would be asked what I was doing, but I was always able to bullshit my way in. I operated with impunity;

walking into screenings, interviews, parties, hotels, you name it. I would talk to anyone who would listen. I approached bathers on the beachfront, chatting with all kinds of nationalities, hung out with film crews who were interviewing the stars of the competing movies, and even got to meet some of the actors and models scattered throughout the city. I watched them all work their magic and was both intrigued and in awe of everything I saw. It was a world away from the life I had led until that point.

A few days in, with a Quick Burger sticking out of my mouth, something on the beach caught my eye, and no, it was not boobs. It was a large book. A few of the sunbathers appeared to be flicking through its many pages. It was about half the size of the yellow pages, with a painting of an ocean liner on the front accompanied by the festival logo. I approached the best-looking woman who had one and asked what she was reading. She explained that it was the Cannes festival guide, a programme containing every event during the film festival. Apparently they were giving them away for free in the Carlton Hotel.

Ker-ching. An idea immediately formed in my scammer's brain. Just to be absolutely certain I asked her to confirm: 'Gratis?'

'Oui,' she replied. This news made me a very happy bunny.

Although it is easily the grandest hotel on the seafront, the Carlton was relatively easy to gain access to. I had already been inside a few times and knew my way around reasonably well. The last time I had been in there I saw Faye Dunaway having her photo taken on the main staircase and brazenly wandered up to her and casually said hello. She replied, 'Hello to you too, young man,' while peering down at me questioningly.

However, this time would be more difficult. I had to somehow sneak into the Press Lounge. It was a dining hall that had been temporarily converted into an events space and was now full to the rafters with festival merchandise and goodies. I was sure if the books were anywhere, they would be in there.

Surprisingly, I wasn't stopped and gained access to the Press Lounge by simply walking in. The moment I set foot inside I could see festival guides everywhere; they were piled high on trestle tables throughout the room. I then noticed full boxes behind the tables that contained ten books each. Audaciously I picked up a box and walked off with it, right out of the room and through the lobby. The doorman asked where I was going and I told him I was going to help distribute them on the beach. He smiled and opened the door for me as I staggered across the busy road and out onto the promenade.

My plan was simple. I was sure that most people would be unaware that the guides were free. Although they didn't display a price on the front, they didn't say they were free either. My plan was to sell as many as possible for ten francs a pop, which was about a pound at the time. It wasn't long before I had some takers and I emptied my box within half an hour. I was surprised at how easy it had been. I went back to the hotel and got another box. Again, nobody said a word and off I went to sell more. In fact the more times I returned, the more official I started to appear. I, too, began to believe I was working for the hotel in some way and got to know some of the staff in the process. No one suspected a thing; it was brilliant. At ten pounds per box I was raking it in and sold more than I can remember. I did this for a few days until I was inevitably rumbled.

Someone must have informed the hotel that I was selling their free books on the beach, because while walking across the lobby with a box of guides in my arms I was finally accosted. A tall, thin man shouted at me to put the box down and leave the hotel immediately. I feigned innocence, telling him I was helping to distribute them for the Carlton. During this dialogue one of the staff I'd chatted to previously ran over to defend me, but the man ignored him, reiterating his demands for me to leave. I left the hotel and that was the end of it. I was just glad that they didn't call the police. I guessed it would probably be a little tricky to prove.

Although I could no longer get full boxes of programmes, this didn't stop me finding used ones around town and selling them on, sometimes at 'half price'. It was a great little enterprise and it was all my own idea. I already had plenty of cash stashed at my 'riverbank' (get it?). But I couldn't stop. The hustle was addictive. If I was saving purely to run away, then I already had more than I needed, but I wasn't going anywhere, not just yet.

For my next trick I started asking tourists for foreign currency. I simply told them I was a coin collector and they started handing over money. I would accept coins or notes, I didn't mind. At the time bureau de changes accepted some larger coins, so it was no trouble turning it all into usable francs. I also continued my 'late-night fare' begging and even started a new racket to complete the hat-trick, whereby I would go into various shops, pick up something really fast and walk straight up to the counter, where I'd blatantly ask for a refund. Because I didn't speak a word of French, I would perform these cons in English, but still add in the pan-euro accent for effect. I have no idea why this helped, it just did. I would tell them I'd bought the item the previous day, before throwing in an accompanying lie, like 'my mum already bought it for me' or some such. This very much relied on 'my honest face' more than anything else and worked almost every time.

I certainly had a lot of balls in the air for a twelve-year-old, but I still managed to enjoy the festival and wasn't solely trying to make money. I snuck into a few films here and there, and met a few famous people to boot, the highlight being the English comedy legend Frankie Howerd. I chatted his ear off as we walked along the seafront. He was good value and did lots of his trademark vocalisations, which made me giggle.

My life in Cannes was a blast, mainly because I spent almost all of my time alone and most of it making vast sums of money. However, I nearly came a cropper while out shopping with my parents one tricky afternoon.

They were buying wine at a ludicrously low price when I noticed one of the couples who'd given me money for the bus just a few nights earlier. I was obviously talking in my regular accent and was seconds from being exposed.

I was in quite the pickle. I decided to try something a little left field. I would try to somehow use both accents at the same time. I tried not to speak at all at first, but my mum kept asking me bloody questions. Therefore, whenever the couple got too close, I morphed my answers into the euro accent that I had been using. My mum looked at me puzzled – it must have seemed like I was having a stroke. She asked why I was talking that way, but I refused to explain. I gave the couple a look as if to say, 'Please don't say anything.' I think they knew I'd get into trouble for having taken their money, but if they heard my real accent they would know that I'd swindled them as well and I'd be done for. I just had to juggle both accents until they left. Amazingly I got out of there without being found out. My mum was definitely suspicious, but she still had no idea what was really going on!

Our time in Cannes was drawing to a close when my dad suggested I take a trip to Monte Carlo. The Grand Prix was taking place the following day and he thought I should go and check it out. Again he reminded me that I should be spending more time on my own and not hanging around them so much. I have no idea why they wanted me out of the way all the time. I wondered if they were up to no good themselves. He gave me some money for the train and told me not to come home too late, as we would be leaving the next day and needed to pack.

So the very next morning I got up bright and early and jumped on the first train to Monaco. It took about an hour and the money my dad gave me stayed firmly in my pocket as I decided to travel the entire way in the WC. The vibe in Monte Carlo was electric; it was even more exciting than Cannes. As soon as I got off the train I could hear the whizzing of Formula One cars twisting up and down through the hills and tunnels of the city below; it was all very impressive. The organisers had formed a route from the station down to a public viewing area, but it was nowhere near the action and I was convinced that I could get closer. I therefore continued further into the fray in search of pole position. I managed to sneak through a couple of checkpoints, but once I got to the entrance of the pits there was nowhere else to go. Without a ticket or a press pass there was no way I was going to qualify.

Near to the entrance were a number of publicity stalls giving away free merchandise, much like in Cannes. It was while I was hanging around the Ferrari stand that I got chatting to a sports journalist. The guys at the stand had kitted me out with all things Ferrari including a metal badge and cap, which I instantly adored. I told them that I wanted to get in and see the race, and now that I was a walking advert for their company, so did they. They suggested that the journalist sneak me in with him and, to my continued amazement, he agreed. He told me to stay close as we approached the entrance chatting. He flashed his press pass and I did a random pointing motion as if to say, 'I'm with him', and that was it. I was in. It was so darn easy. There I was, standing in the actual pits of the Monte Carlo Grand Prix. You couldn't write this stuff.

I had a formidable seat and watched in awe as the cars sped by in front of me only to whizz back around behind my head seconds later. I would peer through the bleachers to try to make out who was out in front. I was soon on my own, wandering the press area and tucking into the free food and pop without shame. It was a joy to be eating something other than my parents' gross camping food. It was a glorious experience all round and I did not relish leaving. However, I could hear my dad's voice instructing me not to be late and reluctantly left before the end of that legendary race.

I climbed the near vertical hill to the station, caught the next train to Cannes and got back to the campsite in time to see hot ravioli hitting plastic plates. My parents seemed genuinely surprised to see me and asked why I'd returned so early. I reminded my dad of his warning not to be late. He then told me he meant eight or nine o'clock, not dinnertime.

'Jesus, I didn't want you to miss the end of the Grand Prix,' he declared. Damn it, I could tell that he was being sincere too. Arse.

CHAPTER 30

OUT OF MY DEPTH

My fun in Cannes had come to an abrupt end. The festival was over and it was once again time to move on. I was dreading getting back on those bloody bicycles. Luckily, so was my mother. It turned out I wasn't the only one who despised pushing steel up inclines, so she managed to persuade my dad to transport our bikes back to Marseilles by train. From there we would attempt to cycle to Spain. *What great news!* I thought.

All thoughts of running away had since dissipated and my mood was much lighter following my adventures in Cannes. I now had my own money hidden deep within my rucksack, so if things went awry I could always abscond at a later date. However, before boarding the train back to Marseilles, we had a couple of apparently important things to do.

My dad desperately needed a new pair of trainers. He did a lot of running and his old ones were almost worn through, so, with heavy bags and bicycles, we went in search of a pair of New Balance trainers. It was the only make he would wear; all others were shite, or so he claimed. We found a pair he approved of, but they were quite expensive. Not to worry. Without flinching my dad simply handed over one of our crisp, newly acquired traveller's cheques. It seemed like an awful lot to spend on a pair of fancy plimsolls, considering we still had months of travelling to do and were technically eating rations for dinner, but according to my mum we still had most of our money from Dublin, so it didn't matter.

Something didn't feel right, though. I started to worry that they were up to something.

Opposite Cannes Ville railway station was a phone box and inside said phone box was my father. He was talking heatedly to someone from American Express. I wondered what on earth was going on. I was sure it was something to do with his recent purchase, so I asked my mum. She then casually explained that while I'd been running around Cannes making pennies here and there, they had been devising a scheme to double our money. And all it would take was one solitary phone call. I was all ears.

Their idea was to spend a handful of the traveller's cheques on expensive purchases while in Cannes, which they had apparently already been doing, then report their money belt stolen. They told Amex it had been pinched from the campsite. My dad was on the phone reporting this fact while my mum filled me in. By the time he put down the receiver, American Express had agreed to reissue our cheques in Marseilles that very afternoon. All they had to do was sign a form and the money was theirs. It was that easy. Even though the reported cheques would now be on the fraudulent list, my parents were certain they could still spend the few they had left along the way. There were sure to be plenty of places that didn't do thorough checks where they could offload them easily.

***

Marseilles was just as we had left it. We returned to the same campsite as before and began to organise the rest of our trip. At the end of the week we would be heading to Spain and then possibly over to Africa, where my parents still maintained that they would leave me with a random family. The specifics of this were never made clear, so I suspected it was just a ruse to keep me in line. Still, luckily for me, world events would play their part and thwart my parents' ludicrous scheme.

Three days into our Marseilles stay and everything changed. I had brought my refund trick with me from Cannes and was now making money consistently from news kiosks. I would pick up a handful of postcards from the side of the news stand and take them directly to the seller, professing to have bought them earlier. I would explain that I no longer needed so many and asked to return just a few of them, for cash. Bizarrely this worked more often than not. However, to help with a clean getaway I got used to leaning my bike against the kerb without locking it. This was to be my downfall. I was walking away from one of the little huts when I noticed something was missing: my bicycle.

Oh shit, I thought with a wince. I looked in every direction but there was no sign of my Le Jeune anywhere; it was gone.

The fact that my bike was technically one-third of our transport around Europe guaranteed my parents' displeasure. All I could hope for was that they were in a good mood when I returned without it. Maybe it wasn't such a big deal? After all, we had enough money to buy a hundred bikes. Still, I had to come up with an alternative story; there was no way I was admitting to my father that I had left it unlocked, as he'd have killed me for that alone.

I walked home solemnly with no idea what to expect. I did, however, enjoy the somewhat ironic concept that someone had actually stolen my stolen bicycle.

I thought I had already faced the full wrath of my father over the years and assumed there were no surprises left in store. I was wrong.

Once I arrived back at the campsite my mum and dad were in a bad way. There had clearly been an altercation and I could tell my mum was hurt. He had hit her again. This was not a good omen. It could not have been worse timing for what I was about to tell them. Instead of giving me the benefit of the doubt, my mum noticed that I didn't have my bike with me and made a big song and dance about it, I suspect to deflect my dad's attention away from her. With both parents staring at me, I had to admit that I had in fact lost the bike.

Before I could explain the intricacies of what had happened, my dad was dragging me along the ground towards a wooden cabin. We had a cabin? I thought we were supposed to be sleeping in our tents?

He threw me inside, followed me in and locked the door. He gave me a look that I recognised and I braced myself for a beating that didn't come. He had other ideas. His eyes were wide and in that moment he was a lunatic. I suddenly became afraid of him in a new way.

'I told you to lock your bike,' he snarled quietly.

'I did,' I said, lying. There was no way I was admitting to not doing that now. He didn't ask any more questions, he just told me to roll up my sleeves. I was confused by his request but obliged, albeit nervously. 'What is he about to do?' I wondered.

All I could think about was not pissing myself; that was sure to make things worse. I did, however, begin to cry a little in fear, begging him not to hurt me, but he wasn't listening. Instead he was circling me, finally stopping directly behind my shoulder blades. He instructed me to let my hands hang down, as if I were about to play piano. Suddenly he reached forward and grabbed my right hand. His own hand was pulling my fingers inward towards my forearm, making my wrist bend far more than it was supposed to. He would release his hold slightly, then try again, my fingers getting closer to the inside of my arm each time. He had a devil's grip as I screamed for him to stop. It was absolute bloody torture. I was in agony and could not understand why he was doing this to me. It was too much. I became angry with myself: why didn't I run away when I had the fucking chance? He then changed sides and went for the other hand, pulling it inward until it seemed to almost touch my elbow. I nearly passed out. I tried my best to shut down my senses until it was over, but I just couldn't block it out, the pain was too intense. Instead I began to focus on how much I hated him, fantasising about how I would seek revenge for his savagery. In that moment all I wanted to do was stick a knife in that cunt's chest.

Caveat: I realise that many people have trouble with the C word, but I make no apologies for using it myself here. It is just a word, and one that aptly describes my father in this instance. I do, however, believe it should be used sparingly and not thrown around in the same way Americans use the word 'awesome'. As I also consider myself a feminist, please don't presume that it is used in any lady-hating manner; it is not. In that regard, I also realise that I have called my mum a bitch from time to time, but this can be easily explained by the fact that, on occasion, she was one.

Once my father had inflicted the desired amount of pain, he gave me a few digs and left me squirming. My wrists hurt so badly that I had to assume they were sprained. I was desperate for relief, but the only thing that helped was pouring ice-cold water onto the affected area. I went to the shower block a number of times during the night, but it only gave temporary comfort; nothing could fully quell the ache. When my mum finally came to see if I was okay, I noticed bruises on her arms and knew exactly where they had come from. We were both in the same boat. Years later, when I told her what he actually did to me in that cabin, she casually replied, 'So what? He did the same thing to me, you know.'

As I no longer had a bicycle, there was a new plan. We would buy three inter-rail tickets and travel the rest of Europe by train. The only problem was they were only available for people under twenty-six, which my parents absolutely were not. A bit of forgery on my dad's part, however, and that was no longer an issue. I was of course blamed for the cost of these tickets, even though we could have easily bought a cheap replacement bicycle for next to nothing. It was also decided that my mum and dad's bikes were to be sent to Calais, where they would remain in storage until they returned from Africa without me.

Incidentally the whole 'leaving me in Africa' thing seemed to become ever more real, never more so than after the bike-loss debacle. They appeared deadly serious after that, often talking about how they were going to offload me on some unsuspecting Kenyans. However, I had every intention of bailing before they got the chance. There was no way I was going to be left alone in Africa. Whenever they discussed it, I would give them a look as if to say, 'Yeah, that ain't happening, mate.'

Although I had newfound plans to run away, I seemed to be taking my sweet time enacting them. Whatever was I waiting for, I wonder?

***

And so inter-railing began, with an early morning train to the Spanish border. The bikes and saddlebags were no more, replaced by three enormous, tightly packed rucksacks. I adored train travel and was keen to see another new country. Although France had been full of adventures, I was eager to familiarise myself with the rest of Europe.

With just a few miles to go until the Spanish border our train came to a sudden halt. We had arrived at the small border town of Cerbère, our train's final destination. We did not know this when we boarded in Marseilles, so it came as some surprise that we now had a two-hour wait until the second train into Spain arrived. My parents decided that we should go to the beach to kill time rather than wait on the featureless platform. Even though I was not a huge fan of the sea, it did look rather inviting. It was barely mid morning and the sun was already hanging high in the sky; it really was quite beautiful. That would have been a lovely memory, but we can't possibly leave it there, can we?

My dad had decided it was time that I learned to swim. He was not wrong. I had tried many times, but the constant changing of schools and abodes hadn't led to the structure needed to learn such things. The last time I tried to learn was in London when I was overweight. I had despised taking my shirt off to get in the pool; it was embarrassing. In order to float I had to wear armbands and inevitably the other kids would laugh at me for this. I felt like such an idiot in those situations. I had already decided that when it came to things like swimming and football I had probably missed the boat.

My dad, however, did not agree with my prognosis. He asked me to trust him, which I found laughable. How could I possibly trust him of all people? Was he demented? I wondered if the man possessed the ability to recall past events.

As I secretly longed to be able to swim, though, I figured I had nothing to lose. My dad promised that he would have me flapping about in no time and for a split second I actually believed him. He told me that all we had to do was make our way to a floating platform fifty or so metres out to sea and he would teach me from there. I was pretty scared to have to swim so far out from the beach, but he assured me that he would have my back, so I put my faith in him.

He told me to hold onto his shoulders as he swam and we would be there momentarily. My hands still ached from the Marseilles incident, so I struggled to hold onto his slippery torso. I don't think I'd ever held on to my dad before, it was a brand new sensation and one that was to be short-lived. A few metres shy of the platform he vanished. I felt something around my feet and then I was alone, flailing about in the actual sea.

I was unable to keep my head above water and instantly became terrified. I was convinced I was about to drown. I was taking in water and finding it hard to breathe. I knew I had to get back to the shore, but how? I decided my best hope was to emulate the motions of those around me, but I wasn't sure if I was doing it correctly. My dad was now on the beach; he had joined my mum and they were both waving at me. What the hell? I flapped my feet uncontrollably and mustered just enough strength to propel myself forward, my hands burning. I certainly wouldn't call it swimming, but by some miracle I ended up back in the shallows, eventually flopping onto the sand, choking. My dad ran over, visibly proud of himself. 'See,' he said, 'I knew you could swim.'

CHAPTER 31

A DOG'S DINNER

We had taken the train from the border to Barcelona and arrived too late for lunch. We were just passing through, apparently. My parents were keen to catch another train heading south that same afternoon. Going to all these places without actually seeing them was starting to irk me and I had to wonder if their idea of travelling around Europe was simply ticking cities off a list. Sometimes we didn't even bother to stay the night. Therefore, my only recollection of Barcelona is of taking the bus between two railway stations. It was the hottest and loudest bus that I'd ever had the displeasure to board. In my left ear lived a Spanish woman who loved to shout, and I prayed to whichever god would listen to strike her down. I could not wait to get off that humid, rattling mess. Once we disembarked from the bus, my mum took one look at our gear, then asked my dad. 'Where's the tent?'

It transpired that my dad had left it in France. He had rested it against a pillar on the platform in Cerbère and forgotten to retrieve it. I was carrying my own body bag of a tent, but they would now either have to sleep under the stars or fork out for a hotel room, heaven forbid. It was a huge error on his part and he was not best pleased.

There was a double standard here. A few days prior I had lost my bike and was forced to face my dad's wrath, but for him to lose the roof over their heads was somehow amusing, at least to my mother. I, on the other hand, considered that I should perhaps take him round the back of the station and smash his hands with a hammer – all in the name of fairness, of course.

There was no chance of us heading back to France for the want of a cheap tent. Instead we boarded the train, found some acceptable seats and tried to get settled. My mum was teasing my dad; she clearly enjoyed having the upper hand and he remained vexed for much of the journey.

We were on the first of two trains, our final destination being Algeciras, the most southern tip of Spain. The carriage was modern and comfy but nowhere near as sleek as its French counterparts. Luckily I managed to hog the Walkman, drowning out my parents' quibbling with the sounds of David Bowie.

I awoke around three hours later with a start. My mum was tapping me to get a move on. It was time to change trains. I was ravenous but there was no time to eat: the connecting train was already waiting and we had to make a run for it. I was a little exhausted from the constant travelling and therefore felt out of breath as I clambered up the steps of the new carriage. Although I was in something of a daze, it was still apparent that the train was noticeably superior to what we were used to.

Once we had departed, a rather well-dressed butler-type conductor appeared, immediately making us feel like we didn't belong. On seeing our tickets he informed us that we were prohibited from travelling on that particular locomotive. We would have to get off at the next stop and wait for the regular train, which was some hours behind, apparently. This was not good news and I could see my dad's temper rising. At least we had half an hour of luxury to enjoy before having to alight and I was going to make the most of it.

Eventually the train slowed down and we pulled up at a remote station named Andújar. It looked like something out of the Wild West. We were the only people to get off the train, which wasn't particularly surprising, as it appeared to be in the middle of nowhere. There was an adjoining town nearby, it turned out, though nothing in the station alluded to that fact.

As it was getting dark my parents decided it was a good idea to walk into Andújar town to see if there was a cheap place for us to stay, just in case the late train didn't materialise. They also wanted to purchase some much-needed supplies. My dad ordered me to stay put and prepare dinner; they would be back in an hour or so and they expected the ravioli to be ready upon their return. I gave him a sarcastic 'Yes Sir' look and off they went in search of life. As they walked away my dad shouted back, reminding me to be wary of rabid dogs; they were everywhere, apparently. He added that under no circumstances should I leave our belongings unattended.

I was bored shitless in that station. There wasn't even a usable bench to sit on along the entire platform; instead I sat on the bare concrete and attempted to study Spanish from my phrasebook. It only had a few phrases of real use, but it was fun all the same. Once I'd learned them, it was time to start dinner. I lit the gas stove and dropped the disgusting mulch into the pot with a squelch. As I began to stir I was overcome with an urge to pee. I tried to stay put as per my dad's instructions, but eventually the need was too strong and I had to leave the wooden spoon to its own devices. I left the ravioli cooking on the stove and ran behind the ticket office. I figured I would be a matter of seconds, what was the worst that could happen?

I returned to see two things: first, a rabid-looking dog with white foam covering its lips eating hot ravioli straight from our pan, burning its snout in the process. And secondly, my mum and dad getting back and seeing said dog.

My dad came at me like a madman. He grabbed hold of me and started pulling me along the dusty gravel away from the station. He dragged me to a nearby patch of earth and threw me to the ground. I noticed that I was just the right distance away from my mother that she might not hear my screams. Then he hit me.

Firstly my torso took the brunt of his rage, but eventually he moved on to my face and limbs. All the while he was telling me how there were no shops open nearby and that I had therefore ruined our only chance of dinner. He was furious about the dog incident and kept reiterating how he'd specifically told me not to leave the food unattended. I explained that I needed to pee and was only gone for a few seconds. In retaliation for that statement he kicked me right in the privates, as if to teach my nether regions a lesson in discipline. I really thought I would just get a few slaps, but this was brutal stuff, and he was just getting started.

We even ended up fighting a little. I hit him back a few times and told him to 'go fuck himself', but he just kept coming at me with a ferocity I had not seen before. I was used to receiving his punches, but on this occasion they felt harder somehow, like he wasn't holding back. I was taking adult-strength blows. Eventually I ended up back on the ground and he started kicking me in the sides. The pain was all-encompassing and this time there was blood. He never usually went this far; he didn't like the idea of people seeing his handiwork on me. Any scars or bruises inflicted could usually be hidden with the right clothing, but on this cold night he didn't seem to care about any of that.

In the middle of the beating he tried to bend my wrists again, but I kept pulling away. I wasn't letting him do that to me again, no fucking way. I was swearing at him throughout, which is also something I never did. I didn't care. He was already doing his worst anyway, so why hold back? The final blow was a punch to the stomach and it knocked the wind out of me. He then stood up, dusted himself off and walked away, swearing as he went. He shouted back towards me, telling me not to bother coming back to the station, adding that I should 'just fuck off' as neither of them wanted me around any more. It was clearly time for me to go.

I lay on the arid ground sobbing miserably. I was crying not just with pain but also with anger. I could barely move. I was bloodied and battered and I wanted to kill him, although I feared that, at this rate, he was going to get me first.

Once he was a safe distance away a couple came over to help me, but I screamed at them to leave me alone; I hated everyone in that moment, including them. I was also extremely embarrassed. I found a suitable place to sit and thought about my next move. Running away was no longer an option, as what little money I had left over from France was now buried deep within my rucksack. I concluded that I would have to board the next train out of there, just not with them. I planned to wait until I saw it coming and then somehow sneak on, alone.

As usual though, after a while my mood softened and I assumed enough time had passed for me to return. I thought perhaps my mum would feel some remorse when she saw the beating I'd taken. She did not. When she finally saw me, the first thing she said was that I had brought it on myself and that I shouldn't have talked back to my father, especially when he was in 'that kind of mood'. Apparently it was my fault that the situation had gotten out of hand. I could not believe her. I was twelve, for fuck sake, and covered in cuts and bruises. Somehow this was considered an acceptable punishment for accidentally letting a dog eat what I considered to be dog food.

The train arrived in the wee hours and all three of us boarded without speaking. I was too sore to sleep that night. God knows what people must have thought of my injuries, although I'm sure my parents had a suitable excuse lined up should anyone have had the courage to ask.

The sun was coming up as we pulled in to the port city of Algeciras, whereby we headed directly to the jetty to board a boat to Morocco.

Inside I had every intention of running away, but for some reason I was still with them, following their every move. By this point I was so tired of the bullshit that I could barely be bothered to kick against it. So what if their plan was to take me to Africa and leave me behind. Whatever. Let them do it, what did I care? I had given up. Luckily a customs officer would put a stop to their idiotic scheme.

As we attempted to board the ferry, my mother was told she wasn't allowed through. The customs officer simply said to her, 'I no like.' It was in respect to her British passport. The Falklands war was reaching its peak at the time and this guy was clearly prejudiced against her Britishness. Although my dad and I had already cleared customs with our Irish passports, my mum was unable to follow. Thankfully, we had no choice but to turn back. If we had ended up in Africa, who knows what nonsense would have occurred?

Later that day, without proper sleep or any discernible plan, we jumped on yet another train, this time bound for Madrid, but, instead of going to the city centre, we ended up at the airport early the following morning. At first I thought, *Oh no! Are we going to try and fly to a different African country?* I tentatively asked my mum and she explained that we would be taking an overnight train to Rome that same night; the airport just happened to be the connecting station. *Phew!* I thought. Hang on. Were they kidding? Were we going to see anything on this trip? Losing the tent didn't mean we had to spend every single night on a bloody train. They could have delved into the cash we were carrying and bought a new one by now, or at least paid for the odd hotel room. I kept my thoughts to myself, however, as I was keen to see Madrid. It turned out they were keener.

I was ordered to stay with the luggage while they went into the city for a jolly. I was again instructed not to leave the bags under any circumstances. I should have just chucked the whole fucking lot in the bin and disappeared, but, like the good little scoundrel I was, I endured yet again. It was late morning as I plonked my exhausted self down into the most plastic of chairs.

That day was a long one. I was tired and hungry and found it difficult to stay alert. However, I didn't want to wake up to find our rucksacks stolen, so I tried my best not to nod off completely. It was evening when my parents returned. They were in a good mood, having clearly enjoyed their day out. They proceeded to tell me about all the great sights they had seen. I had rather foolishly expected them to bring me back a meal of some sort, but this had not occurred to them. All I received was the usual attitude from my mother when I asked about food. Apparently I was still fat in her eyes and could stand to miss a few meals.

CHAPTER 32

ANCIENT HISTORY

We rolled into Rome's Termini station the following afternoon, just in time to experience the sweltering heat. Once we had arrived at our hostel, which was anything but opulent, my dad became unusually generous. He handed me a 1,000-lire note and told me that I could go and spend it however I desired. A thousand? That sounded like a lot. I thought he'd made an error and snatched it from his crusty hand before he had time to realise his mistake. I headed off in search of confectionery and other treats, but I didn't get very far. There was a kiosk nearby, so I picked up a small chocolate bar and was about to ask when ...

'Nine hundred and fifty,' the man exclaimed with his hand out.

'What?' I asked to confirm. Yep, my dad was clearly taking the piss. It turned out that 1,000 lire was equivalent to about forty pence.

Uncharacteristically, we spent a couple of days taking in the sights together. Rome was a little too big for them to let me loose in, so there was hardly any separation during our visit. My mum and I wandered the Colosseum while my dad waited outside, refusing to pay to go in. We took photos at the Trevi Fountain and my dad got into an altercation at the Vatican after being refused entry on the grounds that his hair was too long. This amused me greatly. I was surprised he didn't just cut it all off; it was such a hot summer. Incidentally, it was in Rome that I first noticed that my mum's belly appeared to be getting a little bigger. I guessed that it was all that delicious square pizza we were eating.

Our next stop was Pompeii. We took a train south and, after a quick wander around Naples, ended up at a campsite close to the ruins. I didn't know much about Pompeii, so that evening I decided to educate myself by inhaling my guidebook and any other accompanying literature I could find scattered around the campsite. However, it was hard to concentrate, as we spent most of that evening hanging out with other travellers in the communal area.

There was alcohol and drugs-a-plenty for the adults in attendance, which invariably led to some very bizarre conversations. One American guy tried to convince my dad that he could make a one-dimensional triangle. He banged on about it all night, boring everyone in the process. Somehow we got stuck with him and my dad inevitably ended up asking him to prove his claim. I was personally expecting magic, but there was to be no such luck. Stoned out of his mind, this guy simply cut a strip of paper and made a fold about halfway down. Once he had made a triangle he twisted the paper and glued it together. He then ran his finger along the flat surface and at the twist his finger, of course, ended up on the other side of the paper. This apparently proved it was a one-dimensional object. He clasped his hands together proudly while my dad exhaled a 'Jesus'.

We were staying in Pompeii for a few days and I was itching to head off on my own again. After Rome I craved time away from my parents and I'm sure they felt the same way. Luckily the next day gave us that very opportunity. My parents were heading back into Naples for reasons never divulged and told me if I wanted to stay in Pompeii, I could. They were going to visit the ruins the following day on their own, so if I fancied having a look around beforehand, I could do so.

I did just that. I preferred to wander around at my own pace anyway. My parents always rushed us around such places and I hated that. After breakfast I headed up to the entrance, paid the minuscule entrance fee and walked around the outrageously impressive ruins for much of the morning. I was in awe of how well everything had been preserved in the ash. To my young eyes the abandoned city resembled a giant movie set. At around midday I headed back to the gate, where I popped into the tourist café for a bite to eat. I was leaning against an ancient pillar eating my sandwich when I started talking randomly in my pan-euro accent again, just sounding it out. I began to mouth the words on the plaque in front of me out loud, just for fun. It was then that a rather large American woman approached me and started asking questions about the ruins. I think she assumed I worked there. So, not wanting to disappoint, I started making things up. She was soon joined by her friends and within a few minutes I was telling a group of onlookers a bunch of lies in a silly accent. This had never been my plan, it just happened organically. And what do they say about looking a gift-horse in the mouth?

I ended up ushering them around most of the ruins, just making stuff up as I went. It was supposed to be funny and I didn't really expect them to pay me, but pay me they did, and handsomely. I had stumbled on yet another way to make money. What a find!

I headed back to the café and picked up another unsuspecting group and began shuffling them around the ruins. With the second group in tow, I decided to read from the plaques a little more, using the smattering of information in English that was available. On top of this authentic information I would add facts that I had learned the night before and mix it all together with a heavy dose of bullshit. It was fun and worked like a charm.

I was harassed by a couple of official guides hanging around the entrance, but mostly I was left alone. I did this for the rest of the afternoon and by the time I returned to the campsite, my pockets were bursting with lire. I enjoyed making my own money, albeit in an unethical manner. It gave me a sense of self-worth and I felt quite entrepreneurial. I vowed to return the next day and do even better.

My second morning in Pompeii was going extremely well. I had a good number of tourists in my first group and was in the middle of my second tour when it all went wrong. I was out the door nice and early that day, avoiding my parents in the process. I knew they would be visiting that afternoon, so I wanted to shuttle as many groups through the ruins before they arrived on the scene and ruined my enterprise. Little did I know, but they had changed their plans and were just metres away from where I was spouting my own particular brand of gibberish.

My mother came around the corner and heard what she would later describe as 'this stupid voice talking loudly' and she immediately knew it was me. I had no idea anything was occurring until I looked up mid-sentence to see my dad's bearded face in front of me. I was horrified and he was furious. He grabbed hold of my arm and dragged me to one side. My tour group was puzzled by the turn of events, so my mother stepped in to explain; she informed my congregation that they'd been duped by a child who was making everything up as he went along. Suddenly I had two-dozen resentful eyes upon me. My mum promptly apologised on my behalf and we vanished down a stony verge.

I was escorted by the scruff of the neck back to the campsite and given quite the thrashing. My parents were far angrier with me than I expected. I didn't quite understand it. I thought they might even be proud after seeing me make money like that, especially as it was all my own idea. But they were not impressed, only embarrassed. I handed over my spoils and we left the following morning.

***

I awoke to a flash of white light. The most violent of thunderstorms had engulfed the train and it was unspeakably loud. Lightning surrounded us as heavy rain bombarded the carriage, which was now rocking from side to side in an alarming manner, made worse by the fact that we were travelling between two bodies of water. We were coming into Venice along a thin strip of land that linked the Italian marvel to the mainland. It was still dark outside and barely six in the morning.

The storm was still in full force when the train eventually pulled into the station. Most people decided to stay put in the carriages, waiting for the weather to break. All of a sudden there was an almighty crack followed by a metallic crashing sound. A bolt of lightning had struck a clock in the station and it now lay on the concrete with its face spinning to a stop. There were sparks coming from underneath and I think it was safe to say it was probably kaput. It was bloody scary. I had no idea storms could be so powerful.

Once the sun rose, the weather improved dramatically and it was time for us to go in search of our elusive campsite. We stepped out onto the bank of the main canal. The view was breathtaking; it resembled every James Bond film I'd ever seen. It also looked exactly like I'd imagined, only busier. The water was jam-packed with boat taxis ferrying commuters up and down the bustling canals. My nostrils imploded slightly. 'What the hell is that smell?' I wondered.

As it was rush hour, my dad decided to hire our very own private water taxi. He approached a ramshackle ticket office and asked to be taken to 'Piazza di Roma'. He then proceeded to hand over bricks of lire before walking down a wooden plank to a waiting boatman. My dad again asked, 'Piazza di Roma?'

'Sì, no problem,' replied our private sailor. He was very affable and we boarded his boat, taking our seats excitedly. From the 'Piazza di Roma' we were to take a bus to the campsite, which I had gathered was quite far away. My dad was clearly proud of himself, having managed to convey our needs to the boatman.

No sooner had we sat down than the man said, 'Okay, we here.'

My dad asked him again, 'Piazza di Roma?'

'Sì, Piazzale Roma, we here,' he said, finally correcting my dad. We had only travelled a few metres upstream and crossed to the other bank. It was clearly a scam. We could have easily walked over the bridge like everybody else, and for free. My dad became irate while my mum burst out laughing. This, of course, put him in a terrible mood, which would last for much of our stay.

The following day I wandered the streets of Venice alone, taking in the sights and hanging out with other foreign tourists. By mid afternoon, however, I was hiding under a café table trying to avoid my parents. They were out shopping for tat while I was chatting to a couple of pretty English girls in a nearby eatery. The moment they appeared I dived under the table, not wanting to be seen. However, once they were out of sight I decided to follow them. I wanted to observe them in the wild. I was intrigued to see how they behaved when I wasn't around. It was truly fascinating. They seemed to be getting on really well and looked like regular travellers going about their day. It just shows, you never can tell.

***

Once we arrived at the Austrian border I felt the air change. I opened my eyes to see two ferocious German shepherds showing their teeth and growling. They were accompanied by border guards and had clearly picked up the scent of my mother's epilepsy medication. This happened often, as there was an ingredient in my mum's tablets which made them flag up as a class A drug, and it also made those drug-detecting demon hounds go a bit doolally.

Regardless of how much we tried to explain, the guards insisted we get our bags down. So we did exactly that, with savage dogs nipping at our ankles. My mum showed the guards her pill bottles; they were clearly prescribed, displaying her printed name on each label. The guards were studying her passport trying to match up the name when the dogs started going crazy, no doubt due to the close proximity of her medication. It was then that we were asked to get off the train.

Professing our innocence, my mum and dad disembarked while the guards removed our luggage. However, I was told to stay put. I waited inside that compartment for about half an hour while they searched our belongings meticulously on the platform. There was a fair amount of shouting outside the carriage and I suspect my dad's hair length was again not helping, long hair often being associated with drug use. Our sideshow had obviously delayed the train and people were becoming tetchy. After much persuading from my mother, the border guards finally accepted her story and we were once again on our way, to the equal delight and disdain of the other passengers.

It was midnight when we arrived in Vienna, and that meant it was cold, shockingly so. After just a few moments in the freezing night air, my parents again decided that we would have to push on. It was simply too cold to stay. There was a train to Switzerland leaving in the small hours and they planned to be on it. I was so fed up with their speedy travelling. It seemed ludicrous to come to all these amazing places, only to leave.

My dad went off in search of tickets while my mum and I went off to get hot drinks. We found a small café in the station and she proceeded to order a black coffee. When the bill came she was sure there had been a mistake. 'Excuse me, is this right?' she enquired. It was the equivalent of around three English pounds, which was a fortune for a beverage at the time. To my utter dismay she paid it without flinching. She explained that she was desperate for a hot drink and needed to warm up at any cost. She made me promise not to tell my dad about the extortionate price, as he would no doubt be livid. I agreed. Still, I couldn't believe it cost three quid; that was insane.

Later, while on the train, my dad stopped a lady pushing a drinks trolley to ask how much a cup of coffee was. I thought that strange, as he rarely drank coffee, which was very much my mum's cup of tea. The woman relayed a similarly high price and he of course declined the purchase while mumbling, 'Jesus.' Once the woman was out of view he gave my mum a knowing look, his eyes thinning to slits. He knew.

Once we were in Switzerland, my parents, of course, wanted to go on to Germany – Hamburg, to be precise. We hadn't stopped moving since Venice and were in danger of seeing nothing of Austria or Switzerland. I could not imagine another full night on a train, and for what? We would be travelling the entire length of West Germany without ever stopping. This trip was becoming a joke. Were my parents allergic to hotels? I almost wished I wasn't going to all these places, since there was little chance of doing any actual sightseeing. I was promised a few hours in Basel before we moved on, so I made do with that, albeit begrudgingly.

We threw our rucksacks into a couple of lockers and headed out into the city. As we were consuming our Franco-Germanic lunch, my parents told me they had news. We would be going to England for the weekend to visit my dad's brother David in London. However, we would have to be vigilant, I was told, especially at the ports. I was bound to be on some sort of list, so we had to proceed with caution.

To me it seemed foolish to be taking such an enormous risk just to visit relatives for the weekend. I suspected there had to be a secondary reason for our visit.

The trip to London took another couple of days. Once we got to Hamburg we continued into the Netherlands and from Amsterdam took a boat-train combo all the way to London. The only significant event en route was when my dad gave me a thorough beating on the train, all because I couldn't wring out our washing to his usual high standard.

We were somewhere in Germany when I was ordered to clean our clothes using the WC at the end of our carriage. My dad pre-warned me that if I didn't get all the water out of the clothes, including our jeans, I would get a hiding. It was absurd. I did not possess the strength needed to complete the task at hand and was therefore being set up for a fall. Still, I tried with all my might, but I just couldn't manage it. I was twelve and he was a fully grown man. 'Why couldn't he do it?' I wondered.

During this beating he again acted like a coward. When anyone else got close he would stop hitting me, say something like 'How's your hole?' as they walked past, then wait. Once they were out of sight he would resume the violence. I was beginning to realise just how phony he was, especially around others. While he was hitting me I thought about running away once we got back to England. I had to wonder though, where on earth could I realistically go after everything that had happened?

***

I was surprisingly pleased to be back in my hometown of London. I didn't know the area in which we were staying, but it resembled exactly what I had been missing while living in Ireland. The area where David lived seemed to be made up of leafy avenues, parks and large red-brick houses. It looked fantastic to my young eyes.

We didn't stray far from my uncle's house, only venturing out for food to the local shops. The day after we arrived I was left in the company of my uncle and aunt while my parents travelled into Central London for a mysterious 'appointment'. I did not know these people at all, or their children. Although they were my cousins, they were complete strangers, like much of my family, I'm sad to say.

When my parents returned that evening I got to see a very different side to my father. From what I could tell, his relationship with David was far more authentic than the forced brotherly love he felt for Archie. They had a bond. David was taking numerous drugs and appeared quite gaunt. He was suffering from depression, a disorder that would ultimately lead him to reroute an exhaust pipe through his own car window a few years later, causing him to drift off to the next world. It was all very sad and I know his death caused my father a great deal of distress. But in 1982 the mood was lighter and we had a very memorable weekend.

At Charing Cross station on the Monday morning, however, things got weird. We had made our way from David's house with the intention of taking the late train to Dover, where we would catch an overnight boat back to France. My mum had just purchased our tickets, but had returned with only two. 'Okay, what's going on here?' I wondered. My mum and dad then whispered to each other conspiratorially while looking in my direction, before coming back over.

'We've been thinking,' said my mum.

'You're not coming with us,' blurted out my dad.

Excuse me, what? I was dumbfounded. My dad then handed me a five-pound note and told me it was time that we went our separate ways. *Huh? Why? What have I done this time?* I thought, racking my brain.

I had been looking forward to the next part of the trip. We were heading to Greece and I was excited by the prospect. But they had other ideas. My mum explained that I had been losing too many things of late and that those mistakes were becoming costly. It was, therefore, time for me to return to my grandparents. She went on to tell me that 'it just wasn't working out' and how they longed for time alone, without me.

I was mortified. I had planned to run away many times when things got rough, but I'd stuck by them in hope of change. Yet here they were throwing me to the wolves over a few bits of missing kit. I wasn't the only one who lost things. My dad had recently lost the tent, for fuck sake.

Their words hurt me terribly and I began to sob. I could not believe they were abandoning me again. After all we had been through.

Earlier that year my parents had fought a custodial case and lost, and still they didn't give up on me, so why now? What was the point of going through all of that if all they were going to do was bring me back to London and put me on a train a few months later? It made little sense.

My mum handed me a tube map and explained how to get to my grandparents' house. They told me that the fiver should be more than enough to get there. They suggested that I phone my grandparents before I arrived, just to make sure they were home. They began to load up their gear and within seconds were walking off towards the platform, waving goodbye. I stayed glued to a metal bench in total silence, with tears streaming down my face.

A few people came over to ask me what was wrong and as usual I told them to leave me the fuck alone.

My parents had often told me that by absconding with them to Europe I would be forfeiting any kind of future relationship with my grandparents. The fact that they had won the court case and still didn't get me back would have been a death knell. There could be no back-pedalling.

Therefore, I was convinced that my mum and dad hadn't thought it through. I could hardly rock up at my grandparents' door and expect them to take me in after all we'd been through. It was preposterous.

Just as I was about to descend into the bowels of the London Underground, I heard a familiar voice: 'Jesus.' It was my dad. My mum then piped up, 'Listen, we've been talking. If you promise not to lose anything else, you can come with us, okay?' I hastily agreed, sporting the biggest grin I could summon. She then added that if I lost one more item during our trip, I would be sent back to England in an instant. I nodded in agreement, relieved to be back in the game.

***

The next morning I was on a French train running parallel to the infamous beach at Dunkirk. I found myself staring meditatively at the sand as I recalled a story my granddad had told me regarding his experiences during the war. Early one morning he had been on that very beach, talking to some of the other soldiers in his regiment, when he heard a voice call his name just a few metres away. He ran over to see where the voice was coming from, but was instantly distracted by a huge explosion behind him. When he looked back, he could see that the soldiers he had just been talking to were now dead. He was in no doubt that he too would have died had he not investigated the alleged voice.

I was contemplating whether or not to be concerned by my granddad's ability to hear voices, when I suddenly became rather thirsty. I reached down to grab my water canteen but, alas, it was gone. *Oh dear!* I thought.

I decided to keep schtum as we made our way at lightning speed towards what was then the Republic of Yugoslavia.

CHAPTER 33

GREEK TO ME

The final part of our European escapade had begun, although I remained blissfully unaware of this fact. We had endured yet another night aboard a speeding locomotive, this time ploughing through the very heart of Europe before coming to a halt in the city of Zagreb.

There was a short break between trains, so I headed out into the Yugoslavian streets in order to quell my burgeoning appetite. Outside the station I spotted the perfect little food wagon selling copious amounts of unfamiliar hot food. I pointed towards something I deemed edible, a sort of pastry with spinach and what I now believe to be feta. I took a bite. It was revolting. But as I'd already paid for it, I was reluctant to give up and therefore soldiered on. After a few more mouthfuls I found that I wanted more. I had developed a taste for it. Even though the flavour was less than pleasant, I had become accustomed to it, so much so that I even considered buying another. However, there was no time for that. My parents were beckoning me and before I could say 'Croatia' I was on yet another iron horse, this time bound for Athens via Belgrade.

I was in and out of consciousness throughout the journey down to Greece, finally stirring as the train changed engines in Thessaloniki. I awoke fully to the carriage shunting forwards, finding myself in the midst of a heated debate. My dad was in deep conversation with a shifty-looking Greek fellow who had recently boarded the train. He appeared to be holding what I mistook for a stack of colourful envelopes. It transpired that he was offering Greek currency at a black-market rate and my dad was showing a keen interest. The man was pressuring him to part with more of our precious traveller's cheques in exchange for some rather large drachma notes. He mentioned conspiratorially that he had to get off the train before it departed, so my dad had to decide quickly if he wanted in on the deal. This alone should have set off alarm bells, but my father remained in gullible mode and promptly purchased the notes. He got a heck of a deal, apparently, almost twice the going rate. He was very proud of himself.

Once the train was moving, a rickety food trolley could be heard trundling its way into our carriage. On spotting this, my dad waved the pusher of said trolley over; the haggling had clearly spiked his hunger. After selecting a few snacks, he held out one of his newly acquired banknotes. The attendant smiled politely and returned the A3-sized currency with a side order of indifference. My dad, seemingly bewildered, asked why he wouldn't accept the cash, upon which the gentleman in question silently pointed at a date stamped clearly on the bottom of each massive note. It read '1939'.

The dodgy geezer, who had since departed the train, had offloaded some old-ass notes that were utterly worthless. My mum, as usual, was crying with laughter while my dad seethed in his seat. It was pretty funny from where I was sitting, but I dared not laugh. It did, however, feel pretty good to not be the one screwing up. In a matter of moments my dad had managed to lose over 200 pounds.

The train meandered its way into Athens, where we stepped out into the blistering heat of Greece. Our hotel was thankfully close by, so we didn't have to suffer too much at first. Upon arrival I ran to a nearby cold tap and drank until I could drink no more; water had never tasted so delicious. We threw our bags into our rooms and headed out into the white sun in search of luncheon.

My mum spotted a shabby café nearby which would have to suffice. We hadn't eaten a hot meal in days and weren't in the mood to be choosy.

Inside it was even more decrepit than the outside suggested. The menu was basic and the entire place seemed to be run by one old lady with extremely hairy arms and very dirty hands. As she took my order I noticed that grease had somehow accumulated in every visible crevice of the woman's skin. I felt a little shiver of disgust. Unfortunately that wasn't the only place I was going to see that particular substance that afternoon. When my meal finally arrived it was floating on a sea of the stuff. I had ordered eggs, which were delivered atop a bubble of thick greasy fat accompanied by a weird sooty black frosting, which I can only assume was ash. None of us could quite stomach the fayre on offer, so instead we decided to bail and go in search of alternative nosh. It was then that my dad spotted cake.

Without warning, my dad's hair took on a life of its own. With pastries shoved in our faces, my mum and I watched as his curly locks floated high into the air. It was a few seconds before he realised something was amiss, but, once he did, he started freaking the fuck out. It was beyond funny. From what I could tell, some kind of tropical flying beast had become entangled in his natural perm and was fighting to escape. Meanwhile my dad was hitting his own head as my mother looked on, trying not to wet herself. My father was far from amused. Once the creature was released, we headed back to the hotel in silence, my dad sulking while my mum and I tried to hold in our giggles.

When I got back to my room I unpacked my rucksack and began making up my bed. While tucking in the provided ripped sheet, I noticed something glistening beneath the headboard. I reached down to retrieve the shiny object, pulling it up between the slats. In my dusty palm sat a fluff-covered watch. I didn't recognise the brand but it looked relatively old and was quite dishevelled. One of the hands had come loose and was floating around underneath the glass. I popped it on my wrist, lay on my bed and attempted to sleep, none the wiser that I was in fact wearing a Rolex.

The room was like an oven that night and I could barely get a wink of sleep. However, the next day the hotelier invited everyone to relocate to the roof due to the intense heat building up inside the hotel and I, for one, took him up on the offer. I slept up there every night after that. It was much cooler and therefore more comfortable, even if it was a little noisy.

A couple of days passed before my dad spotted my watch. He seemed very keen on getting a good look at my find. He told me that it was the same kind of watch that James Bond wore and that it could well be worth something. He promised that once we got back to England, he would take me to a jeweller to get it fixed.

England? Ha! So we're not going to Africa then, I thought gleefully. He'd finally let it slip. All this time my mum had still been adamant that we were going to Kenya, but I'd had serious doubts about that for quite some time. Something was afoot; I just knew it, but what exactly? I had recently heard my parents talking about returning to England, but never Ireland. That seemed to be off the table altogether. It was all very mysterious.

***

Athens was a great city in which to wander, and I did just that. After a few days at my parents' side, I was off on my own again, exploring the ancient metropolis, often travelling to the port of Piraeus where tourists arrived in droves from the islands. While chatting with the new arrivals, one thing kept coming up: the confusing layout of the city. This led me to come up with a rather nifty plan to acquire some drachma notes of my own, though mine would belong in my pocket and not in a museum, like the ones my dad had stupidly purchased on the train.

I started offering my services at the port by accosting travellers and promising to guide them around Athens for a small fee, mostly shuttling people to and from the main train station, but occasionally visiting tourist sites such as the Acropolis en route. I was soon able to direct backpackers to most places with ease, utilising the old wooden underground trains as they wound their way through and under the ancient city. It was the best of times and for once I was actually earning an honest buck.

We stayed in Athens for about two weeks before we too headed off to the islands. My mum had bought the wrong tickets, apparently, but after a very long, violent and seasick journey we arrived in Mykonos. It was something of a party island and quite popular with the gay community. There were beaches assigned to almost every kind of sexual persuasion.

On Mykonos there were hoards of topless women as far as my eyes could manage to see. Even the mother of a kid I hung out with exposed her breasts right in front of me mid conversation. I was still a child and didn't really understand why I found topless women appealing, but I could barely keep my eyes to myself on that island. It was an intriguing time for a young chap. However, it soon became quite normal and it wasn't long before they were just bodies on a beach.

I would occasionally wander into the main town via the roasting hot beach. The sand would actually burn the soles of my feet, which was a new sensation for a boy from the cloud-covered islands of Northern Europe. While in town, I would often end up talking with the old codgers who sat around playing board games and guzzling Ouzo. They were a mixture of Greeks and ex-pats and were always up for a chinwag. I even got to try a little Ouzo myself. I was given a wee dram by an old fellow who taught me how to play backgammon. We played the entire afternoon, but, unfortunately, once I stood up all memory of how to play the game left me.

In Greece, my mum and dad continued their misplaced guidance when it came to water activities. After I got up the courage to snorkel, my dad snuck up behind me and held his hand over my breathing pipe. He thought it was hilarious that I was choking on salt water and swam away laughing. It did not exactly instil the confidence needed for me to continue with such things.

Around the same time my mother also developed an obsession where she would force me to dive into the sea from rocky cliff tops. I couldn't even swim properly, but she insisted I do it anyway. In her words, if I didn't dive 'I was a fucking coward'. If there were people close by, she would use them like an audience to egg me on. I hated her for making me feel so exposed.

We ended up leaving Mykonos in the smallest of planes. My mother tried to convince me that we were returning to Athens, but I was suspicious. I had never been on such a small plane before and it made me nervous from the outset. I could see that my dad was also not exactly keen on our chosen vessel. He seemed jittery and was clearly perturbed.

This was brand new information. I wasn't aware that my father even had fears, especially since he would often profess that no real man should ever be scared of anything. It was refreshing to know I wasn't the only one feeling anxious, I just wished I didn't have to share my misgivings with a hypocrite.

It was only my third-ever flight, and although I was still in awe of flying, this time I realised it may not be the safest way to travel. The idea of flying through the air in a tiny metal tube suddenly filled me with dread. Shortly after take-off, the plane banked dramatically to the left, then continued to head south. I had studied maps of the islands and could tell from the shape of the land below that we were not going to Athens, so I asked my mum where we were really heading.

'It's a surprise,' she said.

It better not be bloody Africa, I thought.

The plane almost hit the outer fence of the airport as it landed, giving us all a pretty good scare. I was relieved to be off that clown plane and back on terra firma, although I didn't know exactly which terra firma I was on. My mum soon informed me that we were now on the island of Crete, where we would be staying for about a fortnight before continuing our journey by boat. I suspected my dad had made that decision due to our bumpy ride in the sky, not that he would ever admit it.

***

My mum had some bad news; we were out of money. Apparently we could no longer afford to go to Africa. *Quelle surprise!* Therefore, we would now return to London and settle there instead. *Really?* I thought. *We've spent the whole six thousand pounds?* I couldn't see how. We had been living on bread and cheese and inedible tinned concoctions for months. Our tents almost guaranteed cheap accommodation and our travel was effectively pre-paid. I didn't believe a word of it. Don't get me wrong, I was delighted that we were no longer heading to Africa, but I remain convinced that we were never actually out of money. Although I myself had managed to spend every cent of my own booty.

I did have misgivings about living in the same city as my grandparents; surely that would be an issue? But I was keen to return to London regardless, mostly so that I could practice my newfound scamming skills. I was certain I could make a small fortune there. So, as we had effectively run out of road (and money?), we boarded a boat for the twelve-hour ride back to Athens. Our journey back to England had begun.

My mum explained that from Athens they planned to take a bus known as 'The Magic Bus' all the way back to London. *A bus? Are you mad?* I thought. The journey would take three days.

It was anything but magic. The dilapidated 1950s-style bus looked so out of place as it pulled up in the middle of Athens with 'KING'S CROSS' scrawled across its windscreen. My mother told me that the decision to take the bus was my father's. Ha, suspicion confirmed! It was four hours by plane or three days by bus; it would seem that he who looked down on fear was scared of something after all.

Within hours we were hurtling through the Yugoslavian countryside when there was an almighty bang, followed by a bit of swerving across lanes of traffic. The skilful driver somehow regained control and thankfully brought the bus to an abrupt stop, albeit in the middle of a busy motorway. The cause was a blown-out tyre. He informed us that it would be a while before we could resume our journey, as he had to raise the rear of the bus using only jacks. He then suggested that all passengers take refuge at a nearby restaurant he'd spotted on the other side of the road. I thought it fortunate that we had broken down so close to a hot-food option and was looking forward to checking out the cuisine; unfortunately my dad had other ideas. He refused to leave our belongings and insisted that we stay on the bus. He later revised this to 'if we wanted to eat something, then it would have to be beside the bus', giving us the opportunity of a take-away meal. It was then decided that my mother and I should wait by the coach while he went in search of suitable refreshments.

About twenty minutes passed before we heard my dad's potty mouth. He was using various expletives as he attempted to dodge Yugoslavian traffic, all the while balancing three plates of spaghetti bolognese about his person. The food looked awful but I grabbed my plate and dug in with gusto.

'Urgh!' It was stone cold.

My dad spat his first mouthful straight onto the tarmac. With his face crumpled in disgust he let out a solitary 'Jesus.'

He had no interest in walking all the way back to the restaurant, so I was nominated with the task of getting the food reheated. Off I shuffled with three cold spaghetti meals across a foreign motorway. I could not understand why we weren't just eating inside like normal people. All the other passengers were in the restaurant enjoying presumably hot food. It was all very avoidable.

I asked the people running the café to heat up our food, but I wasn't entirely sure they understood me. I didn't speak their tongue and they certainly didn't speak mine. When I got the plates back they did seem a little warmer, but by the time I was back at the bus they were somehow even colder than before. My dad was furious. Like the comedy sketch that it was, my mum was next in line to get our street dinner reheated. However, when she returned with the plates, she too appeared confused. The spaghetti was getting colder each time. They obviously didn't understand us. Perhaps microwave ovens in Yugoslavia operated in reverse? We realised the entire exercise was a waste of time when the driver piped up. He explained to us that in certain parts of Yugoslavia they ate pasta cold, even bolognese. He told us that they probably thought we were asking for it to be cooled down further each time. 'How would they do that?' I wondered. Upon this realisation my dad exclaimed that the Yugoslavians were indeed 'quare hawks'.

The bus continued its journey northward, working its way through Italy, Switzerland and France, getting ever closer to the land I once called home.

**

The final day of our European adventure may have been upon us, but there was still time to squeeze in one final plot twist. As the bus made its merry way towards Calais my mother dropped a bombshell. She told me that both her and my dad would be getting off the bus somewhere in northern France and I would have to travel the rest of the way alone. They wanted to go to Paris for the weekend before travelling back to Calais to pick up their stolen bicycles. They planned to join me in London the following week, but they weren't sure exactly when. 'What the fuck?' I mouthed.

My mum then tried to sell me on the idea by professing that I had less chance of being spotted by immigration officers if I was travelling alone. She suggested that, when I got to England, I should walk alongside a middle-aged lady whom they'd befriended on the bus. If I stuck with her, she said, I had a good chance of passing through undetected.

My dad then reached across the aisle of the bus and handed me a ten-pound note and a scrap of paper. The paper had a series of indistinct numbers scrawled upon it. My mum explained that it was my uncle Archie's telephone number. I was to call him as soon as I arrived in London. He would tell me what to do from there. My dad explained that Archie would probably arrange to meet me, so everything would work out fine. 'Probably? What if he doesn't answer the phone?' I pondered. Clearly forethought was not my parents' forte.

The bus soon pulled up at a remote bus stop somewhere in northern France and my parents jumped ship. They grabbed their bags, gave me a nod and vanished into the French countryside.

The fact that I was flying solo was exciting, in one way, but scary in another. I was also pretty apprehensive about going through customs. I was alone with a ten-pound note and a phone number. It was not ideal.

Once we arrived in England I disembarked from the ferry and entered immigration. This was the real test. I stuck close to the older lady, as my mother had suggested, hoping they would think we were together. My initial plan was to talk to her the entire time, but I was too nervous to speak and instead walked alongside her without muttering so much as a word.

When it was our turn the woman went to the kiosk on the right and I proceeded to the one on the left. I kept looking at her throughout and, although she was done first, she was kind enough to wait for me. The officer asked, 'Are you with her?' to which I replied with a rather high-pitched 'Yes.' He then stared at me for about as long as it takes to soft boil an egg. Just as I was getting worried – THUD! He'd stamped my passport, muttered 'There you go', and waved me in.

I couldn't believe it. I was back in the UK and everything was suddenly tip-top. However, as we left the outskirts of Dover the bus's destination was abruptly changed; we were now set to terminate at Camden Town. Although I'd heard of it, I had no idea where Camden was in relation to

Archie's flat and became concerned about how much further it might be.

As The Magic Bus wound through the London streets I felt both elated and apprehensive. I was happy to be back in the city of my birth and excited by the prospect of living there once again. Although, I was worried about the close proximity of other family members and about effectively being a runaway living in the very place I'd run away from, this fear was soon overshadowed by my urge to explore. I did not know London at all, really, and was eager to find my way around. It seemed impossible to comprehend ever knowing one's way around such chaos.

The bus pulled up alongside Camden Town tube station and we were asked to alight. It had driven me nearly 2,000 miles across Europe, but now it was time to say *adieu*. I grabbed my rucksack, thanked the lady who'd helped me and disappeared into the London night. It was Friday and the city looked exceptionally lively. There were hoards of drunks roaming around, shouting and smashing pint glasses, couples arguing and tramps in doorways with nicotine-stained beards talking to themselves. I soon realised that I would have to be on my guard in a place like this.

After making change, I found a pay phone within the station concourse and, with my fingers crossed, called the number I had been given. I was praying that Archie was home. It rang a few times before he answered. All my fears dissipated as soon as I heard his voice on the other end of that receiver. He instructed me on the best way to get to him and I followed his directions implicitly.

I descended into the London Underground system and negotiated the trains with ease, surfacing just twenty minutes later. As I exited the turnstile I could see a man who resembled my father wearing a flat cap. I hadn't seen Archie in years and he looked much older. He patted me on the back and seemed genuinely pleased to see me. We chatted excitedly as we walked towards his flat, which happened to be situated in a small high-rise close by.

On arrival I met his friendly wife, Helga, who showed me to my room and left me to get settled in. Later, over dinner, I watched in equal parts awe and dismay as they downed an enormous bottle of vodka between them; I was to find out later that this was quite the norm in their household.

Later that night, I sat on the bed and contemplated my newfound situation. I was back in mighty London – not Africa or Ireland, but bloody London – and it felt great. Best of all, my parents would not be returning for a few days, giving me ample time to explore and get up to no good. The city would be my playground until their arrival.

Let the games commence, I thought.

LONDON

1982-83

CHAPTER 34

LAND OF MILK AND HONEY

My European escapades may have been over, but London felt like a blank canvas on which I was eager to make my own mark. Archie didn't seem too fussed about what I got up to, so off I trotted, out into the wild summer sun in search of a little skullduggery.

From day one I carried on in much the same way as I had in Greece, talking to tourists and sneaking into attractions around Westminster. I was mesmerised by all that London had to offer and was finally old enough to fully appreciate how beautiful it was.

It was July and the city was alive with bipeds. The streets were awash with flag-toting, camera-wielding tourists, and Londoners who were trying to manoeuvre themselves around said tourists without becoming agitated. There was a constant buzz, and although I had visited many of Europe's premier sightseeing spots, I had never before witnessed such a density of people as this.

London was far bigger than I remembered; even the West End was tricky to navigate. In those early days I would get lost often, sometimes finding myself completely turned around. I made it my mission, however, to venture down every street and alley I came across just to see where it went, until I could find my bearings and form some kind of mental map.

As it was a scorcher of a summer, I often became thirsty and subsequently developed a penchant for Slush Puppies. I was pretty low on funds, having spent the remainder of my European spoils in Crete, so I could not afford to pay full price. Instead I struck a deal with a vendor who ran a machine close to the foot of Big Ben. I asked her if I could purchase the slush on its own without the added flavour and she happily agreed. From that day forth I would start my day by guzzling a non-flavoured slush for a mere five pence a pop, while strolling the streets looking for a way to make some moolah. I became pretty friendly with that vendor; she was the one welcoming face in a sea of strangers.

In addition to the West End, I also spent a fair amount of time hanging out in Camden. I was drawn to the neighbourhood via one of my favourite bands: Madness. They happened to be from the area and referenced many nearby locations in their lyrics. Even their album covers depicted places in the vicinity and I went in search of those sacred sites in earnest.

Camden Lock Market was a bit more ramshackle in those days and certainly less commercial than it is now. I would roam the stalls in awe of their varied stock from all over the globe; it was eye-opening to see so many random objects all in one place. I wasn't doing any kind of scamming, I was just observing and learning. I had a whole city to take in, and it was, in the true sense of the word, awesome.

North London was awash with used record stores and, although I wasn't exactly flush, the temptation to buy an album was too great. My dad had lent me his Walkman for the remainder of my journey from France and I would parade around Camden Town with that boxy oblong clipped uncomfortably to my hip, listening to his cassettes. However, because they were all his tapes, the experience felt somehow borrowed. I had therefore decided to purchase my very own copy of what was then, and still is, my favourite album: *Scary Monsters* by David Bowie. I listened to it constantly during our travels and it was very much the background score to my young life. I placed three pounds on the counter, popped on my orange headphones and walked out of the shop listening to the very first album I ever bought with my own coin.

My dad would later reprimand me for buying that tape, saying it was a waste of money as I could have always listened to his cassette. He couldn't comprehend why I would want my own copy. Funnily enough, he then started to denigrate the album, telling me how overrated he thought it was. He even tried to convince me that he didn't like Bowie, a ridiculous claim considering that he owned many of his albums and always professed that 'Heroes' was the best song ever written. This became a pattern. If I happened to like something he introduced me to, he would later deny that he'd ever liked it and try to convince me that it was rubbish.

***

It had to happen. Eventually, a few days later than expected, my parents returned, arriving at Archie's flat early one evening. I was relieved. Although I was having a grand old time in London on my own, I had wondered if I had perhaps been 'dropped off' at Archie's until further notice. I guess by this point I had abandonment issues. But here they were in the flesh, smiling and happy. They'd obviously had a good time in Paris, as my mother was positively glowing. That night there was a party atmosphere in the flat and out came the hard stuff. My dad had a couple of drinks, but I noticed that my mother was abstaining, which was unlike her.

It turned out that my parents had very big news. They explained to me that after years of trying in Ireland, my mum was finally pregnant. She had all but given up after many miscarriages led the doctors to believe she would never conceive again. But here she was with a little miracle baby in her belly, due just after Christmas.

I was overjoyed. I had little concept of what it would be like to have a younger sibling, but at least I would no longer be alone. Finally I would have someone else to relate to. We had turned a corner at long last, it seemed, and I began to look forward to the promise of better times.

Within days I accompanied my parents to a housing office, where they managed to get relatively close to the top of the list for emergency housing.

It was a major concern due to my mother's pregnancy. We desperately needed somewhere to live, and fast. Luckily, we were soon leaving Archie's flat, bound for temporary accommodation in a particularly swish part of North London where many rich and famous people lived.

I was impressed at being given such a prestigious area to live in by the council. I even had my own small room separate from my parents, complete with all necessary amenities including a pull-out bed. It was amazing. There were many varied people living in the house, all in their separate sections. My parents' room was one floor above mine, so we effectively lived apart, much like in Dublin. I preferred this arrangement, as it gave me a degree of privacy I desperately needed.

My mother soon became obsessed with baby purchases. Although they had quite a small room, she was already stocking up merrily. I would accompany her every other day to help carry her motherly bargains home.

My dad also took my Athens Rolex to be appraised and fixed. He asked me for it shortly after moving in, promising to return it as soon as it was repaired. Rather predictably, I never laid eyes on it again. He later told me that it was accidentally damaged, but not to worry as it was found to be worthless.

Hmmm, I seriously doubt that, I thought.

***

Even with the incessant shopping trips around North London, I still managed to find plenty of time to visit Central London. I was also about to devise my least ethical, but most effective, money-making scheme to date. It was simple and would work flawlessly.

While hanging out in Covent Garden I noticed quite a lot of volunteers collecting money for various charities. They would shake their collection tins under the noses of cappuccino-swigging tourists as they sat around eating overpriced sandwiches. The charity worker would ask for a small donation and I watched curiously as almost every person they asked gave them something. They would set aside their posh coffee and dig around in their linen pockets until they found an amount they were willing to part with. All this occurred to the backdrop of whichever street performer happened to be on the cobbles, no doubt up a ladder while singing and juggling.

I was strangely drawn to the milky froth that said tourists were gulping down, thinking how odd it looked. *My mum would never drink that*, I thought. She was an avid fan of post-war powdered milk; apparently, it kept her weight down. I then noticed that the collection boxes people were rattling bore an uncanny resemblance to the containers in which my mother's beloved milk came. It was then that I had my eureka moment.

I ran home, grabbed one of my mum's discarded powdered milk tins from the bin and headed down to my room. The moment I saw it I knew it was perfect. I would, however, need to make some kind of wraparound for it to be truly convincing. I placed it on my shelf and pondered my next move.

The following week I was accompanying my mother to a local building society, where she was intending to withdraw monies (this time legally, I might add). While we were waiting, the woman behind the counter asked if I would perhaps like a bookmark. I thought it was a bit of an odd question in what was essentially a bank, but I took one regardless. The bookmarks were to promote a lifeboat charity. I noticed that there were piles of the things on every counter. I then asked, 'Are you only giving these out at this branch?'

'Oh no,' she said. 'We're giving them out all over.'

Oh my goodness, eureka moment complete!

It was a rather unscrupulous plan, I know, but I wasn't thinking about the consequences of my actions or considering the ethics. All I wanted was to come up with the next way of making money and possibly impress my parents in the process.

Therefore, the very next day I returned to the same branch of the building society and asked the woman behind the counter for the form needed to open a child's account. As she reached for the form, I used my right arm in a sweeping motion to slide a large pile of bookmarks into my waiting bag. She did not see or suspect a thing.

I thanked her and left with a huge smile. I ran up the hill to our temporary home and retrieved the milk tin from the shelf, attacking it with a glue stick and scissors. It wasn't long before my collection tin looked pretty authentic. I was ready.

My plan was simple. I would visit busy tourist areas throughout Central London and ask for donations. Whenever I received money, I would give that person a bookmark, in the same way as you might get a sticker. This was the convincer. If I wasn't collecting for the lifeboat charity, how could I possibly have so many of their bookmarks? Also, the building society wasn't big enough for everyone to be aware of the promotion. It was a good scam and, I'm ashamed to say, it was executed perfectly.

I began by putting some of my own small change inside to get the traditional rattling sound up and running, then headed off into the fray. On the very first day my tin was full to the brim within a couple of hours. Once I emptied the tin, I was astonished to find that I had collected almost twenty pounds. I could not quite believe what I had stumbled upon.

I made so much cash that summer that it was hard to know what to do with it all. I would only ever rattle my tin for a few hours each day, mostly in and around Covent Garden, and only ever in the morning. My afternoons were spent solely in the company of a group of street performers who had, over time, befriended me. I thoroughly enjoyed watching their shows, as many of them seemed to possess superhuman skills. They attempted to teach me how to juggle and eat fire, but I was not a natural and what I did learn I soon forgot.

I continued this wicked practice without a hitch. The only real problem I encountered was acquiring more bookmarks. I began to travel further afield to smaller branches, but often they would only have a handful scattered around the countertop. Our local branch was still my best bet, so I continued to pop in often, using distraction techniques and hoping for the best. I always wondered if they noticed the missing bookmarks, as sometimes I would take every last one. How could they not?

I received donations from every spectrum of society. On one occasion even a young policeman approached me. As the blood rushed to my face, he simply reached into his pocket and pulled out a fifty pence piece and popped it into my souped-up tin. My heart was racing, but within seconds he had vanished back into the crowd. Even Archie spotted me one day and gave me a small donation. I was sure he would rumble me and tell my parents, but he never did. My only real mistake was sticking to one area. I adored Covent Garden and, as the footfall was huge, I felt no inclination to move on. I guess I just got lazy. Then the obvious happened.

I was collecting, as usual, when I heard an angry voice shouting. I looked up to see a man pointing in my direction. He then started to run towards me, which led me to bolt at speed. I threw my tin on the cobbles, hoping to slow him down in a cartoon-like manner, running through the back streets towards Leicester Square, ducking in and out of alleyways to evade capture. Thankfully I managed to lose him, but I had also lost my moneymaker.

I'd had a blast hanging out in Covent Garden, but clearly it was too dangerous to return. I reckoned a change of location would make little difference, as the police could well be on the lookout for someone of my description collecting money in exchange for bookmarks. It had been fun while it lasted, but evidently it was time to stop that particular con.

Eventually I told my mum about my exploits and admitted to making quite a lot of money. I explained exactly how I'd done it, in the hope that she might be impressed. I wanted her to know that I too could come up with great ideas. She wasn't mad at me as such, but she did think I was nuts to have done something so blatant. She promised not to tell my dad if I agreed never to do it again and to avoid Covent Garden for a while. I agreed. In fact, I didn't return to that area for at least a year. I also stopped most of my scams, keeping only my 'fifty pence jobs' in the mix.

For this I would hold a fifty pence coin in full view as I perused the frozen treats on display in various ice-cream fridges. Then, just as I was about to pay, I would throw a washer or a two-penny piece under the fridge and profess it was my now-pocketed fifty pence piece. I always got another one from the till or a free ice cream, as most shopkeepers were reluctant to move the heavy fridge. They would also nearly always feel sorry for me, mostly because I would turn on the waterworks if they didn't oblige.

Still, for now, I had money in my pocket and set about enjoying the final days of summer in a more stress-free way. I decided to spend a fraction of my ill-gotten gains on a small Russian television. It was made by a company called Vega and was total rubbish. The body of the TV was ridiculously long and its black and white screen was just four inches wide. There were two dials for tuning, and reception was generally terrible, but I wanted it nonetheless. Bizarrely it had a built-in radio on top with an aerial that stretched to the ceiling, so I was also able to listen to music in my room. I felt like I had a nice little set-up in my North London bedsit.

***

During this period I developed a couple of worrying tendencies. One was the throwing of knives. Although I'd been hanging out with jugglers and street performers throughout the summer, this odd practice was unrelated. It was different. I was testing myself in some way.

I would throw a large, sharp knife high into the air above my bed and then try to catch it. However, I would always throw and catch it by the blade. If I didn't, it was a fail and didn't count. I practised an awful lot and miraculously I never cut myself once. It was pure luck, I'm sure. It was a mad way to spend my evenings, but alas this was not to be the only incident involving knives to occur around this time.

Late one night, while standing at the foot of my bed, I heard a scraping sound. It was coming from beneath me. I looked down to see an enormous knife moving violently from left to right under the door. I was terrified and jumped up onto my bed, where I waited for it to stop. It was a massive blade and I was surprised it hadn't caught my toes. After a few more rounds of knife tennis the blade simply retracted and disappeared. I dared not go outside that night, instead opting for the safety of my duvet.

I suspected this was a mind game executed by my father, although he always denied it. He reckoned it must have been the guy from Trinidad, who lived in the next room, practising some kind of 'voodoo shit' on me. The guy next door had indeed befriended me and I would talk to him about all manner of subjects. I don't doubt that I drove him crazy with my incessant chatter, but he was a friendly fellow and I liked the way he used to always call me 'boy', but with an accent that made it sound like 'bai'. My dad didn't like me talking to him, or anyone in the house for that matter. He didn't want anybody knowing our business. The knife under the door, I am sure, was meant to reinforce this.

The other odd practice in which I used to indulge is a touch more embarrassing, but, as my dad used to say, 'any truth unspoken is a lie'. I therefore have no choice but to put it into words for your reading displeasure.

I was now rather annoyingly hitting puberty, and with that came a certain awakening. Why it couldn't have happened while I was in Greece surrounded by naked women I will never understand. Instead, it surfaced later that same year in a shoddy bedsit in fancy-pants North London. Without being too graphic, I noticed something arise one afternoon while ogling a semi-naked girl in *The Sun* newspaper. This led me to collect as many varied copies as I could muster in order to enjoy my newfound pastime. I must say, as an adult, I find the idea of page-three models abhorrent, but for a twelve-year-old boy it was a bloody godsend.

The most bizarre element that accompanied this practice was something I used to do in the dark of night alone. It didn't last very long and I only did it a few of times, but in a way, I became a little addicted to the thrill.

I would wait until I was sure that everyone in the house was asleep, then I would creep out of my room and head for the front door. Once I was sure there was nobody around, I would disrobe down to my birthday suit. I then stuck one of my shoes in the doorway to keep it open, as I didn't have pockets for keys, obviously. I would then make a run for it. I would run around the local streets completely nude. I didn't venture very far and I did not want to be seen. I would jog in little spurts and hide behind bushes or post boxes. It was cold at night and I liked the way the air felt against my skin. It felt freeing and natural, although it was anything but natural to be doing such a thing in the leafy confines of North London. I don't know what I was thinking exactly and I always reprimanded myself afterwards for having done something quite so strange. I was fully aware that dodgy characters could well be lurking nearby, but I didn't care about that. I also don't think it was sexual per se; it had far more to do with being invisible. I was approaching thirteen and was beginning to feel all sorts of strange urges. I guess this was just one of them.

CHAPTER 35

TENTERHOOKS

I thought my parents had mellowed, especially with a new baby on the way. However, once we got settled in our new house, things soon got back to normal and punishments were dished out in much the same way as they had always been. I was getting older, so my dad had to come up with new ways of debasing me. His new method was nothing less than vile.

He would knock on my door, which meant that I had to 'let him in', as if he were a fucking vampire. He would then stand there, with that half smile on his face, and give me his speech: 'This is going to hurt me far more than it will ...' blah, blah, blah. Then he would ask me to remove my shirt and lie face down on my bed. Only then would he begin. This punishment was all about my back. He would punch me full-fisted into my middle to lower back area until I could take no more. The pain was excruciating and he would pound my spine so hard that I would have trouble walking afterwards. Due to my mattress being so narrow and thin, my nipples would often slam into the raised wooden frame of my bed, causing them to bleed. This has led to me having a very sensitive chest area throughout my adult life. I cannot bear anyone to even brush past my nipples, let alone touch them, even now. And it's all because of that fucking monster.

My mum's punishment tactics were less brutal but equally disgusting. She had started to cook with a horrid, inedible vegetarian mince substitute. I could not stomach it. The taste was awful, never mind the smell. I detested it so much that if I consumed even a morsel, I would almost certainly throw up. My mother noticed my aversion and decided to use it against me.

She and I would play card games such as gin rummy most afternoons, often for money. If ever I lost the game and couldn't pay up, my forfeit would be to eat a bowl of the aforementioned disgusting foodstuff. All I can say is, I'm glad I wasn't vegetarian in 1982. And as far as the card games went, I'm pretty sure I still owe my mum around fifteen pounds.

***

Summer gave way to autumn and with it came the prospect of yet another new school. This was to be the roughest institution I would ever attend. The kids were both street-smart and hard as nails. Entering that environment as a stranger was never going to be easy, but the level of physical and mental abuse I attracted was overwhelming. As soon as I stepped through the main gate it was as if I had been transported to the inside of a penitentiary, a comparison enforced by the high fence that followed the entire perimeter of the school. Each section was topped off with barbed wire and a CCTV camera mounted on the highest of poles, adding to that Big Brother/watchtower feel.

I had a truly awful time in this school. At first, I was constantly referred to as a 'batty man', a slur that I soon found out meant gay. However, compared to the rest of my day, that was merely a mild irritation. It was a thoroughly unwelcoming institute where allegiances had clearly been formed over a number of years, which meant that I had no chance. Although I was also pretty street-smart myself, I failed to gel with a single attendee of that school.

One kid seemingly offered the hand of friendship during my first lunch break, but even that turned out to be nothing more than a prank. As I was from a poor family, I received free school meals. This meant that each day I was given a blue plastic disc, which I could present as alternative payment for food. So I asked the semi-friendly kid if he knew how much the disc was worth. He told me I could have anything I wanted, it didn't matter; my lunch was free regardless. I greedily piled my tray full of goodies and made my way forward down the line. I handed my solitary blue disc to the dinner lady, who snatched it, popped it in the register and asked for extra money on top. I was confused, but not for long. I looked around to see the other kids laughing. The little shits! I had to put most of my grub back, as I was only entitled to the most basic of lunches, which inevitably happened to be the worst food available.

The top arsehole of the entire experience was a tall Jamaican kid who would throw my pens and pencils on the floor during lessons and wait for me to retrieve them. Once I bent down to pick them up, he would stand on my fingers with all his weight, pinning me down while laughing at me from above. He was my age, but he looked about eighteen. That prick made my life a fucking misery.

One memorable afternoon a stink bomb was detonated inside the cafeteria during lunch, causing the school to be evacuated and many meals to be ruined. I somehow got the blame for this, even though I was not on school property at the time. The perpetrators had got together and set me up. Upon my return I was dragged into an office, whereby the deputy head began accusing me, telling me I could be expelled for my actions. I tried to explain, but he'd already picked up the phone to call my mother. My heart dropped. Later that night my dad administered a thorough beating for something I absolutely did not do. By this point I was the boy who cried wolf in my parents' eyes, so my denial meant nothing. Not content with making my school day a hellish experience, those little fuckers were now affecting my home life as well.

Something my dad did not find out about, thank the Lord, was a crime I did commit. Yes, I realise the irony in this. I was up to my old tricks again and was now partaking in what I liked to call 'money-back jobs'. I would go into local shops and, in much the same way as I had done in France, pick up an item quickly, walk straight up to the counter and demand a full refund. I would state that I had bought the item previously and had subsequently changed my mind. What I liked about this scam was that I could never be accused of shoplifting per se, as I never actually took the item from the premises. All the shop assistants could legally do was deny the refund and throw me out. At that point I would simply leave the disputed item behind, feign outrage and skedaddle. No harm done.

One fateful afternoon, however, I became careless. My golden rule was 'never hit the same place twice'. But I was running out of shops to exploit locally, so I decided to make an exception. There was one particular shop where I thought perhaps enough time had passed for me to have another crack. It was a huge lapse in judgement. Within seconds of walking in I was caught red-handed. The shopkeeper was also now aware that I had scammed him previously, which meant I could technically be charged with stealing.

Luckily, the police weren't called. The shopkeeper merely escorted me back to school, where I was once again taken to the deputy head's office. I was of course banned from the shop and ordered to reimburse him for my previous indiscretion, but that was all.

So there I was in the same office in a similar predicament, only this time I was actually guilty. I was told that they were going to call my parents again and at that point I broke down. I pleaded with the deputy head not to phone home. I wasn't trying to garner sympathy or anything of that sort, I simply did not want to get hit any more. I had taken my fill.

Somehow my tears got through to him and he hung up the phone. I had been given a final reprieve. It was agreed that, as a compromise, I would spend all future lunch periods on school premises and avoid the nearby high street altogether. I happily agreed and thanked him for his mercy.

***

When I wasn't at school or wandering around Central London, I would frequent a local youth club. Many troubled kids hung out there, so I fitted in surprisingly well. The downside was that the club attracted skinheads. They would often play pool in a separate room out back, and it was in this room that, one afternoon, I found myself in danger of getting a good thrashing.

A couple of shaven-headed fools approached me and began shoving me around. I reacted by calling them a bunch of wankers, which resulted in the leader of the pack coming right up into my face. Then, just before the first of what I assumed would be multiple punches, he said, 'Hey, do you like Madness?'

Huh? I thought.

He pointed to the little two-tone badge on my lapel. 'Yeah, I love them,' I replied nervously. Suddenly I had the arm of a violent skinhead around my shoulder while we discussed the merits of their new album versus their last. The incident was soon forgotten; even one of the boneheads who'd originally pushed me around came up to me afterwards and said, 'You're alright, mate.' High praise indeed.

The youth club was set to be knocked down in order to make room for yet another beige office block. All of us in attendance were opposed to this atrocity, some more than others. I took such personal offence that, once the bulldozers arrived, I planned a little payback. I had spotted a pay phone within the site and decided to smash it open. I had a fondness for relieving machines of their booty, having recently worked out the exact spot in which to strike a certain tube-station vending machine to guarantee a platform coin spill. I figured I could possibly do the same with the phone box.

I gathered a few like-minded souls and climbed the fence. We tried a number of ways to open up the coin box, all to no avail. Even with our combined might, it just would not budge. We didn't want to hang around long enough to be discovered, so we decided to remove the entire thing. I picked up a nearby pickaxe and swung it at the phone. It took some effort, but after a few good blows the entire contraption was hanging by a thread. I had seen a couple of guys in Dublin run out of a pub with a complete phone box earlier that year and thought that we could perhaps do the same. If we severed it, we could always empty it later. Still, no matter how hard I tried, the bloody thing just would not separate from its thick cables.

One of the other kids handed me a hacksaw and I began cutting in earnest. It took a while to chop through the dense cables, but eventually we had the whole thing on the deck. Before committing to carrying the heavy metal box over a high fence, I thought I'd try one last lunge of the pickaxe while it was still on the floor. With a huge effort I swung the axe. On impact the beast finally flew open, sending bronze and silver in all directions. It was mostly small change and many coins were green with mould, but we swept every last one up regardless, shoving them into our pockets before absconding. It was a heck of a thrill and I felt like a vigilante, when in truth we were actually just being vandals.

**

The festive season was on its way, as was the baby, but first it was time to pick out my own Christmas present. I had my eye firmly fixed on a stereo. I had recently bought a couple of cassettes but had no real way of playing them. Access to my dad's Walkman had diminished somewhat, so my parents offered to buy me a boombox, but only if I paid half. They explained that if I gave them fifteen pounds, I would receive exactly what I wanted. So, begrudgingly, I handed over the dosh.

Once Christmas rolled around I was given my present. I immediately thought it was a bit small. Still, I ripped at the packaging enthusiastically, excited at the prospect of owning my very own ghetto blaster. Unfortunately what I got was definitely not that. It wasn't even a stereo. It only had one bloody speaker! I was so disappointed. My mum said it was all they could afford and I soon realised my 'one speaker jobbie' had probably been bought solely with the funds I had provided. They were always so tight when it came to presents for me. The impending arrival of my sibling had made them stingier than usual, it would seem.

I realise that many children have jealousy issues surrounding the birth of a sibling. However, I did not experience any of this, perhaps because I was older. I could not wait to be a brother and was on tenterhooks wondering who might be coming. It felt very much like a new dawn and I remained convinced that the life of my immediate family was about to vastly improve.

My baby brother arrived on New Year's Eve, just in time for lunch. I was waiting anxiously when my dad delivered the good news. He resembled a different man entirely; he was elated and seemed light on his feet. He told me that he'd arranged for me to stay with Archie for a few days while he wrapped things up in North London, as we were moving to a flat in the south-east of the city the following week. He would drop me off at Archie's flat and rejoin me later that evening, so we could bring in the New Year together.

I finally had a sibling and it felt strange. I could not wait to see the little fella, but that would have to wait until the following morning. 'Jesus, come on, let's go,' said my dad hurriedly, as he grabbed my belongings and bundled me into the car.

Admittedly, we didn't get very far at first. My father had a penchant for automobiles and, having acquired yet another model, he took me for the shortest of rides. We had come to a complete stop just up the hill from our flat. He turned off the engine and told me he had something very important to impart. He explained how everything was going to be different from here on out; for one, there would be no more beatings: I was too old for that now, apparently. But more importantly, it was imperative that my little brother became the main focus in my life and that I vow to protect him, no matter what.

It was welcome news that I would no longer be physically abused, but why was he telling me this stuff? I already possessed these feelings towards my just-born sibling and did not need to be told, especially by someone who never seemed to show empathy towards another living soul. Although I was yet to see my brother in person, my protective impulses were already in overdrive. I was also acutely aware that his mere existence had indirectly saved me from a terrible fate. I no longer believed my mother's story regarding us running out of money on our European trip. It was clearly the pregnancy that had brought us back to London and finally put a stop to their crazy African plans. As a result, I was thankful to him long before I ever met him.

It later transpired that my mother had taken my father to one side before she was ever admitted to hospital, hence our roadside summit. My dad was told in no uncertain terms that he was not to touch a hair on my brother's head. She told him straight that if he ever hit him, she would leave in a heartbeat.

My dad agreed to her terms. All beatings ceased immediately and my dad tried his best to change. Although he came close a couple of times, I can honestly say that my father never raised his hand to me again. The violence was finally over.

On the night of my brother's birth, an impromptu party broke out at Archie's flat to celebrate his arrival. As it was also New Year's, alcohol was plentiful and the vibe was very merry indeed. My dad, while trying to stay sober, kept passing his glasses of Pernod on to me. He would later try and convince me that he thought Pernod was non-alcoholic. It was not. I got completely wasted, blind drunk in fact.

I was in great spirits when I eventually went to my room. I stood upright on the bed and let myself fall forward onto the pillows. I laughed as I hit the mattress at full force. I did this many times while giggling. I was inebriated, happy and relieved. I went to bed that night confident that the birth of my brother had changed all our lives for the better.

On New Year's Day I visited the hospital to see my baby brother for the very first time. I was immediately struck by how tiny and red he was. It was abundantly clear that my mum loved him with every ounce of her being. I saw something new in my parents that day which gave me hope, and I looked forward to us moving on as a family. I was convinced that – after many false dawns – we had finally reached a turning point.

CHAPTER 36

A STONE'S THROW

With a babe in arms we moved into our new flat, which was situated within a vast ugly housing estate in South-East London. The complex was an interwoven labyrinth of concrete blocks and overpasses made up of damp walkways, flaky railings, overfilled high rises and all manner of dodgy-looking nooks and crannies. It was very much an environment that seemed to cultivate crime and substance abuse. A walk home would mean enduring numerous unlit stairwells that smelled solely of urine, even more so than the putrid metallic lifts that sat abused at each end of every corridor. Luckily, we were on the first floor of one of the newer blocks. It was served by a wide concrete ramp that led down to some of the raunchiest-looking shops I had ever seen. It was nothing short of horrid and a far cry from idyllic North London, but as that accommodation had only ever been temporary, our new abode would have to do. According to my mum, it was the best of a bad lot.

My dad used his renovating skills to make the flat liveable. I had my own bedroom complete with Coca-Cola lampshade and various items from Habitat, which just so happened to be my favourite store. I particularly liked the bendy desktop lamp for which they were famous, and my dad had bought me one in jet black. I loved it.

My brother was still incredibly small, and once we'd moved in I posed for a couple of photographs with him in my arms. It was odd to be holding your own sibling as a baby, looking down into his innocent little eyes, wondering who was in there. 'Can he see me?' I wondered. 'Does he know

I am his brother?' I became acutely aware of just how delicate and precious he was in that moment and promptly handed him back to my mother. She was extremely attentive towards him in those early months; she was positively smitten. Incidentally, until he was born I had no idea just how much my mother loved babies and everything to do with babies! It was a side of her I had never seen before. Although it was wonderful, I barely recognised the woman.

For once I was hoping to move schools. Once we'd moved across the city I was certain a new school would be on the horizon. My parents, it turned out, had other ideas. They thought it would be far easier for me to take the Underground the ten or so miles each way, rather than disrupt my education further. They had finally taken into account my hatred of constantly moving schools. Great, now they listened to me! When I was in the worst school ever. Brilliant.

In the early 1980s, children in London who lived a certain distance from their school were given a free travel pass, which could be used seven days a week. This was not limited to the school route either; it covered the entire city. At first I was reluctant to commit to the two-hour round-trip, but after a while I realised the tube was a pretty cool way to travel to school, and having the pass was a massive bonus.

A new year had arrived and with it came my need to be a better me. I therefore decided that my scamming days were over. My exploits were causing me way too much grief, plus now that we lived in London there were too many added dangers. I also had visions of becoming like my parents and I didn't like that idea one iota. I had a little brother now and couldn't risk being taken away from him. I had made my decision; I was going straight.

I managed to secure a paper round close to our block, which I hoped would enable me to earn a decent wage and therefore become an obedient member of society. I was used to filling my pockets with cash without breaking a sweat, but those days were behind me. I would have to get used to having a lot less. It was backbreaking work for very little reward and I loathed it, but I refused to give up. The sheer amount of newspapers I had to deliver was ridiculous. My route seemed to cover the entire estate, making me wonder if I might be the only person delivering papers in the area. It was exhausting stuff and for my trouble I received a meagre four pounds a week, an amount I could usually raise in a couple of hours.

The absolute turd in my glass was Sundays. Although the newspapers weighed twice as much due to supplements, I didn't receive a single extra penny. Also, as it was double the weight, it took twice as long to deliver.

I may have disliked the work, but I did enjoy the legitimacy of it. Earning my own money made me feel like 'more of a man' than simply stealing it, regardless of how low the wage was. I kept that stupid job the entire time I lived there, which, as it turned out, wasn't very long.

My dad, too, avoided the easy route of making money by illegal means, instead opting to return to full-time work as a bricklayer. It was the responsible choice and I took my theoretical hat off to him for doing so. My mum, however, more than made up for it by claiming every social benefit she could put her name to. She used a combination of our real names and some fake monikers, even claiming money for me using my actual name. How nobody made the link and came looking for me is a wonder.

***

I developed another short-lived addiction while living on the estate. I had never slept in the shadow of such tall buildings before, and although they made me nervous and triggered feelings of vertigo, I couldn't help but ascend them. I used to travel in the rickety lifts up to the twenty-fourth floor, alight all jelly-legged and peer down at the buildings below. I liked it up there; it was private. I have always found a place to go, wherever I have lived or been schooled, that is solely mine, a hiding place if you will. It was therefore important for me to have a sanctuary during this period, and that place was the top floor of a high rise.

Even though the experience of looking down would make the backs of my knees tingle and give me a feeling akin to falling, I couldn't help but go up. I liked the confused feeling of fear and excitement that it triggered within. I even had a favourite tower. Above this block's highest reachable floor was a kind of half floor, which I assumed was used by janitors and such. It was on this section of staircase that one of the windows had been either removed or broken. I would perch on the edge of this particular frame and look directly down, daring myself to lean over the edge. In addition to simply going up there I eventually added an extra thrill to the mix.

I had previously noticed a large amount of overfilled bin bags near the lifts. So, for reasons I still don't quite understand, I took one with me all the way to the top. Once I got to the missing window I paused and took in the moment – something special was about to happen. I hung the bag over the edge and held it outward. I wasn't sure if I would actually let go, but before I had time to think about my actions it was falling through the air. I watched as it circled around the entire tower, going out of view on its way down. Once it got to the bottom I heard a loud crash and watched as dust rose from the impact. I waited to see if anyone would react or if perhaps the police would be called. Nothing happened.

I got such a thrill from this pursuit that, instead of running away, I went back down to the ground floor to get another heavy bag. I continued this bizarre behaviour for a number of days before I realised the potential dangers of what I was doing. What if the bag landed on someone? At that velocity it could easily kill them.

Although I never threw another bag, I did continue to visit my secret staircase. It was a place where I could escape the world and watch other people's lives play out beneath me. I felt a bit like a cat stuck up a tree, except I wasn't stuck. I wanted to be there.

***

We hadn't been living in South-East London very long before my actions caused a tectonic shift. I had lived with my baby brother for barely two months when I set off for school on a crisp, pivotal winter's morn.

It was a bit of a trek to the tube station, but I liked my morning walks; they gave me valuable time in which to think. It was nearing the end of a cold spell and I was looking forward to warmer times. Life at home was improving and I was enjoying spending time with my little brother. My parents had softened since my brother's arrival; even my father was showing signs of tenderness. I loved my tiny sibling for many reasons, but mostly for bringing us all closer together.

Usually I was in a rush to catch my train, but on this particular day I didn't have quite enough to eat for breakfast, so I decided to grab a snack from a newly opened shop within the station. I opened the door to the shop, prompting a bell to ring loudly above my peckish noggin. I continued to the back of the shop towards a mountain of potato snacks and picked up a packet of cheese and onion crisps before heading for the counter. As I approached, a thick Scottish accent bellowed the words, 'You. Out!'

I was convinced that the shopkeeper was talking to someone else and ignored him, continuing towards the register. The man became further enraged and started hurling abuse in my direction while insisting I leave.

I had no clue why this nut job was accosting me in this manner. It was the first time I'd set foot in his stupid shop, what was his problem? Getting someone mad at me before they've even met me was a skill I did not know I possessed. I tried to reason with him, explaining that it was clearly a case of mistaken identity, but his mind was made up. He came around the counter, snatched the packet from my hand and manhandled me out of his shop. That pissed me off royally and I began to see red.

Once outside, my anger surfaced and before I knew it I'd picked up the first stone I could find. I grabbed a perfectly rounded pebble from the pavement and launched it at the shop's window. I didn't give any thought to what I was doing at the time; it was as if it was happening to someone else entirely. To my horror the pebble hit the window in the sweet spot, shattering it instantly. Glass poured out into the street right before my eyes and I quite literally shat myself.

My response was to run like the wind. I legged it back into the station with the intention of jumping on the first train out of there. Unfortunately once I got down to the platform I could see via the display that the next train wasn't for four minutes. I looked for somewhere suitable to hide and noticed that behind some of the benches were recesses resembling alcoves. I threw myself inside the closest one and huddled in the corner trying not to make a sound.

Then I heard him; the commotion of an angry Scot on a platform. He was mad as hell and wanted blood, my blood. I stayed still, hoping I could make a run for it once the train arrived. I even considered running across the tracks but was concerned about getting electrocuted in the process. The shopkeeper was walking down the platform in my direction, spitting expletives, when I noticed an Underground worker on the opposite platform point in my direction. I was screwed.

The next thing I felt was the tugging of my hair. The angry shopkeeper dragged me kicking and screaming up the staircase solely by my bonce. Once we were through the turnstiles and back in his shop he threw me down on the floor and locked the door. The whole experience was dreadful and I found myself in a right pickle. Making a run for it was out of the question. I lived locally and travelled to school along that route daily. Even if I managed to escape, I was sure to be spotted eventually. I was mad at myself for being so reckless. Why did I respond by throwing a bloody stone? I was also furious at him for starting the whole kerfuffle in the first place.

I tried one last time to explain that I had never been in his shop before and couldn't understand why he'd thrown me out. It dawned on me as we both stared out of the broken window that none of that really mattered any more. He informed me that the police were on their way, so it was too late to try and talk my way out of it. He subsequently became calmer and a tad reflective. Perhaps he realised that I wasn't the kid he originally thought I was.

A squad car came screaming past at high speed complete with flashing lights and piercing siren. My heart skipped a beat, but luckily it went by without stopping. 'Phew!' I was relieved. Then it backed up. I saw it come back into view as it reversed and my insides tightened. Shit! It *was* for me. The severity of what was happening became crystal clear and I gave in to the fact that I was probably not going home that day.

A police officer took me to one side and demanded my name and address. I was reluctant to admit to where I lived and attempted to hide my travel pass, as it contained my full name. I figured if they discovered my name it would trigger an instant alert and I would be sent back to my grandparents.

I gave the officers a modified version of my name and they began relaying the details via their radios. As they bundled me into the panda car it all got a bit real. Until that point the whole experience had been a little dreamlike, but now it was turning into a waking nightmare. I had a newborn baby brother at home and my mum was no doubt getting him ready for the day as I sat in the back of that squad car. She would have been feeding and changing him with no clue that her eldest son was about to come home with the police in tow.

Somehow they knew where I lived. Even though I gave them only a vague clue pertaining to my identity, we were whizzing our way towards our flat within minutes. I can only assume that they knew my address by virtue of my mother's child benefit claims.

We pulled up outside the block where I lived and I nearly wet myself in fear. I was so bloody scared. I prayed that my dad wasn't still home – that would be so much worse. I was told to stay in the car while the police went to knock on my front door. It has to be reiterated that my dad warned me regularly to never bring the police to the door under any circumstances. It was the cardinal sin. Time froze as I sat in that cop car. It really was the most terrible of all mornings.

The police finally emerged with the worst possible person beside them, my father. I was absolutely mortified. He got in the back of the car and sat down next to me. Before I could say a word he gave me a look of pure hatred. Once the vehicle was moving he muttered a phrase under his breath that sent a chill down my spine: 'I'm going to fucking kill you for this.' I tried to explain that I didn't really do anything that bad, but he cut me off saying, 'Shut the fuck up, you little cunt.'

And that was that.

We were driven to a police station and taken to an interrogation room. However, it soon became apparent that my dad was the person under investigation, not me. The police seemed to know both of our names. Still, I continued to deny my identity until they brought in a picture of my face that had been supplied by my grandparents and the jig was up. They asked me if I thought they were stupid and I badly wanted to say 'yes'.

(I later found out that I was looking at my Interpol picture. Apparently they knew that we had been travelling in Europe the previous summer as I had been spotted in both Italy and France. How exciting!)

My dad had no choice but to admit to his identity, whereby the police produced a pair of handcuffs and ushered him towards the cells. As they led him away he appeared less threatening, pathetic even. Of course, I still had no idea why they were arresting him. I assumed that it was for kidnapping me. Perhaps they knew about Dublin? It was all very troubling and I was sure that I too was headed for the cells.

This was how I found out that my dad had skipped parole in 1976. Until that day I had no idea that he had technically been on the run the entire time. I thought I had been the only one in that category. Due to my dad's short-sighted move seven years earlier, he was sent back to prison to finish his term. Initially, I thought I had managed to get him sent down for his remaining years, but luckily they decided that five weeks would suffice. Years later, he maintained that I still owed him five weeks of his life, but I wasn't the one to jump bail, was I, dear father? Still, I did feel terribly guilty about it, mostly because my mother had the worst day she had probably endured in years.

After this incident I was faced with the fact that I probably wouldn't see my brother for quite some time and that my own mother might never speak to me again. To me, the unfair element in all this was that I was actually innocent. Well, apart from my foolishly throwing a stone in retaliation, it had simply been a case of mistaken identity, a misunderstanding.

***

Next up was a trip to the superintendent's office, where I was to be cautioned for running away from my guardians and absconding to Ireland. As well as my parents getting into trouble, I was now deemed old enough to receive my very own punishment. Although my dad was about to do jail time, my mother escaped without charge. She could easily have been arrested for kidnapping, but she was deemed unfit for prosecution due to my brother being so young. This was surprising, as I was convinced that she too would be sent to prison and he'd be taken into care. It was technically the second time she'd abducted me and taken me off to Ireland, so by my reckoning she got off pretty lightly. This time, however, it was my turn to receive a thorough dressing down and I was nervous from the outset.

I had been cautioned before in Ireland, but the police there had been very relaxed and more amiable. Getting a caution from an Irish policeman consisted of a pat on the shoulder accompanied by a 'hope you'll do better next time' smile. But here it was a very different affair.

The superintendent entered the room with an air of authority I had only seen in military types. He immediately started shouting in my direction, 'Stand up straight lad! Legs apart! Hands out of pockets!' Unfortunately my response was to giggle. He then screamed, 'Is this funny to you, boy?'

After a few minutes it dawned on me that someone else had entered the room behind me. At first I thought it was another policeman, but it wasn't. It was my nan. She was seated and seemed to be hovering between joy and melancholy. She remained quiet throughout, although I could tell from her facial expressions that she too thought the policeman was being particularly harsh.

I was told in no uncertain terms that if I ran back to my mother I would be arrested and put into care. I would then be kept away from all family members until I was eighteen, by which time they probably wouldn't want to see me any more. It was all a bit much, but for some reason this guy really got to me and I took him at his word. The truth was I didn't think I could run back to my mum after this anyway. Why the hell would she want me? I was a one-person disaster zone. Trouble always found me, even when I tried to behave. Somehow I always managed to mess things up, regardless of my intentions.

It was time to stop running, I realised. This time I would have to stay put and deal with the consequences of my actions. If my mum should ask me to return, I would decline. It wasn't worth the pain. It was time to end the cycle.

After receiving the caution I was released into my nan's custody and we left the police station, albeit awkwardly. The first thing she mentioned was how upset she had been when I ran away, and how hurt she was by the nasty thing I'd said to her on the phone from Ireland. I apologised and tried to explain that I never meant to hurt anybody, I just wanted to be with my parents. That was all.

I sat on the train next to my nan in silence. I could not comprehend how I had gotten myself into such a mess, when just a few hours earlier I had been making my way to school as per usual. Home life with my parents and brother had become as close to normal as I had ever experienced. It was incredibly ironic that the bad times had ended at the exact same point in time that I had managed to screw everything up. It was bloody typical.

This day was a turning point in my childhood. Because of my actions that day, my dad was back in jail, my mum was alone with a newborn and I was heading back to a life I had already left behind. The knock-on effect of going into that shop for a bag of crisps changed the course of my entire life. It was quite the quagmire.

EPILOGUE

BESPOKE AL FRESCO DINING

With a pint of Guinness in one hand and a packet of Tayto crisps in the other, I set about writing this conclusion of my tale. I was in the town in Ireland where I'd spent the worst year of my life; this was at the end of a week-long research trip, conducted after the completion of the initial draft.

I had decided it would be a good idea to take a short trip to some of the more relevant locations mentioned in this book to see if I'd accidentally left something out or had perhaps forgotten crucial details. I also wanted to experience some of these places first-hand one last time, to see what feelings, if any, they might bring up.

Although I still have family in Ireland, I chose to remain completely anonymous while conducting my research, as contact with them would have no doubt clouded my judgement. An example of how strictly I stuck to this method occurred while wandering around my dad's hometown twenty miles north. I was scribbling in my notebook when I looked up to see one of my aunts walking directly towards me. I stared down at the ground until she passed by, saying nothing. She was none the wiser and I was relieved to have avoided a stop 'n' chat. I was truly committed to being invisible. I felt akin to a ghost while walking along those forgotten pavements of my youth.

I experienced a myriad of emotions during this trip, from hate to guilt, and anger to sorrow, all of which was part of an accidental therapy that emerged during the writing process. I doubt I fully understood what I was getting myself into at the start, but this project has easily been the most difficult endeavour I have ever undertaken. The emotional revelations that surfaced throughout were extremely hard to deal with, as they often appeared out of nowhere. Perhaps the most surprising of these was a sudden outburst outside the horror house that had been my home during that terrible year. 'Fuck you, house,' I shouted, with tears streaming down my face. After that I refused to look in its direction any longer. We were done.

***

It is difficult not to feel like a time traveller when visiting former homes and finding them in a state not dissimilar to a relic. Our first house in that town, for example, barely resembled itself. The woodland behind was no more, having been replaced by a housing estate that inherited its name. Even the narrow lanes where I used to throw coins above drains have become wide avenues with mansions on either side. Any space that was empty when I was a child has been deliberately filled in; only the edges remain the same. It seems to be a pattern. By comparison the homes I lived in seem so small to me now. It's hard to comprehend that three people lived in such tiny quarters. Perhaps the claustrophobic nature of our various abodes somehow contributed to a build-up of confinement and stress, which surfaced as cruelty.

It is somewhat amusing to me that I can now enjoy a soy latte in my father's hometown. The town's only international telephone box has been replaced by chairs, fancy tables and a chalkboard menu. In 1981 I called my nan a fish face from a place where you can now enjoy bespoke al fresco dining! Conversely, I always imagined the current era would look somewhat futuristic, but Ireland in many ways still looks eerily similar, especially if you squint.

While wandering around these old haunts, it was hard to pass people by on the street without wondering about their own past and the changes they had most likely witnessed. When passing an old man, for instance, I wondered if perhaps he had beat his own children, or his wife. Maybe he was abused himself by the Christian Brothers? I considered what such a man would make of modern Ireland, a country that had recently been voted the happiest place to live in the world – something I find somewhat ironic, considering it was easily the unhappiest place on earth to me for many years.

You don't have to be that old to have witnessed the change in Irish culture. Even when passing people my own age I can see the differences and can't help but wonder what they would think of me if they knew my tale. Would they be glad that someone spoke out, or would they simply think I was just whining about a life endured by many? 'Cop on,' they might say, or 'What makes your story so special anyway?' Perhaps they would even see me as weak for empowering the past by not letting it lie.

Watching school kids walking home through the town park, however, reminded me that the children growing up in Ireland today are coming of age in a completely different land to the one in which I spent my childhood. I am hopeful that my generation was the last to experience the extreme teaching methods and domestic violence that seemed so prevalent in the 1970s and early 1980s.

I only wish I could have told that little boy locked in the red-lit room that he would one day have a loving wife and children of his own. Maybe he would have been able to better cope with the situation. It would have been nice to know there was a light at the end of what seemed to be a very dark tunnel.

Of course there are far worse tales than my own. Everything is relative. I have travelled to some pretty shocking countries and seen babies crawling around in muck, so, believe me, I know on which side my bread is buttered.

Talking of babies, I do consider it apt to have written this account around the birth of my first child. Now that I too am a father, I naturally see things differently. I cannot fathom harming my child the way that my father did me. My son was born out of, and into, pure love, which will hopefully surround him and protect him throughout his life. He will most certainly never have to fear his father, or worry about being beaten. I will never understand the mentality of people who think it's okay to hit their children, but alas it is still embedded in many of the world's cultures to this day. Thankfully, in the West, at least, such acts are now frowned upon.

***

So, before I conclude I should probably tie up a few loose ends, so as to not leave you hanging – without ruining the plot of any follow-up book, of course (wink, wink).

On returning to my grandparents, I found it much harder to adapt back to their way of life. The teenage years were kicking in and I became something of a troublemaker. Although my dad did not fulfil his promise of killing me, we remained estranged for around eighteen months, after which my parents began visiting once more. This coincided with the beginning of their new criminal enterprise; one that would ultimately involve most of the family and see my mother thrown in jail shortly after giving birth to brother number two. I continued to live with my grandparents until my unruly behaviour hit a peak at sixteen, whereby I moved out of the family home within a week of leaving school and never once looked back.

My parents eventually returned to Ireland, and I continued to visit them often, allowing me to forge a relationship with my brothers, albeit mostly from afar. However, after years of trying to put the past behind us, I cut off all ties with my parents around a decade ago.

While I have recently rekindled my relationship with my mother – mostly due to my being a father and her being a grandmother – my own father remains firmly out of the picture. There, now you are all caught up.

It has been a lot easier to forgive my mother for what she did, as she was also a victim of violence and for way longer than I ever was. However, I am often asked if I forgive my father for his actions – to which I state resolutely, 'No, I absolutely do not.' It would be all too easy to forgive and forget, but I just don't have it in me. I've always thought it a topsy-turvy kind of world that places the act of forgiveness squarely on the shoulders of the victim; but if my father does indeed crave forgiveness, he is going to have to manifest it himself in the next world, I'm afraid.

But, dear reader, do not worry that I am carrying a sort of hatred to the grave; it's all a very long time ago and although this period haunts me from time to time, it no longer defines who I am. It is other people, I fear, who have had to bear the brunt of most of the after-effects.

As I sit here, I am simply happy to have survived to tell the tale. I have certainly been carrying this shit around for way too long.

THE END

P.S. I was all set to wrap it up there, but thought I might leave you with this little nugget instead:

Around the time of my eighteenth birthday, my mother told me something that would change my perspective entirely. It was time to share some brand new information. She explained how close I'd come to having a sibling at a much earlier point. Apparently, she became pregnant about a year or so after I was born but decided to terminate the pregnancy; she didn't even tell my dad about it at the time, allegedly.

I asked her why she didn't keep the baby, mentioning how much I would have loved to have had a little brother or sister to grow up alongside. She explained that, at the time, she was worried that if she had another baby my dad would have done the very same things to that poor mite as he did to me, or perhaps worse. I looked at her, dumbstruck. She saw my reaction, and not quite understanding my horror, hastily volunteered: 'Oh, no, I could never have let it happen to *two* of you.'